THE POLICY PARADOX IN AFRICA

THE POLICY PARADOX IN AFRICA

Strengthening Links between Economic Research and Policymaking

Edited by
Elias T. Ayuk and Mohamed Ali Marouani

Africa World Press, Inc.
P.O. Box 1892
Trenton, NJ 08607
P.O. Box 48
Asmara, ERITREA

International Development Research Centre
Ottawa • Cairo • Dakar • Montevideo • Nairobi • New Delhi • Singapore

Africa World Press, Inc.

P.O. Box 1892
Trenton, NJ 08607

P.O. Box 48
Asmara, ERITREA

First Printing 2007

Jointly Published by
AFRICA WORLD PRESS
P.O. Box 1892, Trenton, New Jersey 08607
awprsp@verizon.net/www.africaworldpressbooks.com

and the
International Development Research Centre
PO Box 8500, Ottawa, ON Canada KIG 3149
info@idrc/www.idrc.ca
ISBN (e-book) 978-1-55250-335-5

Book and cover design: Saverance Publishing Services

Library of Congress Cataloging-in-Publication Data

The policy paradox in Africa : strengthening links between economic research and policymaking / editors, Elias T. Ayuk and Mohamed Ali Marouani.
p. cm.
Includes bibliographical references and index.
ISBN 1-59221-576-9 (hardcover) -- ISBN 1-59221-577-7 (pbk.)
1. Economic assistance--Africa. 2. Africa--Economic policy--21st century. 3. Africa--Economic conditions--Research. 4. Economic development--Research--Africa. I. Ayuk, Elias. II. Marouani, Mohamed Ali.

HC800.P633 2007
338.96--dc22

2007013117

TABLE OF CONTENTS

PART II
EVERY COUNTRY HAS A STORY TO TELL—ECONOMIC RESEARCH AND POLICY-MAKING THROUGH NATIONAL EXPERIENCES IN AFRICA

PREFACE

During the past three decades, the African continent has faced a wide range of challenges, amongst which are those related to its economic development. Finding solutions to these development challenges has received considerable attention within the international donor community, regional organizations and the individual countries themselves. On the international front, the Millennium Development Goals set a timeline of targets to be attained by 2015. The Bretton Wood institutions, in particular, and other initiatives such as the Commission for Africa that British Prime Minister Tony Blair launched in 2004 have played varying roles in the search for appropriate answers. Structural adjustment programmes, poverty reduction strategies, plans for debt cancellation and the G8 promise to focus on Africa are just some of the examples of the effort.

A key issue associated with addressing the continent's development problems has been the degree of local participation in the design of these solutions. While it is recognized that homegrown solutions have a higher probability of success than those developed off the continent, the lack of availability of local capacity has been identified as a major stumbling block. However, even when there is the capacity available, policy-makers have not adequately exploited it, generally preferring to defer to the opinion of external foreign consultants.

Strengthening the capacity of economic research institutions so that they can play an effective role in the design of economic policy has been one of the key objectives of the Secretariat for Institutional Support for Economic Research in Africa (SISERA). SISERA was established in 1997 as a Secretariat of the International Development Research Centre (IDRC). It provided technical and financial support to economic research centres in sub-Sahara Africa (SSA) so that they can undertake policy-relevant research with the goal of influencing economic policy-making.

In January 2005, the Secretariat organized an international conference in Dakar, Senegal, during which participants from key economic think tanks presented their experiences in the policy development process in Africa. Of particular interest was the role of economic research and economic researchers in policy-making. The authors examine the extent to which economic policies that are formulated in the sub-continent draw from research based on local realities and undertaken by local researchers and research networks in Africa. Other relevant issues that received attention include: the main channels and mechanisms through which economic research influences policy-making in Africa; the degree to which policy-makers rely on economic research in their decision making; the level of incentives for economists to feed the policy debate; and the impact of donor behaviour on the policy-research relationship. The participation of policy-makers at this conference provided a unique opportunity for vibrant discussions. The presentations were supplemented with roundtable discussions that allowed exchange of ideas.

This book brings together selected papers that were presented at the conference. These papers are based on the individual experiences of the researchers and their institutions in working with policy-makers on policy relevant issues with the goal of providing useful input in the development of economic policy. An important conclusion emerging from the available evidence is that there is a disconnect between policy-making and economic research. Research institutions have to build their credibility, develop a communication strategy and remain attentive to the needs of the policy makers. The underlying reason for remaining attentive to the needs of policy-makers is the fact that the link between policy research and policy-making is non-linear. Researchers must therefore be flexible and agile in the timing of their interventions.

There is an urgent need for a concerted effort by all stakeholders involved in policy development in Africa. The economic researchers and institutions have the necessary skills to provide useful input into the policy debate. They must continue to undertake credible research that addresses the needs of the policy-makers. Policy-makers should understand that foreign consultants do not have any comparative advantage over local researchers. As for the donor community, they must strive to draw more from the local research community than they have done in the past.

Recent developments seem to indicate that the various stakeholders are becomingly increasingly conscious of the need to work together if policies in Africa are to reflect the needs of the countries for which and in which they are being developed and applied. These efforts must be pursued so that domestic policies can provide the necessary impetus for economic development. The following pages offer some invaluable suggestions for how that can be done.

ACKNOWLEDGEMENTS

The papers in this book were presented at an International Conference that the Secretariat for Institutional Support for Economic Research in Africa (SISERA) organized in Dakar January 28-29, 2005. We are grateful to the people who helped run the conference. Many thanks go to Mrs Catherine Cherrier-Daffé who provided excellent leadership in the organization of the Conference. Miss Marie-Jeanne Diouf, Mrs Safietou Tall, Mrs Grace Fokam-Sarr and Mrs Edwidge Mampassi ably assisted her. Mr. Moussa Drame looked at the documentation aspects of the conference. Our colleague, Dr. Diakalia Sanogo, also provided very helpful comments throughout.

As for any endeavour many other people were involved in this work. First, we would like to thank all the presenters, discussants of the various papers and those who led the roundtable discussions for the excellent quality of their work. The following discussants provided comments that were useful to the authors of the various papers. They include Olugbemi Agbola, Lambert N'Galadjo Bamba, Mesfin Bezuneh, Innocent Butare, Jean-Pierre Cling, Jan Isaksen, Francis Kern, Wafula Masai and David Sahn. Secondly, we thank Amadou Bah, Eric Eboh, Fred Carden, Dirk Hansohm, Sana Faty, François Resneaud, Jean-Christophe Boungou Bazika, Taladidia Thiombiano, Bernard Decaluwé, and Mrs Gnouka Diouf who agreed to take additional responsibilities by serving as chairs and rapporteurs for the various sessions. Thirdly, our appreciation is addressed to the Directors of SISERA partner institutions or their representatives who shared their experiences in different forms and shape. The lessons presented in this book could not have been possible without their readiness to share the rich information at their disposal.

We would also like to thank SISERA's main donors during the past eight years. They are the United States Agency for International Development (USAID), the Canadian International Development

Agency (CIDA), the International Development Research Centre (IDRC), the French Ministry of Foreign Affairs, the Dutch Ministry of Foreign Affairs, the European Union and the Ford Foundation. The Foundation made a generous grant to SISERA to enable the publication of this book. A final thank you goes to Mrs. Joan Baxter who read the entire manuscript and edited the text to make the presentations as concise and precise as possible.

PART I

ASKING QUESTIONS, FINDING ANSWERS

IMPROVING AFRICAN RESEARCH TO IMPROVE AFRICAN POLICY-MAKING

INTRODUCTION

Mohamed Ali Marouani and Elias T. Ayuk[1]

It is becoming increasingly clear that without sweeping changes to domestic policies and international ones we well, Africa will not reach the Millennium Development Goals by 2015. This is probably why so many recent international development initiatives focus on the continent—the Commission for Africa launched by the United Kingdom with its plan for debt cancellation for the poorest countries and the declarations in 2005 by the incoming president of the World Bank, Paul Wolfowitz, that he wants to focus on Africa.

Donors also say they will favour democratic countries that adopt sound development policies. This raises several questions. What constitutes a sound development policy? And who is making that policy? What role does economic research—and economic researchers in Africa—play in the existing process of policy development on the continent? Are policy-makers and political leaders cognizant of the research on-going in their own countries and that being done by research networks across the continent when they formulate policies intended to promote sustainable development in Africa? And if they are not taking research findings into account when deciding on key policies that can make—or break—developing efforts, how can the relationship between research and policy be strengthened to remedy this weakness in the links between the research and policy process?

During the 1980s and 1990s, a majority of countries in Africa and in Latin America implemented structural adjustment programs (SAPs) prescribed by the World Bank and the International Monetary Fund (IMF). These programs consisted of profound and severe economic reforms. Given the generally dismal state of African economies, there was clearly need for economic restructuring, but a major criticism of the SAPs was that they did not bring about the expected positive results because they invoked policies that did not take into account the social, economic and political realities of the countries concerned.

During this period and until today, most countries in sub-Saharan Africa (SSA) suffered from a common weakness in their institutions that meant there was a lack of capacity to carry out economic reforms (Toye 1993). As a consequence, African governments relied heavily on external agencies and foreign consultants for research that was to be the foundation for policy decisions. Dollar and Svensson (2000) also found that over a third of the programs failed because they were implemented in a poor policy environment.

To try to improve the policy environment, there were numerous efforts to strengthen local African capacity. But this raised an important issue: could and did research results from within Africa actually feed into and improve the policy-making process in Africa? For many years, Africa's policy agendas had been set outside the continent and it was not obvious that the international financial institutions (IFIs) were willing to consider any views in variance with their pre-set convictions.

It became increasingly important to try to establish the much-needed link between research and policy-making *in* Africa, and to examine a number of questions. First, *does* economic research on the continent play any role in its process of policy development? Second, to what extent do African policy-makers and political leaders take into account the on-going research in their own countries when they formulate policies? Thirdly, is there any evidence of the links—or opportunities to forge or expand them—between research and policy-making in Africa?

These were the important questions that we sought to answer when we at the Secretariat for Institutional Support for Economic Research in Africa (SISERA) organized in January 2005 the international conference to examine the contribution of economic research to policy development in Africa. The conference brought together over 100 participants mainly from SISERA member economic research institutions, government and other research and development institutions and funding agencies. The participants came from 20 African countries, Canada, the United States of America and Europe. This book builds on a coherent and cohesive selection of papers presented at that conference in Dakar, Senegal, that cover a range of interlocking issues: the main channels and mechanisms through which economic research influences policy-making in Africa and elsewhere in developing countries; the degree to which policy-makers rely on economic research in their decision-making; the level of incentives for economists to feed the policy debate; the impact of donor behaviour on the policy–research relationship, and how improved indigenous research–policy relationships can help strengthen democracies in Africa.[2] The contributions in this book have been written by economists belonging to the leading economic research centres in Africa, regional research networks, well-known development research institutions in Europe and also the International Development Research Centre (IDRC) in Canada, which has supported SISERA. The chapters that appear here evolved from the papers by incorporating resulting discussions and comments from both researchers and policy-makers working closely with the research community at the country or regional levels in Africa.

Our aim is to offer an African perspective on the relationship between economic research and policy development both generally and specifically in Africa. While it includes numerous analyses of research–policy relationships and linkages in a theoretical framewok in developing countries, this is a book that is primarily *about* Africa that comes largely *from* Africa. Most of its contributors belong to SISERA's network of institutions involved in policy-relevant economic research on the continent. Moreover, the authors reflect both francophone and anglophone views, cutting across and eliminating the language barrier that often dislocates regional development efforts in Africa, where neighbouring countries are often divided along linguistic lines—depending on whether French or English is their official language—although they share similar ecosystems, cultures and economic indices and outlooks.

The book is divided in two sections. Part I provides an overview of the main themes, concepts and methods used to analyze the economic research–policy nexus in Africa. It also talks about regional experiences and about donors' involvement and impact on the policy-research relationships. Part II brings these themes "down to earth", offering practical insights and case studies from distinct national experiences in Africa to show how economic research and policy-making are currently linked and how better research and policy-making could become mutually reinforcing, thereby attempting to answer the theoretical research and policy questions presented in Part I. This book includes fascinating insider views of the research–policy nexus past and present in countries as diverse as Côte d'Ivoire, Kenya, Madagascar, Namibia, Nigeria, Senegal and South Africa, while also examining experiences of regional research networks on the African continent and providing an overview of current trends in strengthening the research–policy link throughout the developing world, concluding irrevocably that independent and strong research is a prerequisite for development policies that will have the desired outcomes.

Even if the research–policy relationship is treated from an economic viewpoint, the conclusions of the books are broader and could help in shaping the debate for other disciplines related to sustainable development in Africa—and beyond.

BACKGROUND: ECONOMIC RESEARCH AND POLICY DESIGN IN AFRICA

For an African policy-maker, an economist, a development practitioner or a student in the field of development, there is a general perception that indigenous economic research contributes only a little—or not at all—to policy design in Africa. This difficulty is closely related to the complex nature of the policy–research relationship.

To determine whether or not research is a significant input into policy-making in Africa, it is first important to look at the three main paradigms that have been advanced to try to define and describe the link between economic research and policy design. First is the classic, purist and knowledge-driven model. It suggests that research generates knowledge, which leads to a policy decision in a linear sequence (Hanney et al 2003). This positivist or "technicist" approach assumes that researchers find solutions for developmental problems and policy-makers simply have to implement them. However, such knowledge-driven research faces many challenges in Africa, where we know the limited capacity and funding levels of its research institutions. This model also fails to take into account the fact that some policies are driven solely by politics. Where political considerations are the overriding concern, some have cast doubt on the usefulness of research as an input for decision-making. According to some cynics (Haas and Springer 1998), "if everything boils down to questions of politics, why bother to conduct research?"

The second paradigm is the problem-solving, engineering or policy-driven model. This begins with the identification of a problem by the client, which could be the government, and the researchers' role is to identify and assess alternative solutions (Hanney et al 2003; Gewirtz 2003). Although this model also follows a linear sequence, it takes into account the interaction between suppliers and demanders of policy research (Caplan 1979). The bi-directional flow of information ensures that the research community undertakes research that is relevant and in response to the actual needs of government. This model subsumes that mechanisms are in place for this two-way exchange of information. In the African context, however, and also in the developed economies, the fact is that social scientists do not have the solutions for policy problems. Rather, they can contribute to the policy process by helping policy-makers understand the problems and show the possible effects of various policy scenarios, but they cannot determine what the best choices are because these best choices depend on many other factors that researchers do not control. A variant of this model, the social interaction model, includes a set of interactions between researchers and a diverse group of users and stakeholders besides the government. The move from research to policy is not linear in this configuration.

A third paradigm focuses on the enlightenment function of research (Weiss 1977; Hanney et al 2003). It posits that research is more likely to be useful through the gradual "sedimentation" of insight and theories as well as concepts and perspectives. For the African economic research institution, this means having the ability to explore second-generation problems and issues, a research exercise for which funds are difficult to find.

Finally, Hanney et al. (2003) have described the tactical paradigm in which research is used when there is pressure for action to be taken on a specific issue and policy-makers respond by announcing that they have commissioned a research study to examine the matter. This type of commissioned work usually provides the political system with some time to reflect and therefore avoid irrational policy-making. The recent case of antiretroviral drugs in South Africa is an example of such a process. The government "used research as a delaying tactic by commissioning research on the costing of antiretroviral drugs" (p.194, Setswe,G). The study was commissioned in October 2003 and the decision on the introduction of antiretroviral drugs was made in August 2004.

Economic research institutions in Africa therefore face many tough challenges as they strive to influence policy. They must address the technical considerations of the issues, put them in their proper context and be pragmatic (Casey and Brugha 2005) in the type of options they propose.

POTENTIAL CONTRIBUTION OF RESEARCH TO POLICY-MAKING

The main driving force for economic research—particularly for applied economics—is for use as an intermediate input for decision-making. A number of potential contributions of research to policy-making have been proposed. First, one introduced by Weiss (1977) is that research can influence the policy arena by feeding it with new ideas and concepts. A good example is the concept of "equality of opportunity" brought to the international development debate by Sen (1992) and transmitted to policy-makers by international and national policy research institutions. This concept has been playing an increasing role in the development of poverty reduction strategies. However, the danger is that policy-makers select only the ideas that are compatible with their policy discourse (Nutley, Walter and Davies 2002).

Secondly, a concept on which most authors agree is that policy research improves decision-makers' understanding of many policy issues, especially complex ones. Researchers have the skills and time that policy-makers lack to investigate in great depth issues behind policies.

Third, research has strong positive effects on capacity building, which is a very critical issue in Africa. Chapter Seven that deals with the impact of research on trade policies is a good illustrative example. Technical issues discussed during World Trade Organization (WTO) negotiations are very complex. Researchers who work on these issues for a long period develop capacities from which decision-makers can draw and benefit through their joint participation on various technical committees, or in training workshops for the representatives of those countries in international negotiations, for example.

A fourth way that research can contribute to and improve public decision processes has been developed by Haas and Springer (1998), who suggest that applied research can reduce uncertainty. When policy-makers want to launch a program or a policy they need to assess the risks and opportunities associated with the measures proposed. Public policy evaluations, especially prospective investigations, are devoted to this task. Economic policy research has developed a set of tools precisely for this purpose. Even if the models used are still far from being perfect for various reasons (technical capacities, availability of data, and so on), they can be very helpful in identifying the main potential effects of a policy decision.

The final consideration deals with the contribution of research to improving the quality of the public debate. Chapter Two discusses this issue extensively. This idea is particularly interesting, given the new focus in Africa on improving accountability and participation in the design of development policies. The role of research will necessarily increase with the democratization of African countries, and indeed contribute to it, as several authors point out in this book.

DIFFICULTIES OF LINKING RESEARCH AND POLICY-MAKING

Although research can contribute to policy design in many ways, there are practical problems for both researchers and policy-makers. Even if the research–policy alliance seems desirable, it poses some threats for both communities (Rein 1983). Researchers who spend a significant amount of their time on policy research risk lower performances in terms of their academic research, which results in less recognition and sometimes suspicion within the research community. Policy-makers who rely heavily on research evidence risk endangering their political support base.

Why then do researchers involve themselves in policy-oriented research if it could be so risky for their academic career? What are the motivations of policy-makers?

Researchers' motivations could be financial, better access to data, the prestige associated with proximity to the reins of political power, the preparation of a future political career, or just the desire to have a greater impact on the main decisions concerning a country or a region.

For all those incentives researchers may have to work closely with policy-makers, Edwards (2004) notes that there are several potential difficulties involved. They can face an "anti-intellectual" attitude among some policy-makers; overly-high expectations from others. The access to data is not always easy, even when researchers work for the government. The findings can be controlled by policy-makers or censored by the authors themselves to avoid embarrassing decision-makers. In this regard, the nature of the financial arrangements plays a crucial role. Consultancies or short-term focused grants are always more constraining than long-term financings.

There are similar dilemmas for policy-makers. Their motivation to engage researchers can vary from a true belief in the virtues of research-based decision-making, to the need to legitimate their decisions with research-based evidence. The individual background of policy-makers can also affect their attitude to research: the more education they have, the keener they tend to be to work with the research community.

Another significant problem in the research–policy nexus is the difference in the time frames of policy-makers and researchers. While governments need quick evaluation of the policies that they want to implement, research often requires long-term investigations. As stressed by Phillips and Seck (2004), if research wants to influence policy, it must precede it, even if during implementation assessments can also help adjust non-performing programs or policies. Think tanks in the United States and other anglophone countries have developed the capacity to anticipate issues that will be central in the policy-makers' agenda.

Moreover, applied research cannot be devoted only to the issues that are of direct interest to policy-makers. A good example is the focus on poverty by the vast majority of the studies commissioned by national and international policy-makers during the last five or six years in Africa. If the entire research community worked only on poverty-related subjects, this would endanger any future investigations on many other important subjects.

Two other related crucial issues are those of research financing and the independence of research. Government or other interest groups can have their research institutions, but there is still a great need for independent research institutions with long-term vision and financing. Sustainable financing schemes can guarantee greater independence for African economic research institutions, which would allow them to produce research characterized by greater objectivity. However, objectivity alone is not enough if researchers are to earn the respect of policy-makers; for this the researchers and their institutions must ensure their reputations are built on the quality and credibility of their work (IFPRI 2002).

Research centres can gain a good reputation by hiring well-known researchers (especially those who have worked previously in established American or European research institutions), by cooperating with recognized international or foreign research institutions, by organizing significant events (international conferences, etc.), and by feeding the public debate with timely and rigorous studies. Research institutions staffed by researchers—at least some of them—with good communication skills and the same understanding of the issues as policy-makers will also have a better reputation within the policy arena.

The final difficulty relates to the considerable weight that donors exert over policy in Africa. Given the critical role that donors play in the decision-making process on the continent, especially in its poorest countries, clearly it is important that African institutions examine the impact their interventions have on research–policy relationships.

DONORS' ROLE IN POLICY-MAKING IN AFRICA

A recurrent theme in this book is the influence that donors have on policy-making in Africa and the various channels through which this influence passes. The first is obviously "money aid" to governments. Donors very often link their aid to conditionalities that recipient countries need to respect, such as the implementation of SAPs to obtain Breton Woods Institutions loans and the preparation of poverty reduction strategy papers (PRSP) to obtain debt relief through the Heavily Indebted Poor Countries (HIPC) initiative. How strictly imposed these conditions are depends on donors' objectives, their influence (on the recipient countries or on other donors) and on their culture of development aid.

The second channel is "ideas aid". Donors' research policy units produce this kind of aid, which is generally developed by commissioning experts and research centres or think tanks in developed countries to do the research and come up with the "ideas". This kind of aid aims not only to directly influence policy-making in developing countries but also indirectly by influencing other donors (especially those who invest less in policy research) and policy research institutions (in developed and developing countries). The latter, especially in Africa, are very often dependent on donors' money and ideas, and are thus a good channel for donors to strengthen their influence on policy-making and research agendas in Africa.

The third channel for donor influence is capacity-building for African civil servants and policy-makers. Training and internships allow donors to have counterparts with a common or similar perspective of the issues in the recipient countries. Sometimes donors hire researchers after they become highly trained and decide to leave their ministerial offices, and help contribute to the brain drain from Africa. The more channels donors use, the more influential they are in setting the international development agenda and the more impact they have on national decision-making in Africa. The three channels are obviously mutually reinforcing and all can place research institutions in difficult situations.

But there is one other aid channel that actually promotes national policy research institutions or regional policy research networks. This form of aid requires the supply of money and capacity building, and helps contribute to independent and competent research capacity within and for Africa, as detailed in Chapter Five. Institutions that have developed on the basis of this kind of donor support include the African Capacity Building Foundation (ACBF), the African Economic Research Consortium (AERC) and SISERA. While the AERC is an independent African network that promotes individual researchers, the ACBF and SISERA support institutions. This channel of aid seems the most promising in reducing the monopoly power of donors on economic policy research, even though the money still comes from the North and the main development concepts are still elaborated there.

STRENGTHENING ECONOMIC RESEARCH CAPACITY FOR POLICY-MAKING IN AFRICA

The poor policy environment of the SAP years and the need to build a critical mass of qualified economists to spearhead economic research that can effectively feed the policy-making process led to the creation of a number of initiatives in Africa in the 1990s, including AERC, the ACBF, SISERA, and the Global Development Network (GDN), all of which figure prominently in this book and thus merit a few lines for background in this introduction. The African Development Bank (ADB), the United Nations Economic Commission for Africa (UNECA) and the Council for the Development of Social Research in Africa (CODESRIA) are also important partners but are not examined here in greater detail.

AERC started as a special project of the IDRC in 1988. Its main goal was to involve individual African researchers in the research–policy linkage. Through its small grants program, annual conferences, direct technical support via the organization of methodological workshops, publication series, a joint Masters in Economics program for anglophone countries and a joint PhD program, the institution has been playing a major role in enhancing the quality of research output and in establishing direct links with policy-makers on the continent.

ACBF was created in 1991 as a multi-donor initiative with the primary objective of building institutional capacity on the continent rather than that of individual researchers. The program therefore funded and facilitated the creation of new think tanks and also invested considerably to enhance the skills of African researchers. The African Capacity Building Foundation is a major donor to AERC and to the Programme de Troisième Cycle Interuniversitaire (PTCI) for francophone Africa.

The GDN was spearheaded by the World Bank and launched in 1999. It has put emphasis in internationalizing the policy debate. It supports and links research and policy institutes involved in development with the aim of generating and sharing knowledge for development and thereby bridging the gap between the development of ideas and their implementation. By organizing international forums at which African researchers are well represented, it has helped establish a mechanism for dialogue not only with national (local) policy makers but also international ones.

SISERA was created in 1997 as an IDRC Secretariat with support from the United States Agency for International Development (USAID), the Canadian International Development Agency (CIDA) and IDRC. Its main objective is to provide support for African economic research institutions to enable them to play a major role in the design of policy grounded in the realities of the respective countries and to facilitate their participation in the policy debate. SISERA provides technical and financial support, enhances the managerial capacity of the institutions, links researchers to policy-makers and helps develop networks. SISERA supports 20 research centres in 18 countries in sub-Saharan Africa. It has also facilitated the creation of two sub-regional networks, one for Western and Central Africa and the second for Southern and Eastern Africa, the latter of which is discussed in Chapter Six.

For all this progress in establishing and building independent research capacity with the competence and expertise to greatly enhance decision-making in Africa, research and researchers on the continent remain for the most part, left out of and marginal to the main policy-making process on the continent. This book delves into the reasons why this is so even half a century after political independence in Africa, examining examples of successful and unsuccessful attempts to develop stronger links between African researchers and research institutions and decision-makers in a cross-section of countries on the continent, and then using these lessons learned to develop recommendations on how best to build on the growing research base and draw on this invaluable resource in policy-making on the continent to strengthen Africa's new democracies.

BOOK CONTENTS

Chapter 1 analyses the contemporary policy process in Africa, at what kinds of research are being carried out by international financial institutions and well-endowed donors, which permits them to dominate the policy-making processes for and on the continent. It concludes with an important list of recommendations for how the playing field could be levelled to reflect real needs and public consensus and lead to sustainable development.

The second chapter examines the increasing importance of public participation in formulating and then implementing policies in Africa, as democracy continues to spread on the continent. The authors describe how the production of statistical data, economic analysis, and the dissemination of results can have a major—positive—impact on the public debate, particularly when the press are mobilized to expand the audience for "economic news".

Chapter 3 focuses on the complexity and multiple dimensions of all policy processes, highlighting practical work carried out by Great Britain's Overseas Development Institute (ODI) under a programme known as RAPID (Research and Policy in Development) and the Global Development Network (GDN) project, which has been bridging research and policy over the past three years to improve policy processes.

In Chapter 4, the author describes a study done by the International Development Research Centre to better understand the influence of IDRC-supported research on public policy. This study examines 22 case studies of research supported by the Centre, exploring the nature of policy influence, offering lessons for researchers on how best to target their work and results for maximum effect on sound policy. It utilizes different aspects of the market model described earlier.

Chapter 5 describes modalities that SISERA has adopted in the past seven years to strengthen and build the capacity of Economic Research Institutions (ERI) in Africa, which enable them play an effective role in the policy-making process on the continent. It shows that ERI have a long way to go to become real players in the policy process in their respective countries and regions, and examines areas in which more efforts are needed.

Chapter 6 presents strong arguments for more economic research with a regional approach and scope in Africa. The authors note that there has been growth in the number of research networks on the continent. Drawing on the experience of the Southern and Eastern Africa Policy Research Network (SEAPREN), they examine the potential of the policy-making process on the regional level and the role that research networks play in this process.

In chapter 7, the author illustrates the way research and trade policy interact in his native Nigeria. He assesses to what degree research provides essential analytical support for trade policy-making in Nigeria within the context of the Doha Development Agenda of the World Trade Organization (WTO). The author concludes that there is no identifiable source of, or structure for research and analytical support Nigeria needs to develop sound trade policies. This chapter presents an example of the Direct Transmission Model.

According to Chapter 8, despite the existence and activities of policy-oriented research organizations in Nigeria, public policy decisions seem not to have benefited from relevant research input. The author found major pitfalls in the research–policy nexus in Nigeria, and proposes concrete measures to solidify the research–policy partnership and strengthen the influence of research on public policy decisions.

Drawing from a South African experience, Chapter 9 attempts to develop a set of discrete roles that a policy research institution in a developing country should aim to achieve in trying to fulfil its mandate. The author sets out specific arguments—in the form of "nine commandments"—to elucidate the various activities in which research institutions should engage to ensure quality research and impact on policy in the developing world.

In Chapter 10, the authors use three examples to show how the Centre for Research in Applied Economics (CREA) has evolved from virtual anonymity to being a highly visible and persuasive actor in Senegal through close partnerships with public and private sector decision-makers. They show how CREA has been able to influence key government policies, such as the all-important Poverty Reduction Strategy Paper (PRSP).

Chapter 11 reviews the policy-making process in Namibia and the relative importance of economic research in this process. Specifically, it examines the role that the Namibian Economic Policy Research Unit (NEPRU), the country's lead institute in this area, plays in policy-making. It analyses the different channels through which economic researchers can influence policy, and compares their rates of success in two policy areas.

Chapter 12 examines the policy-making process in Kenya, highlighting the divergence between theory and practice in policy making. The authors conclude that for a research institution to play its rightful role in influencing policy, it needs to recruit and retain highly qualified researchers, have adequate financial resources and establish a good working relationship with various stakeholders without compromising its independence.

Chapter 13 focuses on the way the major economic research institution in Côte d'Ivoire, the *Centre Ivoirien de Recherche Economique et Social* (Ivorian Centre for Economic and Social Research or CIRES), has found a compromise with a new social contract linking the centre with the Ivorian public in general and the decision-makers in particular. This is crucial in a rapidly changing world, where the major economic trend is globalization and Africa's research centres are confronted with a dilemma—choose between their original raison d'être, namely research and publishing research findings, or consulting.

A brief concluding chapter synthesizes the main findings of the book and the lively roundtable discussions during the conference. This chapter also identifies key areas for future work.

Notes

1. This paper was prepared when Elias T. Ayuk was Acting Executive Director and Senior Program Specialist with SISERA
2. It is important to note that the views expressed in this book are those of the authors and should not be attributed to institutions to which they have been or are currently affiliated.

References

Caplan, Nathan. 1979. The two-communities theory and knowledge utilization. *American Behavioral Scientist* 22 (3): 459–470

Casey D and Brugha Cathal M. 2005. Understanding the situation of information systems development failure: a role for pragmatism. Paper presented at the 3rd International Conference, Action in Language, Organisations and Information Systems (ALOIS) 2005:15–16 March 2005, Limerick, Ireland

Phillips LC and Seck D (eds). 2004. *Fixing African economies: policy research for development.* Colorado and London: Lynne Rienner Publishers

Dollar D. and Svensson J. 2000. What explains the success or failure of structural adjustment programs? *The Economic Journal* 110 (October): 894–917

Edwards M. 2004. Social science research and public policy: narrowing the divide. Policy Paper 2, Academy of the Social Sciences in Australia, Canberra

Gewirtz S. 2003. Enlightening the research-policy relationship: issues and dilemmas for educational researchers. European Conference on Educational Research, University of Hamburg, 17–20 September

Haas PJ. and Springer JF. 1998. Applied policy research: concepts and cases. New York: Garland

Hanney SR, Gonzalez MA, Buxton MJ and Kogan M. 2003. The utilisation of health research in policy-making: concepts, examples and methods of assessment. *Health Research Policy and Systems* (1):2

IFPRI. 2002. Assessing the impact of policy-oriented social science research. Issue Brief N°5, International Food Policy Research Institute

Mohammedbhai GTG. 1992. Review of training activities in anglophone universities in Africa, Higher Education in Africa: Trends and Challenges for the 21st Century, UNESCO Dakar Regional Office (BREDA), Dakar

Nutley S, Walter I and Davies H. 2002. From knowing to doing: a framework for understanding the evidence-into-practice agenda. Discussion Paper 1, Research Unit for Research Utilisation, University of St Andrews

Rein M. 1983. *From policy to practice.* London: Macmillan

Sen A. 1992. *Inequality re-examined.* Oxford, UK: Oxford University Press

Setswe, G. 2004. Bridge over troubled waters: The research-policy implementation gap, Development Update, vol 5 no. 3: 183 -208

Toye, R .1993. Structural adjustment: context, assumptions, origin and diversity. Paper presented at the DGIS/ISSAS Conference on Structural Adjustment and Beyond, The Hague, 1–3 June 1993.

Weiss CH. 1977. Research for policy's sake: the enlightenment function of social research. *Policy Analysis* 3(4): 531–545

Chapter One

LEVELLING THE PLAYING FIELD—STRENGTHENING THE ROLE OF AFRICAN RESEARCH IN POLICY-MAKING IN AND FOR SUB-SAHARAN AFRICA

Olu Ajakaiye

ABSTRACT

A brief literature review suggests that in sub-Saharan Africa, there has been a disconnect between the policy-making process and the considerable base of knowledge that policy researchers are producing on the continent. That is, full use is not being made of research findings generated in Africa when decision-makers formulate policies that affect the lives of millions of people on the continent. The contemporary reality is that policy-making process is iterative. It involves interaction amongst three broad streams of activities, namely: problem definition; solution proposals; and choice of the line of action through political consensus. However, that interaction is dominated to a large extent by donors, led by international financial institutions, and even African governments use only limited input from African-generated research. This chapter identifies challenges and opportunities that this situation presents. It concludes that policy research organizations should seek to insert their ideas into the streams of activities in the contemporary policy-making process, which involves several players in the executive and legislative arms of government, the private sector, labour unions and civil society organizations. International organizations involved in the supply of policy research should also change tactics. Instead of deploying their leverage to force African policy-makers to adopt their externally-generated ideas, they should collaborate with research organizations in African countries. African governments that adopt externally-imposed policies often do so out of fear of repercussions and not because they are seriously committed to them, which inevitably leads to disappointing outcomes. This can be avoided if all those involved in the policy process work together, so that policy research suppliers *within* Africa can enhance their influence on policy-making *within* Africa.

INTRODUCTION

In the first decade of political independence in Africa, the supply side of the market for policy research was the exclusive preserve of international financial institutions (IFI) such as the World Bank (WB) and International Monetary Fund (IMF), United Nations (UN) agencies and the donor community at large, most of which operated through expatriate consultants. But by the beginning of the new millennium, governments of several sub-Saharan African countries had at least one policy research organization. Certainly, each central bank has a research department of some sort. In several countries, special interest groups such as labour unions, manufacturers' associations, chambers of commerce and bankers have internal research departments or have set up their own external research organizations. There has also been a mushrooming of consultancy outfits and non-governmental organizations (NGOs) that are owned and operated mainly by retired scholars. This is in addition to a relatively few civil society organizations with research departments or research outfits as subsidiaries. So the situation—and supply side of policy research focussing on Africa—is more competitive now than ever before.

The demand side of policy research has also become more competitive as Africa is freed from autocratic leaders by the democratization on the continent. The termination of military rule and the collapse of authoritarian civilian regimes in an increasing number of African countries have meant the demand for policy research is no longer restricted to the executive arm of government. In many African nations, the legislatures are now fully functioning. Political parties, civil society organizations, business associations, labour unions and other special interest groups are gaining considerable influence in the policy-making process.

Despite these reforms, there is general agreement that knowledge generated through policy research still rarely influences policies directly. Simply put, the considerable capacity of policy researchers on the continent is being under-utilized. Before this can be changed, there is a need to examine how the contemporary policy-making process works, the challenges it poses and the opportunities it offers, and then determine the actual demand for research input in policy-making. This involves a look at the models of policy-making, the nature of today's policy research organizations in Africa and their influence on the decision-making process. This analysis leads to recommendations likely to enhance the utilization of policy research in Africa on African public policy-making.

MODELS OF POLICY-MAKING

The body of literature on policy-making models is already quite vast and still growing. Some of the impetus for this growth has come from activities such as those of the Global Development Network (GDN). The theme of the first GDN Conference, held in 1999, was "Bridging Knowledge and Policy" (Stone et al. 2001). Earlier reviews of the literature on models of the policy-making process include Weiss (1981), Sutton (1999), and Garret and Islam (1998). Among the plethora of more recent works in this area are those of the Evaluation Unit of the International Development Research Centre (IDRC), especially the works of Neilson (2001) and Maessen (2003). While there have been a few studies focusing on the relevance of social science research in policy-making within Africa (Ajakaiye and Roberts 1997; Sanda 1981), there is a dearth of work on the policy-making process with specific reference to sub-Saharan Africa. Therefore, the work of Porter with Hicks (1995) is highly pertinent in shaping the following discussion.

There are several classifications of models for the policy-making process, but the following classification is considered pertinent for the present purposes:

- the stages (linear) model
- the iterative, interactive model

The stages model of the policy-making process

This model has been variously referred to as rational, comprehensive or linear (Porter with Hicks 1995; Grindle and Thomas 1991). A variant of this model has also been called "incrementalist" or the "muddling-through" model. According to Ajakaiye (1992), the basic premise of the model is that policies, like drugs, have three types of effects:

- intended and desired
- unintended but desired
- unintended and undesired

Therefore, the primary goal of the policy formulation is to arrive at the most efficient policy or battery thereof that will maximize the first two effects and minimize the last one. Thus, in the model, decisions are made sequentially in the following stages:

1. identifying a problem, issue or phenomenon
2. articulating plausible alternative policies; identifying, assessing and comparing the significance or otherwise of each of the three possible effects of the alternative policies
3. selecting the most efficient one for implementation (Stone et al. 2001:5; Sutton 1999:9; Porter with Hicks 1995:3)
4. implementing the chosen policy
5. evaluating the effect, impact or outcome of the intervention

It should be mentioned that it is the last stage of this model that qualifies it as a policy-making "process" rather than an activity, for even the most effective policy that is efficiently implemented will inevitably have certain undesired effects. As these are identified during the final evaluation or impact-assessment stage, they invariably constitute at least part of the problem, issue or phenomenon, taking the process back to the first stage.

Over the years, donors have offered substantial support to efforts to strengthen policy analysis in developing countries, using the linear model of analysis. The expectation has always been that good policy analysis will translate into good decision-making and subsequently into good policies. With that rationale, donors aimed to build and utilize capacity for policy research and analysis in several sub-Saharan African (SSA) countries by providing technical assistance and support grants to the institutions such as African Capacity Building Foundation (ACBF), the Secretariat for Institutional Support for Economic Research in Africa (SISERA) and African Economic Research Consortium (AERC).

It has also been suggested by Porter with Hicks (1995) that a roughly linear model of the policy-making process underlies many analyses of the reforms proposed to the developing countries by international financial institutions. With their financial leverage and exploitation of the precarious debt situation of African countries, a proposed reform from the powerful IFIs inevitably finds its way onto the agenda for government action in African countries. Such "proposed" policies or institutional arrangements tend to be adopted and implemented—

not always successfully (Grindle and Thomas 1991:121; Grindle and Thomas 1990). Under the "dollar diktat", elaborated by Ajakaiye and Roberts (1995), the influence of indigenous society-centered forces within the country—interest groups, political parties and voters— are either ignored by technocrats, bureaucrats and other non-state stakeholders who are likely to gain from these IFI-proposed policies. Or worse, African civil societies and their views are suppressed by state-centered forces of the security apparatus. This is a possible explanation for the various protests and strike actions that so often accompany the implementation of IFI policies in Africa.

Given the existence of quality policy research institutions on the continent, it might be assumed that there is a demand from policy-makers for the research findings they produce, indeed that they would deem it essential to consult closely with these research institutions. Certainly, a prerequisite of this is to increase the supply capacity of policy research within Africa. But experience in SSA and evidence from elsewhere suggests that it is by no means inevitable that a good supply of policy research will ensure policy-makers utilize it. Indeed, several writers have observed that policy-makers seldom used knowledge gained through research in formulating policies because the reality is a lot more complex than this linear model assumes (Phillips and Seck 2004:3; Neilson 2001:6; Caplan 1979; Weiss 1977). The policy-making process can be conceived as a market for ideas (Phillips and Seck 2004). A policy research organization is, therefore, in the business of producing and contributing high-quality policy relevant information to a pool of knowledge that policy-makers can access when they need it, and then use as—or if—they see fit (Garrett and Islam 1998:4).

As ideal as it may seem and inevitable as it appears, there is really nothing compelling the effective utilization of policy research in the policy-making process in Africa and, indeed, anywhere in the world, especially when countries are operating under the influence of the IFIs. It is reasonable to assume that the undesirable outcomes of many policies in SSA can be attributed to the excessive attention paid by the IFIs to the first three stages of the linear model of policy-making process, and the subsequent deployment of their leverage to secure the adoption of their preferred policy options over whose implementation they have only limited influence. Such has been the fate of Structural Adjustment Programs (SAP). Their proponents from the IFIs may step onto their planes to return home feeling fulfilled by the pledges made by African leaders to adopt the strict fiscal regimes of the SAPs. However, it is the governments in Africa that must confront the serious protests and civil unrest that often result from the SAPs, which may threaten their own political futures and the stability of the country. This may partially or completely derail the implementation process of the SAP reforms.

It is important not to mistake a policy-maker's decision for an authoritative policy decision, which is one that is actually implemented (Porter with Hicks 1995). Just because a high-level policy maker announces a policy decision does not mean that policy will be implemented, or "authoritative". Donor community members tend to fall for this "official announcement illusion", only to discover that despite the announcement made to appease them, the political authorities within a country may not intend to implement the policy effectively—or at all if they regard it as political suicide.

The iterative interaction model of policy-making

The iterative interaction model assumes that as a policy initiative moves through the stages in the linear decision-making process; several actors are involved and their actions determine the fate of the policy at any of the stages. For the purposes of elucidating this model, the stages of the linear model can be grouped into three:

1. problem identification or the *agenda-setting stage*
2. articulation and analysis of alternative policy options or the *solution stage*
3. the *implementation* and *evaluation stages*

During each of these stages, at least three groups of actors are at work:

1. *the government policy-makers and implementers,* made up of politicians in power and the bureaucrats
2. the *special interest groups outside government,* encompassing politicians not in power, business interest organizations, labour unions and sundry interest groups
3. the *international donor community* led by the IFIs

During the agenda-setting and solution stages, the government and international donor community, especially the IFIs, tend to dominate the process in virtually all African countries. The influence of the IFIs tends to over-ride even that of the government in countries that depend heavily on foreign aid and/or have a high debt burden. Such countries are required to undertake certain reforms prescribed by the IFIs before they will be eligible for financial assistance from them or before they can support their pleas for debt rescheduling. In short, the influence of African governments at the first two stages tends to be severely limited, despite the claims by both government and the IFIs to the contrary. In such a situation, to save face the government maintains that the policies are "home-grown" while the IFIs claim that the policies enjoy "national ownership". The reality, however, is that these are the imperatives of the conditionality imposed by IFIs on further financing for the country. During these stages, the influence of the special interest groups tends to be minimal.

The last stage—implementation and evaluation—is when real contestation and negotiations between the government policy-makers and the special interest groups ensue. Special interest groups can be further divided into two sub-components: the sub-group that finds the policy to be beneficial to them and therefore supports it; and the sub-group that sees the policy as detrimental and so opposes it. Experience in Africa abounds to show that governments frequently deploy their powers to suppress any opponents of controversial policies while promoting those who favour it.

Where there is relatively little popular support for a policy, it is usually easy to suppress and perhaps permanently silence the minority among the special interest groups that may oppose it. If, however, the opponents are in the majority or politically powerful, any effort to suppress them may have only short-term success. They will likely persist in their criticism, and resist by organizing protests and civil unrests. Eventually, especially given the democratization on the continent, governments will have to choose from a difficult range of options: concede and abandon the policy; continue to implement it without any desirable effect because of a negative response of the stakeholders; or find themselves removed from or voted out of office, after which the policy will be reversed or modified beyond recognition. There are many examples in Africa to illustrate each of these three possibilities.

The experiences of several African countries under the SAPs, the emergence of multi-party democracy and the termination of authoritarian regimes have opened the door for more active engagements by the hitherto passive special interest groups in the problem-identification and solution stages of the policy-making process. This means the simplistic, sequential linear process no longer suits the real needs of policy-makers in Africa. They must engage in policy debates that will involve diverse and increasingly vociferous groups of actors in all stages of the process. However, till now, governments in league with the IFIs still tend to dominate the first two stages, while special interest groups and the non-governmental actors and organizations tend to be more influential during the last stage. It follows that a policy cannot be authoritative, as defined, unless it enjoys the support of the majority and/or the relatively more powerful sub-component of the non-state actors because such policy decisions will be difficult—or downright impossible—to implement.

Nature of demand for policy research in the iterative interactive policy-making model

Characteristics of Policy Research Organizations

To appreciate the nature of the demands for policy research inputs in the policy-making process described in the preceding section, it is necessary to examine the diverse nature of policy research organizations themselves. It is important to note that each of the three groups of actors—government, IFI and non-state—now actively participate in each of the stages of the iterative interactive policy-making process. Quite a number of non-state actors now have a research organization or they have a department devoted to research within their organization. In any case, they can afford to hire a consultant or commission a study to analyse the impact of a particular policy on their interests. Undoubtedly, the IFIs have the most elaborate and best-endowed research outfits in the world. The UN agencies and other donors, particularly bilateral ones, also either have a research outfit and/or they regularly engage consultants for this purpose.

Thus it is reasonable to assume that each of the three groups of actors that interact in each of the three stages of the policy-making process either own or can acquire policy research output for their use in influencing the process. For those that own a research outfit, it can be assumed that their outfits can either respond to the demand for policy research or receive research outputs from their organizations as a matter of course. In that case, such research organizations are necessarily sympathetic to the philosophy and world view of their owners. In fact, to retain the attention and continued support of their owners, some of these organizations exhibit greater dogmatism than their owners. Of course, owners of research outfits can outsource policy research outputs through consultancies or commissioned studies and they do so for various reasons, including when they are seeking an independent opinion. Actors that do not own a policy research outfit can only receive research output they require by commissioning a study, provided that they are groups or segments of the society with the means to do so.

A typology of policy research

There is not just a wide variety of research outfits at work in Africa, there are also different types of policy research, which need to be identified to understand the nature of the demand for this research. Each type of policy research has its own challenges and opportunities.

Put simply, policy research can be defined as scientific inquiry into a phenomenon or subject that is intended to produce facts that translate into policy advice to feed into the process. This is distinct from advice based on tradition, convention, intuition, hunch or rule of thumb, and is known as "evidence-based policy advice". The following list identifies four main types of policy research:

1. *surveillance/monitoring research* is designed to systematically and constantly track developments in the economy and society with a view to identifying potential opportunities and challenges well in advance of their emergence to allow for the design of appropriate policies and programmes to effectively deal with the situation. This type of research is normally carried out by a research outfit owned by a parent organization or within a research department of an organization.
2. *evaluative research* is designed to analyse and evaluate the impact of specific policies and programs against the background of the intended effects and identify the unintended but desirable effects which should be consolidated, while also identifying the unintended and undesirable effects that must be ameliorated. Evaluative research may be *ex-post* or *ex-ante.* While evaluative research can be procured through consultancies or commissioned studies,

a research outfit owned by a parent organization or within an organization's research department can also conduct it.

3. *prognostic research* is designed to analyse the developments in the relevant aspects of the economy and society at regular intervals with a view to predicting the future direction the system may take under alternative policy regimes and/or evolving circumstances. Prognostic research is invariably carried out by a research outfit owned by a parent organization or within a research department of an organization.
4. *prospective research* is designed to analyse the developments in the relevant aspects of the economy at regular intervals with a view to predicting the future direction the system may take under plausible circumstances that are largely outside the control of policy-makers. Prospective research is also carried out by a research outfit owned by a parent organization or within a research department of an organization.

Obviously, non-state actors and donors without their own research organizations or departments are likely to demand more evaluative research than the others. Experience shows that in Africa, the few non-state actors that own research outfits are engaged essentially in surveillance/monitoring and evaluative research. Given their limited size and resource endowments, they have difficulty sustaining these research activities and seldom have the capacity to carry out prognostic and prospective research.

Similar constraints limit government-owned research organizations in Africa. Like non-state actors, they are also essentially engaged in surveillance/monitoring and evaluative research. In addition, they tend to operate under the prevailing paradigm that is averse to long-range planning as a strategy for development management.

Donors have bona fide and well-endowed research outfits capable of engaging in all types of policy research. The World Bank and IMF are the global leaders in this respect. The African Economic Research Consortium (AERC), through its thematic and collaborative policy research projects conducted by its large network members, is perhaps the only regional organization that engages in the four types of policy research to produce outputs in all four categories.

Demand for policy research in policy-making

Having looked at the characteristics of the actors in the policy process, the features of policy research organizations as they relate to ownership and the associated predisposition to accessing and using policy research, and with a typology of policy research in hand, we now have the full context in which to examine the nature of the demand for policy research input in the policy-making process in SSA.

First, it is important to recognize that the demand for policy research by non-state actors and donors without policy research organizations of their own is likely to be episodic, induced by the need to respond to an urgent problem or crisis. Research is required when these actors want to argue for a change in policy or draw attention to a problem that threatens their interests, or those of their beneficiaries. Such research, which is mainly evaluative, is demanded when this class of actors want to intervene at the agenda-setting or the implementation stages of the policy process. They meet this demand for research findings through consultancies or commissioned research. Non-state actors are not particularly effective participants at the agenda-setting stage, while the donors are not particularly effective in the implementation stage. Accordingly, it appears that the demand for research by non-state actors and donors without their own research outfits is unlikely to have a profound influence on the iterative interactive policy-making process.

Non-state actors with their own policy research outfits tend to concentrate on surveillance/monitoring and evaluative research. Expectedly, this class of non-state actors tends also to have greater influence on the policy process than their counterparts without research outfits. They are, therefore, likely to demand and effectively use the research findings from their own organizations for agenda-setting, and challenge implementation of policies that have undesirable effects on them. Examples of non-state actors in this group are chambers of commerce, bankers' groups and manufacturers' associations. In several African countries, these associations submit policy memoranda to government and engage in effective and persuasive lobbying and advocacy activities on the basis of the evidence obtained from their research outfits. As one interviewee from a non-governmental organization put it succinctly in Coe et al. (2002:6) "Research does empower groups, you have to have it to make your case; you just can't shout slogans."

State actors generally own at least one policy research outfit, either as a department within a ministry or as an autonomous organization outside the government bureaucracy. Invariably all central banks have a research department. However, because of the precarious financial situation of these government branches and organizations, and also the dominant neo-liberal paradigm of the IFIs, they are constrained to do only surveillance/monitoring and evaluative research. Indeed, these organizations have considerable difficulty sustaining even these two types of research activities. They must attract donor funding, which is never guaranteed. The result, therefore, is that government demand for research is usually a result of a crisis caused by the implementation of a policy, or to defend and justify a particular policy action, or simply as a delay tactic to temporarily still critics (Coe et al. 2002; Porter with Hicks 1995; Stone et al. 2001).

The dearth of prospective and prognostic research carried out by government organizations in Africa suggests that governments do not and cannot demand a continuous supply of knowledge generated by their own departments and agencies. This in turn puts them in a no-win "Catch-22" situation; their lack of capacity prevents them from doing the prospective and prognostic research to produce outputs needed to shape policies. They become marginalized, essentially reactive and defensive rather than proactive, and state actors then tend to undervalue them and their outputs. This is especially the case if the policy-makers cannot lay their hands on research evidence to help them win a policy argument with other actors during any of the three stages of the process. This failure may not be a reflection of defective research output, rather it simply reveals the relative weaknesses of some actors—and the enormous powers of others.

The IFIs have the best endowed research outfits in the world. They engage in each of the four types of policy research. As a result, they monopolize the markets for prognostic and prospective policy research outputs, which in turn allows them to dominate the agenda-setting and solution stages of the policy-making process in Africa and elsewhere in the developing world. Their surveillance/monitoring research produces enormous amounts of data with which they construct numerous indicators that enable them identify problems well before they emerge. Through the subsequent prospective research, they are able to initiate discourses on imminent problems *and* solutions, even before the other actors have recognized the problems. Through prognostic research, they are able to influence—if not dictate—the development paradigm and the associated philosophical underpinnings of development policy. Their monopoly of these two important markets for policy research creates a "no alternative" syndrome, as no organization in Africa is in a position to produce similar research outputs that may—and also may *not*—confirm the findings of the studies by the IFIs.

The research outfits of these IFIs, like their counterparts owned by government and non-state actors, normally articulate the problems and solutions in ways compatible with the mandate and interest of their owners. It turns out that there is nothing guaranteeing that proposals that are consistent with the interests of these organizations will necessarily be in the interest of their client countries. It is, therefore, the primary responsibility of the other actors to break the monopoly that the IFIs currently hold on prospective and prognostic policy research output, if they too are to be effective participants in the agenda-setting and solution stages of the policy-making process. It is up to the other actors to strengthen their own research capacities to balance the playing field by reducing the excessive domination of the policy-making process by one set of actors. This does not imply that increasing the influence of other actors throughout the policy-making process, the outcome will necessarily be different. Rather, the resulting policy decisions and choices will be genuinely participatory and broadly owned by all stakeholders, including the development partners. This will help ensure that policies do not result in perverse and destabilizing responses among national organizations and stakeholders within Africa, thereby creating the necessary conditions for successful and effective policy implementation, with less disappointing outcomes.

CHALLENGES, OPPORTUNITIES AND RECOMMENDATIONS

Main challenges

There are clear challenges to improving the policy-making processes—and thus policies—in Africa by better using research to analyse the prospective and unforeseen impact of those policies. First, an iterative interactive policy-making process is a better reflection of the reality in the African context than is the linear model. However, it has been difficult for this process to produce authoritative policies—policies that are effectively and efficiently implemented—on the continent. This is because the influence of donors and IFIs, and to a lesser degree the state actors, dominate the agenda-setting and solution stages of the iterative interactive policy-making process, while the non-state actors exert greater influence on the implementation stage. And as has been shown here, policies that do not enjoy the support of a majority of the socially powerful and politically influential non-state actors are not likely to be effectively and efficiently implemented.

Second, the research organizations owned by African governments and non-state African actors are chronically short of resources and they tend to concentrate on evaluative, and to a lesser degree, monitoring research. They rarely engage in prognostic and prospective research, making them essentially reactive research organizations. The result is they cannot initiate discourses on issues of development in setting agendas and finding solutions.

Third, only the research outfits of the IFIs produce the four main types of policy research: surveillance; evaluative; prospective; and prognostic. They therefore dominate the agenda-setting and solution stages of the iterative interactive policy-making process. However, they have limited influence on the implementation stage so the efficacy of their ideas in enhancing development is severely hampered because the IFI-generated policies that African governments find it expedient to adopt are often not implemented. In short, their policy proposals are not authoritative.

The upshot is that African policy-makers seldom use African-generated policy research when they formulate policies, not only because of Caplan's (1979) "two community" arguments but probably even more importantly because of the uneven power relations of the various actors in the stages of the policy-making process and the inability of national research organizations to engage in prospective and prognostic research. The donor community, led by the IFIs, uses financial and other leverage it possesses because of its relative power and influence, as a strategy to persuade African governments to adopt the agenda and solutions proposed by the IFIs. And yet, these solutions are rarely implemented effectively or with the desired outcomes. This is a major challenge that must be addressed.

Opportunities

There are major opportunities for enhancing the utilization of policy research in policy-making in Africa, not least of which is that the international community is now actively promoting an enabling environment for participatory development. At the national level, African governments are becoming more tolerant of alternative view points. The era of massive suppression of different perspectives and opinions is fading away. The space for participation in the policy- making process is expanding systematically. There are cases where governments have reversed unpopular policies and there are a few cases where governments have been changed partly on account of the lack of authoritative policies.

At the institutional level, in virtually all African countries a significant number of policy research organizations now exist and produce outputs with enormous potential for improving the policy process on the continent. The capacity-building activities of the African Economic Research Consortium over the past fifteen years have increased the supply of high-calibre economists capable of doing high-quality and highly relevant policy research. The activities of SISERA in institutional development and core funding for institutional research have created opportunities for these organizations to initiate surveillance/monitoring and also prognostic and prospective research. The role of the African Capacity-Building Foundation in actively promoting the establishment of policy research organizations where none existed, and supporting the ones that did with institutional development grants, has contributed to the significant increase in the number of countries with policy research organizations both within and outside government. Currently, the ACBF is promoting the establishment of policy research units in the legislative arms of governments to enhance the quality of policy debates and eventually, policy decisions and outcomes.

At the international level, the commitment to a participatory policy-making process through the Poverty Reduction Strategy Papers (PRSPs) creates opportunities for all stakeholders to participate in the agenda-setting, solution and implementation stages of the iterative interactive policy-making process. Also, the global commitment to accountability and transparency creates opportunity for feedback from all stakeholders. Moreover, the IFIs are becoming more flexible and less dogmatic than they tended to be during the final two decades of the last century. The so-called "Washington Consensus"[1] has been toned down at least and the World Bank in particular has been quite receptive to the idea of cooperating with national research organizations in conducting policy research and analysis. Nevertheless, the strategy still remains that of relating to these organizations on a consultancy basis.

Recommendations

To respond to the challenges and take maximum advantage of the opportunities for the utilization of policy research/analysis in policy-making in Africa, there is a need to level the playing fields in the setting of agendas and identifying solutions by empowering the non-state actors as well as the state actors to participate effectively in these stages. One way to do this is to intensify support for African research organizations owned by state and non-state actors to enable them carry out high-quality research in the four categories—surveillance/monitoring, evaluative, prospective and prognostic—like their counterparts in the IFIs. Indeed, the capacity is already largely in place in Africa, with research organizations and networks such as SISERA, AERC and ACBF. What is needed now is adequate and sustained core funding to give these research organizations the jump-start they need to become self-sustaining in flourishing economies on the continent, which will in turn ensure appropriate and sound development policies that feed back into those economies.

The initiative of the AERC to strengthen its relationship with national and regional policy research organizations and research centres within universities would also benefit from increased support and encouragement, especially as this would greatly reinforce linkages between research and policy, and the corollary, between policy and research. Indeed, since AERC has consolidated its capacity-building activities through research and training, it should be encouraged to engage in the type of institutional support activities provided by SISERA. This would complement current AERC capacity-building activities by creating opportunities for effective, relevant and contextually meaningful mobilization of senior researchers to conduct all four types of policy research discussed in this paper.

Also, there is need to intensify and systematize cooperation between policy research organizations of the IFIs and the donors, and their counterparts in African countries. The competition that is desirable among research organizations is the contest of ideas and not the conquest and organizational monopoly of ideas and influence. In this regard, the UN system, World Bank and IMF, as well as other donors should intensify their reliance on national research organizations to carry out country-level research and analysis. As a matter of principle, the research outfits of the IFIs should work in concert with and engage national research outfits in the agenda-setting and solution stages of the policy process. This calls for an extensive and sustained research partnership between research organizations of the IFIs and their counterparts in Africa. In that regard, dogmatism should give way to pragmatism to enable genuine contest of ideas. The IFIs and other donors can then deploy their leverages on government to adopt the agenda and solutions arrived at in collaboration with research organizations within the countries themselves because the policy decision arrived at in this way is likely to be effectively implemented and become authoritative.

Notes

1. The Washington Consensus was a set of rigid policies proposed by John Williamson of the Institute for International Economics in 1989, which was purported to be the recipe for promoting economic growth in Latin America.

References

Ajakaiye D Olu and Roberts FON. 1997. Social science research in Nigeria: the problem of policy relevance. *Journal of Humanities and Social Sciences* 8(2) December: 249–268

Ajakaiye D Olu and Roberts FON. 1995. Social science research in Nigeria: which way forward? *Annals of The Social Science Council of Nigeria* 7(Jan–Dec): 1–22

Ajakaiye D Olu.1992. Marketing acceptance of research findings to policy-makers. *IN:* Sanusi Haroun Usman (ed). *Public policy coordination in Nigeria*. Kuru: NIPSS: Ch. 8

Caplan N. 1979. The two communities' theory and knowledge. *American Behavioural Scientist* 22:450-470

Coe J, Luetchford M and Tess K. 2002. ID21? Tracking routes towards impact. Uganda: UNISE Resource Centre. October

Garrett JL and Islam Y. 1998. Policy research and the policy process: do the twain ever meet? *Gatekeeper Services* No. 74 International Institute for Environmental Development

Grindle M and Thomas John. 1990. After decision: implementing policy reforms in developing countries. *World Development* 18(8):1163–1181

Grindle M and Thomas John. 1991. *Public choice and policy change: the political economy of reform in developing countries.* Baltimore and London: The John Hopkins University Press

Maessen O. 2003. Influence of research on public policy. Workshop Report 2, Evaluation Unit, Ottawa: IDRC

Neilson S. 2001. IDRC-supported research and its influence on public policy: knowledge utilization and policy processes: a literature review. Evaluation Unit, IDRC, December

Phillips L. and Seck D (eds). 2004. *Fixing African economies: policy research for development.* London: Lynne Rienner Publishers.

Porter RD with Hicks I. 1995. Knowledge utilization and the process of policy formulation: towards a framework for Africa. USAID Web page: http://usaid.gov.regions/afr/hhraa/knowledge/utiizataion.htm

Sanda AO (ed). 1981. *Social sciences and social policy in Nigeria.* Ibadan: NISER

Stone Diane, Maxwell S and Kaeting Michael. 2001. Bridging research and policy. Paper presented at an International Workshop held at Radcliffe House, Warwick University, July 16–17

Sutton R. 1999. *The policy process: an overview.* Working Paper 118, Overseas Development Institute, Portland House, Stag Place, London

Weiss CH. 1977. *Using social research in public policy-making.* Lexington, Mass: DC Heath

Weiss CH. 1981. Use of social science research in organizations: the constrained repertoire theory. *IN:* Stein H (ed). *Organization and the Human Services.* Philadelphia: Temple

Chapter Two

ECONOMISTS FUEL PUBLIC DEBATE IN MADAGASCAR—THE MADIO EXPERIENCE

Mireille Razafindrakoto and François Roubaud

ABSTRACT

Poverty Reduction Strategy Papers (PRSPs) are one of the tools being promoted throughout Africa to combat poverty. According to the IMF, these papers "are prepared by member countries through a participatory process involving domestic stakeholders as well as external partners, including the World Bank and IMF". Clearly, if these programs are to be successful, the populations of member countries must participate in the development and follow-up of the PRSPs. However, the success of this "participatory" principle in emerging and young democracies presupposes that the public has access to quality economic information supported by reliable and relevant analyses. Economic research centres thus have a crucial role to play, as shown by the innovative experience of the MADIO Project in Madagascar, which derives its name from its original membership: Madagascar-Dial-Instat-Orstom. MADIO was created to support macroeconomic analysis and the building of a statistical system in the island nation. The project made important links between the production of statistics, economic analysis and the diffusion of these results to encourage meaningful public debate, in particular on political reform. This shows the importance of mobilizing the media to expand the audience for economic "news", and emphasizes the need for quality statistics, information and innovation if populations in Africa are to be engaged in public debate on economic and governance issues that relate directly to reality and the demands of society.

INTRODUCTION

Since the end of the cold war, Africa has been undergoing a process of democratization. To succeed, the emerging and young democracies on the continent require that their citizens are equipped with the information they need to participate effectively in public policy debate—and choices. Civil society has an ever-increasing role in this process, as it becomes better organized and able to exert influence on public policy decisions. The liberalization of the media also offers new opportunities for renewed and re-invigorated public debate.

Such empowerment of the populace in turn promises to make fledgling democracies more accountable to their citizens and offers new prospects to poor African countries. However, these prospects cannot materialize unless there is public debate on the major problems facing society. For such debate, the public must have access to quality information supported by reliable and relevant analyses.

Poverty remains the over-riding concern in much of sub-Saharan Africa, and international institutions such as the International Monetary Fund (IMF) have been encouraging the participation of the population in policy development and the follow-up process of Poverty Reduction Strategy Papers. It is clear that for this "participatory principle" to succeed, economic researchers have a crucial role to play in emerging democracies; equipping the population with the information they require to engage in debate and to contribute to policies that can help solve problems.

There is a need for a linkage—which is today almost non-existent—between analysis outcome and economic policy choices in poor countries. This paper begins with a short diagnosis of the problems and challenges confronting the scientific communities of developing countries and their counterparts in the developed world.

This is followed by a presentation of the innovative experiment of the MADIO Project in Madagascar, to demonstrate how the strategic options taken there have helped arouse the interest of civil society in that country, and bring decision-makers as well as economists and analysts to address key topical issues and economic policy options.

Specifically, it shows how the project created a linkage between statistical output, economic analysis and diffusion of results that in turn evoked public debate and gradually instilled a "culture of numbers" in a country where it barely existed. The paper offers concrete examples that show the importance of mobilizing the press to expand the audience for socio-economic information to restore the legitimacy that economists—and particularly researchers—had lost. It also underscores the need for innovation in introducing to the population new themes that relate directly to their reality and the pressing demands of society.

FINDING THE BALANCE—APPLIED ECONOMIC RESEARCH AND ENLIGHTENED DECISION-MAKING IN POOR COUNTRIES

The communication gap between "scholars" in their proverbial ivory towers and "society" in general is a recurrent problem that is certainly not exclusive to developing countries. The importance of research and the role that researchers must play have been subject to controversy even in developed nations where communication between the scientific community, the public at large and power circles has been more clearly defined and is facilitated by technology and infrastructure. There is indeed a dilemma confronting researchers the world over. On one hand, they need to work independently, without immediate pressure and outside the mainstream to allow for deep reflection over time and with a long-term perspective that takes context and hindsight into account. On the other, their work also needs to satisfy the demands of society by shedding light and understanding on topical themes and problems.

This dilemma is even more pronounced in poor countries, where the socio-political and economic situation can, unfortunately, make long-term research seem like an unaffordable luxury to some who seek immediate and simple solutions and answers. There is simply no linkage between economic analyses and policies; that is, the mechanisms and usual channels for the transmission and diffusion of research findings are either non-existent or non-operational, resulting in the following vicious circle.

- On the one hand, in the absence of any demand, the status of analytical assignments at the national level remains under-utilized. Thus, studies tend to become "grey literature", relegated to desk drawers. Or, if they are published, it is usually in foreign journals. In many African countries, where even photocopying a document is an obstacle course, such analyses are generally inaccessible to potential users.
- Decision-makers, on the other hand, are accustomed to functioning in a context of information scarcity so they tend not to seek or

mobilize the scanty analyses that *are* available, when formulating their policies. Nor do they call upon the economists who are likely to share knowledge or reflection with them on the expected or real outcome of the policies they are adopting.

- The consequence is that research quality cannot be assured if researchers are not trying to meet any demand. In the absence of a platform where outcomes can be debated publicly—with the induced effects of emulation and recognition by merit—there is nothing to encourage or sanction researchers' work. Thus, the best of them will prefer to undertake research on topics and according to international agendas, even though it may not necessarily correspond to national demand and needs.

As a rule, it is not easy for researchers to justify their positions and legitimacy in society; the public at large may not always see or understand the importance of their work. This is even more the case in poor countries where there are so many constraints to manage—limited material, financial and human resources, as well as time—given the urgency of finding solutions to very real and immediate problems related to survival. Chronically scanty resources must then be used in the most effective way. This means that some difficult choices must be made and priorities granted to some central and topical subjects, to some simpler and less expensive methods, and to certain objectives to provide practical lessons that are oriented to practical policies.

For economic research—whether it is done at the national or international levels—to be useful and contribute to policy development and monitoring in poor countries, it must meet two major and closely interdependent challenges.

1. it must ensure the relevance and reliability of the statistical data on which analyses are based so as to guarantee the quality of these analyses;
2. it must take wise and practical choices of methods and tools that take into consideration the limited availability of human and material resources.

The need for relevant and reliable statistical data for sound analyses in Africa

The sad truth is that knowledge about poor economies is severely limited, and nowhere more so than in many least developed countries in sub-Saharan Africa. For many countries on the continent, it is possible only to speculate on the evolution and characteristics of poverty and inequalities over the past decade, simply because the statistical data required for any serious analysis are either of poor quality or non-existent.

The first step, then, would be to increase the reliability of statistical data required for development policy definition and monitoring, after identifying and correcting the reasons for the deficiency of statistics on the continent. Among these are the budgetary crises throughout sub-Saharan Africa as a whole, the financial asphyxiation of individual states and also the lack of human resources, which will be discussed later in this chapter. However, it is also the responsibility of those in charge (statisticians, researchers, political leaders and donors) to break another vicious circle that currently isolates researchers from decision-makers in a system where very poor quality information is accepted as the norm. It is possible to identify three types of undesired effects that contribute to and exacerbate this problem.

1. At the national level, statistical data are often substandard and potential users, notably politicians, do not draw on them. Demand for statistics by potential users subsequently decreases, leading in turn to decreased financial and human resources being made available for data gathering, so statistical supply and quality continues to deteriorate.
2. Within the statistical collection and analysis mechanism itself there is another disconnect. Potential data users (analysts and decision-makers) may participate only very minimally in the design and realization of surveys, and inversely, the data collectors (field operation officers) may play no role in the exploitation and analysis of the information they assemble. This reduces the efficiency and relevance of the overall process of data collection and statistical analysis. Data users may have no control at all of the constraints underlying statistical surveys, nor of the basic criteria that must be complied with on the ground. Data collectors are not sufficiently sensitized to the importance and purposes of statistical analysis, and therefore ignore the importance of accuracy and rigour required for

viable information. To make matters worse, there is an additional problem to be considered: the data production and exploitation phase is usually entirely separate from the process of defining policies that might develop from those statistics. Under these circumstances, it is hardly surprising that statistics are often unreliable or irrelevant to development policy-making on the continent.[1]

3. The third twist in this statistical quagmire is a paradox: while national demand for statistics in sub-Saharan Africa is almost non-existent or not sufficient to promote sound policy-making by individual governments, at the same time and at the instigation of and with the financial backing of international institutions, statistical surveys have been proliferating since the early 1990s. The stock of available and accessible information has clearly increased. Conversely, over time, data quality has also deteriorated (Deaton 1995)[2]. This weakness is largely underestimated. Generally, the publication of derived data or analyses in international journals without any credible or critical diagnosis has led to legitimization of less rigorous practices when it comes to survey result validation. More attention and consideration should be given to field work that makes a clear distinction between quality and unreliable data.

Thus, the current situation manifests itself as a series of contradictions and disconnects adversely affecting the production and quality of data in sub-Saharan Africa.

- First, at the country level, the most fanciful figures are in circulation with almost no possibility of questioning them by returning to the basic data (primary survey processing). Professional statisticians tend to "run after surveys"; even if the surveys are not conducted effectively, they still offer the advantage of providing the statisticians with resources that help compensate for their derisory salaries, regardless of whether there is even a minimum of consistency in the data.
- Secondly, there is a growing gap between data producers on one hand and analysts or researchers on the other. The former are not motivated or encouraged to produce quality data. The latter have little interest in detailing the problems encountered in the field that might jeopardize the validity of their findings. The fact that the analysts may ignore or mask survey shortcomings, and blithely

forge on with studies of dubious quality, does nothing to encourage data producers to seek only reliable and relevant information.

On this second point, we can also note that the exploitation of second-hand information from indigenous African surveys by Western university teams merely aggravates the problem. In addition to their often weak knowledge of field work, as well as of the conditions and basic processing procedures (perpetuated by the absence of documentation), the publication imperative that governs academic spheres and the criteria used to assess scholarly reviews do not encourage Western academics working in Africa to focus attention on data *quality*. In many cases, an only slightly deeper critical analysis would discourage the use of such local surveys. However, such academic integrity could amount to depriving oneself of the comparative advantage of obtaining a database that has not yet been exploited by potential competitors.

Moreover, the over-valuing of formalization and (econometric) instrumentation by development economists often leads them to pay only marginal attention to the quality of the data used. Thus, when this problem is not simply concealed as it appears to be in most of the studies, the usual practice is to mention it briefly in the introduction, and then develop the reasoning and the conclusions, as though the quality issue doesn't have the slightest bearing on the outcome. Lastly, it should be noted that even when an effective data assessment *is* successfully carried out, it does not have any impact on the country of origin because the gap between the two worlds (academic in the North, technical and political in the South) is so wide!

Nevertheless, the growing number of surveys gives the impression that the knowledge base has evolved—albeit a false impression. Too often, the information that is being diffused by these studies has almost no link with the phenomena it purports to measure. This is all the more regrettable as the outcomes of these surveys are later compiled into international databases[3]. From this standpoint, the responsibility of international organizations led by the World Bank and to a lesser degree the United Nations Development Program (UNDP) should not be minimized. By publishing international databases on the basis of often unreliable or even absurd information, these institutions, as well as some renowned researchers, are giving this dubious academic and development practice legitimacy it does not deserve. This does nothing to discourage data users from drawing on poor quality or downright false information to develop policies that affect millions of human lives. This perverse logic was authoritatively highlighted in an article by J-D Naudet (2000).

This raises an important question: is it better to generously publish wrong figures about African economies to fill an information void and guide policy-makers, or not to publish anything at all? While it is hard to maintain a no-publish position, it is also clear that policy definition is a function of the quality of the diagnosis that led to it, which in turn depends on the reliability of the upstream information used to formulate it. This is a major stake, since the fate of many populations—among them the most destitute on the planet—depends on it.

It is time to stop pretending that the knowledge base is there, time to readjust attention on basic information gathering and analysis. The unrewarding and underestimated work of statisticians should be given due recognition and given the status is deserves—as a main priority in Africa.

The need for sound methods and tools especially when resources are scarce

While people in poor countries are well aware of the scale of human and material constraints they face, the international community still has to realize the extent of the perennial problem of weak capacities in developing countries—in administration, in academic circles and in civil society. Of course, donor countries and development agencies continue to support projects of many types: occasional or permanent technical assistance; executive retraining courses; and the establishment of financially-backed teams, units or structures, among others. In most cases, the results are far from convincing. There are many reasons to explain these failures but we would like to dwell only on two of them:

a. the absence of an environment encouraging the development of skills, and
b. the inadequacy of the methods and instruments transmitted, acquired or proposed in relation to the context and priority needs.

a. Fostering an environment to encourage skill development

It is difficult to establish or even to support an analysis or research structure that is likely to be efficient unless there is a public capable of judging, appreciating and mobilizing information the structure produces. The formation of a strong team, large enough to constitute a critical mass or core, might thus be the first criterion that must be met. On one hand, this core helps foster an environment of exchange and emulation among its members, and on the other, it builds the visibility needed to attract the attention of potential users interested in the research and its analyses. An isolated individual working in an inefficient research structure—often falling part—is unlikely to be able to develop his or her skills, whatever those may be.

The second criterion, then, would be to develop a broader audience, trained and sensitized to the importance of the analyses produced, capable of not only recognizing their merits but also providing critical feedback. Of course, this condition presupposes that the research topics addressed correspond to issues that are likely to attract the interest of the general public and their elected representatives. It is therefore necessary to enable and encourage debates around the analyses. Their authors can thus undergo a test in front of a public whose knowledge can feed back into and enrich the research process. These meetings between data producers and potential data users can help create a stimulating environment for quality work.

In the absence of such an environment, there is a tendency to neglect rigour in the collection and analysis of data. To illustrate this problem, one need only look at official documents produced at the national level, and to a lesser degree at the international level, that are frequently riddled with gross inconsistencies—consumption level and structure, poverty incidence, and doubtful extrapolations, to mention only the example of studies on poverty—and then note that these inconsistencies do not seem to trigger any reaction.

b. Finding the right methods and instruments for research that serves policy-makers

In the absence of global reflection and coordination—among various government services, ministries and also among the donors—which is a prerequisite for better management of severely limited human resources, those with research and analysis skills are torn by many and conflicting demands. Given the human and material constraints, there is tendency for researchers to be overly ambitious and unrealistic about what they can accomplish. For example, a single team with only a few members may be charged at the same time with analysing the national census data *and* the data from a household survey, while also carrying out specific surveys at the request of a donor. Through the PRSP initiative, international institutions recommend that African countries monitor a long list of indicators for policy assessment, without taking into account how many skilled researchers are actually expected to accomplish this massive undertaking. In most impoverished African countries, this seems a dubious task, given that it is impossible to decide on the direction of the evolution of even a single indicator such as monetary poverty, the reduction of which is a primary Millennium Development Goal (MDG).

In this context of multiple demands (national and international, short and medium term), it is rare for a team to carry out research over a long period and capitalize on its full potential and use for policy development. The executives who tend to lead the research are either attracted by better remunerating positions or assignments, or mobilized for short-term assignments with tight deadlines.

The definition of priorities becomes a clear necessity. Contrary to past practices that are still in force today, it is obviously important to reassert the importance of the analysis of a few basic indicators, which are easiest to collect with periodically updated light surveys following a consistent methodology. To address the poverty topic, for instance, it would be wise to build a data bank on a specific set of indicators—employment, access to basic infrastructures, the population's perception of their living conditions and policies affecting these—which remain relevant for program follow-up. The capacity of development actors to define adequate policies depends on the availability of two kinds of information: problems as they emerge; and the real or anticipated impact of the options implemented or considered. However, in poor countries where researchers don't have even the basic information needed to take stock of the situation and to understand the mechanisms in force because of the lack of relevant and reliable data, is it realistic to expect them to assess policy impact? Clearly not; the use of sophisticated analysis techniques cannot compensate for shallow field knowledge.

Of course the objective remains: to explore and apply instruments that can be used to accurately assess (*ex ante* and *ex post*) policy impact, notably on poverty. Some innovative research avenues such as micro-simulations constitute some stimulating methodological breakthroughs in that direction. Nevertheless, it is also important to be aware of the difficulties still to be surmounted in setting poverty-alleviation policies according to priority[4]. There is a need for adequate and reliable data if these new assessment methods are to be applied in a useful way and there is also a need to strengthen local technical and institutional capacity so they can handle these complex analytical instruments.

THE EXPERIENCE OF THE MADIO PROJECT IN MADAGASCAR

In the first section of this chapter, we highlighted some important objectives for researchers in developing countries, namely: (1) to base their analyses on reliable and relevant data; (2) to foster an environment that encourages them to develop their skills; (3) to respond to the demands of society by focusing on some key topical issues; and (4) to arouse widespread public interest and make analyses available to the electorate by diffusing their findings broadly. The success of the MADIO Project to support macroeconomic analysis and the building of a sound statistical system in Madagascar illustrates the relevance of this diagnosis. An original linkage between statistical data production, economic analysis and results diffusion characterizes the Project in particular. In this section we describe the original experience of MADIO in this area and demonstrate how the Project strategy to diffuse results has contributed to democratic debate across the country.[5]

The objectives and achievements of the MADIO Project in Madagascar 1994–1999

The purpose of the MADIO Project was to study the conditions for the successful outcome of the dual transition process—economic and political—unfolding in Madagascar. Set up in Madagascar at the end of 1994, its first phase was completed during the first half of 1999[6]. The two scientific partners of the Project were INSTAT (*L'Institut national de la statistique malgache* or the Madagascan National Statistics Institute) and IRD (*L'Institut de recherche pour le développement*, formerly ORSTOM, the French institute for development research). The project was backed financially through agreements with the European Union and the French Ministry of Cooperation, in form of grants amounting to about one million US dollars. Initially made up of a group of eight researchers in early 1995, MADIO underwent a gradual increase in its staff.

In 1998, it mobilized a team of ten, working closely with researchers from DIAL *(Développement, Institutions, Analyses de Long Terme).* MADIO intervenes on two fronts: the promotion of economic analysis in Madagascar and the rehabilitation of the national statistical system. More specifically, MADIO concentrates on five main activities:

1. conducting statistical surveys
2. building macroeconomic models
3. undertaking economic studies
4. developing and promoting policies to diffuse results
5. participating in training

In all these areas, MADIO is considered an exceptional success in Africa; its scientific achievements are many and solidly established, and it enjoys national recognition. Its main partners and its users commend it for its social usefulness.[7] Of course it is difficult to carry out an accurate quantification of any project's achievements because this will be necessarily simplistic given that the most important outputs are also very often those that work in a diffuse way and over time. Within five years, it achieved the following:

- 21 statistical surveys integrated in the national statistical information system
- 300 published studies on a wide range of themes
- created an annual review on economic analysis, four issues of which were published
- organized several public conferences and debates on central economic policy issues
- systematically diffused results of its research for public consumption, resulting in more than 500 newspaper articles
- trained 15 high-level Madagascan statisticians/economists, who are very familiar with survey techniques and economic analysis.

Table 1 provides an overview of MADIO's achievements. It shows that most of the implicit functions that one can expect from a cooperation project were satisfied—high productivity, innovative function, conclusive effect on the environment, capacity to replicate on an endogenous basis, etc.

Table 1. Synthethis of MADIO's accomplishments: 1995–1999

Statistical surveys	Macro-economic modelling	Economic studies	Diffusion, promotion	Training, scientific supervision
5 employment surveys	1 short-term model	300 scientific publications	5,000 studies sold	1 weekly research seminar
4 surveys informal sector & consumption	1 general equilibrium model		500 newspaper articles	17 short "formal" training sessions
2 occasional household surveys	1 input–output model		20 radio/TV programmes	12 on-going PhD. theses
5 industrial surveys	2 projections/ simulations. yearly		creation of an economic review	16 postgraduate dissertations
5 agricultural surveys			18 communications (nat. symposia)	2 memoirs: Final Honours
CPI* Renovation (monthly)			18 communications (internat. symposia)	20 consultancies (nat. or internat.)

* CPI: Consumer price index

Diffusion policy: assessing demands of society and "stimulating" civil society

Many factors contributed to the success of the MADIO Project, too many to discuss here.[8] However, it is useful to emphasize one factor in particular that played an essential role and merits examination here: the outputs diffusion strategy. One of the unique characteristics of MADIO is the way it links the production of reliable statistics with the economic analysis of basic data as well as the promotion and rapid diffusion of results. That is, *statistical production is put at the service of economic analysis, and this know-how is in turn subjected to "let-know", through results diffusion.* Efforts to promote the MADIO survey outcomes (economic studies, public presentations, creation of a review, etc.) paid off by generating a real and virtuous cycle: survey outcomes produced in real time and the thematic analyses derived from them aroused public interest and in turn, brought in fresh resources for new surveys. MADIO succeeded in triggering a strong demand for its outputs and this demand, in turn, became a powerful motivating factor for the executives, and inspired greater self-confidence.

The MADIO Project policy to aggressively promote and diffuse results of its work was a deliberate methodological choice. It emerged from the observation that the ineffectiveness of African national statistics offices is partly due to the statisticians' inability to respond in time and with the required standard to society's demands. In a context of extreme resource scarcity and where the "statistical culture" of decision-makers is limited, statisticians are expected to demonstrate the relevance and importance of the products they are offering. Concretely, four types of instruments made it possible to promote the MADIO surveys:

1. Periodically holding sessions called *Instat-Point Information* (On-the-spot information), at which statisticians present the public with their most salient results whenever an operation has been completed, without waiting for the publication of the final results, which sometimes take a very long time to get to the market.
2. Systematically and rapidly publishing brochures (about 50 pages), entitled *Preliminary Results*, which offer an analysis of the main results of each survey, drafted in an accessible language to non-professionals and in an attractive medium to avoid the indigestible form of conventional statistical products in a succession of tables on gross figures.
3. Diffusing survey results targeted to a limited number of strategic partners that are likely to communicate them to decision-makers (authorities, economic administrations, donors, etc.) and especially to the public through the media. Concurrently, the publications are put on sale in bookshops and made available in libraries in Madagascar.
4. Creating an Annual Review, *Economie de Madagascar*, a quality medium for statisticians and economists wishing to write and diffuse thematic articles aligned with international standards on that matter, which also promotes databases beyond the descriptive commentaries contained in *Preliminary Results*.

The public reacted well to this strategy, as shown by the publicity given to MADIO's activities. Good conference attendance, sales of studies, and press coverage (Table 1) revealed the general thirst for information and relevant analyses—both in the media and civil society.

MADIO took advantage of the surprising and salutary wind of freedom of speech blowing across Madagascar to promote its action and ideas. Since the early 1990s, the Madagascan society has been undergoing profound changes with democratization, political freedom, freedom of the press, and the formation of an active and organized civil society. In this context, MADIO made the most of the freedom allowed it by addressing delicate issues and sometimes even politically charged subjects such as corruption, ethnic issues, weaknesses or failures of some economic policies, and the media then covered its findings. The fact that it expressed itself so openly reinforced the legitimacy of MADIO, as the public increasingly perceived it as a truly independent structure that was not subservient to the state. Furthermore, by diffusing its results and shedding light on these normally taboo subjects, MADIO forced the authorities not only to show interest in many problems they generally prefer to ignore but also to seek solutions for them.

The media were not the only ones to appropriate the results disseminated by MADIO. Employers' organizations proved to be ardent supporters of the project: more than 85 percent of industrialists surveyed said they were satisfied with the mode of delivery of survey results. These organizations called upon MADIO's expertise capacity to deal with specific problems, such as the timeliness of increasing minimum wage in 1996. They also used the results delivered by MADIO and the public debates it organized in their dialogue with the government, as they did when negotiating the credit issue and monetary policy in 1997, and the tax regime in 1998.

Without this diffusion of results, MADIO's research would have remained in desk drawers with no significant impact on the policy-making process. Its appeal to civil society has a double function: (1) subjecting the Project's outputs to a verdict by those who demand information is a measure of its usefulness for society, and; (2) forcing the government's hand on sensitive issues increases its accountability to the public affected by its policies. By introducing in Madagascar a "culture of numbers" and credible economic assessment and by proving their importance to the population as a whole, MADIO created an imperative for data and analysis that could no longer be ignored. MADIO did have a direct impact on decision-making in the arena of economic policy. But perhaps its most important contribution to the democratic process in Madagascar was the indirect and diffuse effect of demonstrating to the public the importance of statistics and quantification (see Box 1).

In its appeal to the civil society, MADIO gave a central role to the *innovative function* of analytical (and statistical) issues. In a society with a chronic shortage of reliable official information, the demand of the population goes far beyond the economic realm. For this reason, MADIO addressed new topics that touched on sociology—social practices, perceptions, opinions. Thus, for example, onto the employment surveys were grafted specific socio-economic modules such as: Antananarivo residents and economic policy (1995); educational policy and structural adjustment (1996); elections, political parties, ethnic groups and religion (1997); reform of the administration, privatization and corruption (1998); subjective approaches to poverty (1998); violence and exclusion (2000). These topics, which in developed countries are generally covered in opinion polls or by specialized research centres, have almost never been studied in developing countries. Yet, it was observed that these issues, in fact, generated more expectations and debates than did inflation or the performance of external trade. Clearly, these touch directly on the daily lives of citizens and favour participation in the democratic process.

With hindsight, it appears that MADIO played a pioneering role in the area of research in sub-Saharan Africa. Today, across the continent, there are growing numbers of surveys on the perception of poverty, governance and democracy issues[9], which prove the validity of the research and analysis options that the project explored.

Box 1, which describes the opinions of a number of strategic partners (public administration, private sector, donors, researchers, media) about the MADIO Project, gives an "outsider" overview of the analyses described earlier of the role that the diffusion of research findings can play in consolidating the democratic process.

How MADIO spawned public debate in Madagascar

The media were an excellent resonance chamber to enhance the reputation of MADIO and the research results it disseminated to them. As noted earlier, MADIO studies resulted in more than 500 newspaper articles between 1995 and 1999. But even more noteworthy is that these project results often made headlines in newspapers, while MADIO members were special guests on many radio and TV

Box 1: The views of MADIO's strategic partners

"As a government official, I must say that the MADIO studies, with the usual few validations, have strongly influenced several economic and social decisions, all the more so as the structure of the project—purportedly independent from the administration services—gives them a credibility felt by public opinion including the business circle" **P. Rakotomavo, former Prime Minister of Madagascar**

"The MADIO Project has allowed GEM and its members not to go any longer fishing for statistics, which are more or less kept secret, often outmoded and requiring a tedious work of verification and consistency between the various sources. It has enabled us in particular to have elements of analysing the socioeconomic context, which has been useful in communicating validly with the public authorities and international financial institutions. MADIO assisted us in the identification and assessment of the various factors that must guide a company's wage policy and subsequently in communicating efficiently with workers' unions." **G. Ramenason, Chair of *Groupement des Entreprises de Madagascar* (GEM, or Malagascan Business Association)**

". . . also founded in its deliberate choice to carry out required diffusion and communication, so that these research papers are not maintained at the stage of a researcher's contribution, but are rather publicized and possibly discussed by all those to whom these results could be useful. Better still, the public at large was also informed since the documents produced had been drafted in a sufficiently clear and accessible language for the major Madagascan dailies to which they were destined to be able to reproduce them in full or in the form of large excerpts in their coverage. In this sense, MADIO has accomplished a pedagogic task: it has largely contributed to driving in a minimum of economic reflection in the Madagascan public opinion." **G. Petitpierre, European Union Delegate to Madagascar**

"The primary factor that strongly contributed to the impact of the MADIO Project is the extreme swiftness with which the results of the surveys carried out within its framework are delivered. The project managers targeted results delivery "in real time", an important objective which was fully achieved . . . The second factor that favoured the dissemination and importance of their results was the existence in Madagascar of a variety of private media—three main newspapers, two credible weeklies, dozens of radio stations, three TV networks—with a tough competition between them and a high literacy rate." **S. Haggblade, economist, Cornell University**

"Personally, I believe that the interest shown in such outputs lies primarily in their very existence. The public is thirsty for research results on their environment. Besides, the topics studied relate directly to daily life. And not least, the vocabulary is understandable. Naturally, the reading of the reports and summaries requires an amount of concentration and spare time, but basically, one feels a real will to be accessible. I do not ignore efforts at the material presentation either: without being luxurious, the MADIO studies are of high standard and one has pleasure leaving them lying negligently on the desk". **R. Ramaholimihaso, Director of the daily newspaper, *Madagascar Tribune***

programs. Our objective here is not to analyse in detail all the press coverage devoted to MADIO research but rather to illustrate with judiciously chosen examples, a number of key issues and also problems raised by this diffusion strategy.

Economic and social information in the press: thirst for knowledge

The first conclusion that may be drawn from the broad coverage of the MADIO studies in the Madagascan media is that there is an *overwhelming thirst for knowledge on the part of the population*, which can be slaked by the press when they are fed solid information by researchers. This runs counter to the common misconception that in developing countries access to information is a superfluous luxury because of the lack of formal education and the low income of ordinary citizens, for whom the priority is only to improve their livelihoods through improved *material* conditions. This is an argument often promoted by authoritarian regimes wishing to concentrate only on economic growth and postpone democratization, and it is fallacious. Even in the most monetarily deprived countries on the planet, there is a real demand for knowledge, and hence of public participation in governance, which relevant socio-economic statistics must satisfy.

The second general lesson concerns the area of *expressed* demand. While economic information on growth, employment, income and inflation is important, it does not tell the whole story that the population wants and needs to hear. Public interests are much broader and cover all issues that impact on their day-to-day existence. In many cases, topics of a more sociological, cultural or political nature—corruption, democracy, social and political identities, etc—have triggered more reactions than strictly economic studies. This is illustrated by the Madagascan press clippings below, with MADIO-inspired headlines about rice prices, health, unemployment, child labour, elections and also a study on the startling gap between rich and poor in the Madagascan capital.

Clippings from Madagascar newspapers illustrate the interest in MADIO work

From left to right - *Madagascar Tribune* (27/06/1997): "Unemployment down"; *L'Express* (2/12/1996): " 'Free rice' prices in freefall!"; *Madagascar Tribune* (6/03/1998): "To your health"; *Dans les Media demain* (*Dossier* 05/03/1998): "One child in three works"; *L'Express* (10/03/2000): "MADIO reveals the magnitude of the gap between rich and poor in Tananarive"; *Madagascar Tribune* (28/11/1997): Who will vote for whom?

MADIO observed that very soon after the initial enthusiasm generated by the provision of structural information (on the labour market, harvesting, industry, etc.), some weariness emerged about these static and strictly economic topics and new areas of interest arose. There was a demand for follow-ups and analysis of developments over time. To meet this new demand, MADIO reoriented its diffusion policy by making available to the media shorter studies in easy-to-read-and-digest four-page documents, which focussed on short-term dynamics and economic prospects. This demand from users highlights the need for real follow-up mechanisms, regular survey systems comparable over time, which unfortunately, are still largely missing in Africa.

The diffusion of all these articles helped develop a very basic economic culture among the populace and also in the media. To fully develop this fledgling culture, however, will be a long-term job.

Macroeconomic prospects—a delicate relationship between MADIO and the media

The MADIO experience with the media was not always fully satisfying, and indeed dealing with the media in any country is a fine art, one laden with pitfalls for the inexperienced. MADIO executives were frequently frustrated by the divergent views expressed in the media. In their articles, journalists did not always reflect the researchers' own conclusions. However, these diverse views are precisely one of the cornerstones of a healthy democracy, which statisticians and economists must accept. Scientific objectivity is not to pre-empt public debate by proposing a single technical solution. Rather, it is expected to enrich that debate by furnishing decision-makers and the public with all the reliable and relevant information necessary to frame the debate. It is then up to everyone to use their data to defend their own proposed options; the final choice will depend on political processes and arbitrations, and will never be purely technical.

Madagascar's media often interpreted MADIO work in their own way.

L'Express (7/11/1997): "Economy: 1998 will be a year full of political dangers"; *Madagascar Tribune* (7/11/1997): "National Economy: still lagging behind"; *Dans les Media Demain (Eco a la une 11/1998):* "An analysis from MADIO Project: Is sustainable growth possible?"

The *Economie de Madagascar* Review and the tax issue—a difficult debate

A public lecture forum usually follows the publication of each issue of the MADIO Review, *Economie de Madagascar,* on its central topic. The third issue, published at the end of 1998, was entitled *Macroeconomic prospects and public policies: the tax issue*" (INSTAT 1998). While any tax issue is a structural, central and recurrent problem of economic policy in Madagascar, by coincidence, it happened that at the time of the publication of the MADIO review that year, tax was particularly topical. An accumulation of concomitant and controversial factors—suppression of the Investment Code, extension of value-added tax (VAT) to free zone companies and medications, denunciation of the customs security contract awarded to Bureau

Véritas[10], a customs service strike, efforts to tax the informal sector, the publication of lists of "bad taxpayers", outcries over the delivery of illegal tax exemptions—had converged and put the authorities on the hot seat when it came to tax problems. The timing for this MADIO conference was delicate, to say the least. In previous years MADIO had felt strong pressure to cancel conferences that the authorities deemed inopportune, and this time the pressure to cancel was even stronger. As one official put it, "You researchers, you don't seem to realize! You are going to throw the country into fire and bloodshed with your studies." MADIO compromised, and agreed to put the public forum debate off for a month, while the finance bill was passed without incident. The conference, which was finally held in January 1999, was a success. The articles published in the Review provided the basis for a cordial but frank exchange of views between the highest competent authorities of the State and the main representatives of the private sector.

Speaking publicly at the time, Madagascar's then Prime Minister, P. Rakotomavo, said, "I can but congratulate the [MADIO] project team for the third issue of the Madagascar Review entitled *Macroeconomic prospects and public policies: the tax issue.* This judicious theme assumes all its meaning in the current economic context and should concern all development actors. Indeed, no one can ignore the great importance of tax revenue, the permanent resources of any modern state and a privileged instrument in the conduct of an efficient public policy."

More generally, MADIO successfully concluded its diffusion policy without any political interference from the administration or the government. Apart from an isolated intimidation attempt while preparing for a TV programme on the country's economic situation, MADIO was not censored at any time. In view of the diversity and very delicate aspects of some of the themes it addressed, this is evidence that a real wind of freedom is blowing in Madagascar. However, it could also be argued that perhaps the lack of censure by authorities may reflect excessive caution on the part of researchers and statisticians, who may not have pushed the limits of an established order, to take advantage of the full freedom that exists in some other democracies.

The winds of change are bringing increasing freedom to Madagascar's media.

L'EXPRESS
"LA QUESTION FISCALE" : AMORCE D'UNE RÉFLEXION CITOYENNE SUR LES IMPÔTS

TRIBUNE
Crise de confiance...

L'EXPRESS
de madagascar
L'ÉCONOMIE SAUVAGE FAIT PERDRE À L'ETAT 1.080 MILLIARDS PAR AN

L'EXPRESS
de madagascar
LA FISCALITÉ À LA LOUPE : DE RÉFORME EN RÉFORME LES RECETTES DIMINUENT !

From left to right - *L'Express (*13/01/1999): "The fiscal question—priming public reflection on taxes"; *Madagascar Tribune* (13/01/1999): "Crisis of confidence"; *L'Express* (25/11/1998): "Economic saving makes the state lose 1,080 billion Fmg, [that is to say US$ 200 million] a year"; *L'Express* (20/11/1998): "Fiscality in the spotlight: reform after reform and the revenue diminishes"

MADIO demystifies free zone companies—and extinguishes a media fire

To attract foreign capital and stimulate exports, in 1990 Madagascar inaugurated a regime of free zone export companies, following the example of many developing countries. However, despite the exceptional dynamism of this sector there was deep scepticism among the public about the timeliness of this strategy. Following some negative international images of the working conditions within these companies (long working hours, poor remunerations, child labour), the media led a movement to reject the system of free zone export companies. Local newspapers were full of articles condemning the companies, with inflammatory headlines: "Free export zones, suffering zones"; "Does slavery still exists in Madagascar?"; "Our female labourers paid starving wages"; "Abusive lay-offs"; "Underage children working nightly" and "Union leaders arrested."

The problem was that there was absolutely no reliable information to support these denunciations, which were at best based on isolated cases amplified by rumour. For this reason, MADIO decided to carry out a study of the economic impacts of the free zone and the wage policies practised there, using the representative data provided by the industrial and employment surveys set up by MADIO (Razafindrakoto and Roubaud 1997). This analysis clearly revealed that the free zone had a very positive impact on the Madagascan economy and that the jobs generated were of a better quality than those generated in other sectors, in terms of wages, services and training. The publication of this study in the media put an immediate end to the smear campaign against companies, mostly run by expatriates, which were operating in the free zone. Interestingly, the unions of free zone companies also exploited this study in their negotiations with the Madagascan authorities. They underline the fact that given the importance of the companies for economic growth and job creation, economic policy should favour their expansion.

The comments of the World Bank resident representative in Madagascar at the time, Philippe Le Houerou, show how the study clarified serious public debate.

> . . . I would like to mention exceptionally the study on the free zones," said Le Houerou. "This is the best example of MADIO's impact on economic debate in the country. This study contributed to demystifying many things. Previously, people would say anything on this issue. In the absence of reliable information, debates looked more like in-fighting or wars of religion. Some perceive free zone companies as hell, others as paradise. Then the study was released. By quantifying the phenomenon, it set the record straight. The controversies ended overnight. This is an important point. More than the direct impact a study has on decision-making—adopting one measure or the other—like MADIO, as I have already pointed out, it is the indirect impact that counts most. With MADIO has been created a reflex which did not exist previously and the idea is making its way: make it a common practice to quantify, to clarify what one is talking about, how to approach problems, to specify the methodology, etc.

Calmer, cooler headlines prevailed after the publication of the MADIO study to demystify the free zone export companies in Madagascar.

From left to right - *Tribune* (18/07/97): "Free export zones in Madagascar: new prosperity or new form of slavery?"; *Midi* (19/03/1998): "Free zones – the motor for exports"; *Midi* 07/97): "158 companies provide 36,000 salaries in 1998"

Corruption—when the truth is revealed, government reacts

Corruption is a recurrent problem in developing countries, although they are by no means the only ones affected by this economic and social ill. It introduces distortions in factor allocations and generates processes of public service exclusion in key social services such as health and education, of which inevitably the poorest are hit hardest. But above all, corruption violates the social contract, discredits the administration, undermines the population's confidence in their institutions and leaders, and eventually weakens the democratic process. Despite its immense scope, corruption remains a statistically opaque phenomenon. While recent research revealed that corruption inhibits growth (World Bank 2001), most of the indicators extracted from international databases remain very weak[11]. They are meant, in particular, to measure the perception of corruption and not its real incidence.

Since 1995, MADIO has tried to develop a methodology that will help capture the scope of the phenomenon through household surveys (Razafindrakoto and Roubaud 1996). Antananarivo residents not only identified corruption as the main single obstacle to the country's development but according to this representative survey, about half their number have been personally victims of corruption. In 1998, the improvement of the economic situation, notably the increase in civil service salaries, seems to have reduced corruption incidence by 30 percent, but it still remains at unacceptable levels. Hardly surprising that the results of this survey generated newspaper headlines, such as the one below from the *Madagascar Tribune* (26/09/1995): "Down with corruption!" and the article from *L'Express* (04/05/1999) headlined, "General mobilization against the roots of corruption".

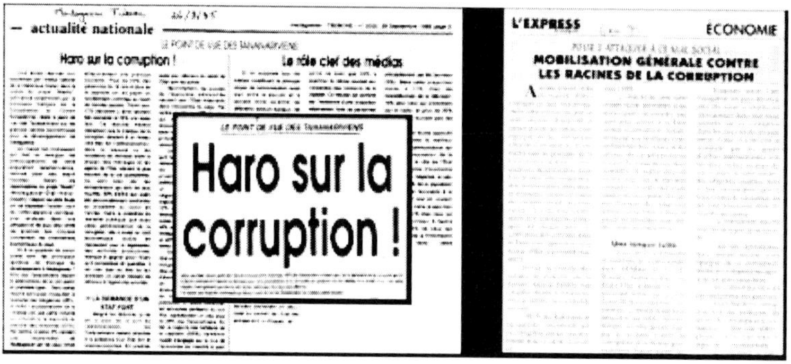
— actualité nationale

Haro sur la corruption !

Le rôle clef des médias

Haro sur la corruption !

L'EXPRESS

ÉCONOMIE

MOBILISATION GÉNÉRALE CONTRE LES RACINES DE LA CORRUPTION

On the basis of the figures released by MADIO, and supported by growing international awareness of the need to fight this scourge more actively, the Madagascan Ministry of Justice took steps to set up a system to suppress corruption. Below is an excerpt from the preamble to the bill against corruption, which, it must be noted, was rejected by Government Council in 1999:

> . . . It is important to recall that according to the results of the statistical survey carried out in May 1995 within the framework of the 'MADIO' Project and co-financed by the French Cooperation Ministry and the European Union: 'The corruption issue appears as a recurrent topic haunting residents in the capital. Ninety-six percent of them consider it a major problem for Madagascar . . . More than 40 percent of the 18-year-and-over age group in the capital have had to bribe a corrupt civil servant in the past year'. Whatever the credibility of this survey and the interpretations made of it, corruption undeniably constitutes

> a social phenomenon in Madagascar . . . therefore the practice must be combated most vigorously.

The delicate matter of ethnicity and castes—should taboos be lifted?

Sub-Saharan Africa is haunted by the spectre of ethnic conflicts. Beyond the paroxysms of outbreaks symbolized by the Rwandan genocide, the history of the continent shows that for their own political ends political entrepreneurs can still easily manipulate ethnicity.[12] Madagascar is a multi-ethnic society, but ethnic tensions have never reached the intensity observed in some other countries. However, they are still present and veiled in a series of past and present incidents that require examination. The ethnic issue is not only political; it is also economic, as recent research tends to demonstrate that "ethnic divisions" reduce economic growth (Easterly and Levine 1997). MADIO therefore decided to address this issue by introducing a specific module on ethnic and caste issues in its 1997 employment survey.

The study derived from this survey revealed that Madagascans had more a cultural than a racial conception of ethnicity and that ethnic origin did not constitute a real problem on the labour market and in city integration, contrary to some alarmist rumours. On the other hand, the castes founded on slavery and abolished near the end the 19th century were still present and people of caste were victims of strong discrimination in terms of their access to employment. These results were widely covered by the media and became the subject of intense public debate, which is indicative of the population's interest in the topic. While the clear majority accepted the conclusions reached by the study, which helped appease latent tensions, a minority of extremist advocates of openly ethno-fascist theses, reacted violently by being virulently critical of the MADIO Project in the local media, and also through a Web forum. The question that arises is whether the "ostrich principle" adhered to in most African countries that prefer to bury ethnic issues in the sand when compiling official statistics, to avoid inflaming rivalries or latent tensions, is the best strategy for dealing with the issue of ethnicity and potential conflict. MADIO's response was a categorical no; rather it chose to address the issue head-on to prevent generally accepted and wrong ideas and stereotypes from continuing to spread under the surface. However, MADIO also recognized the inherent dangers had its results revealed a real ethnic problem in the country, and risked bringing it to the foreground and stirring up tensions.

TRIBUNE

Toujours possibles ?

L'EXPRESS

LA QUESTION ETHNIQUE EST UN FAUX PROBLÈME LES CASTES EN SONT UN

From left to right - *Madagascar Tribune* (10/10/97): "Ethnic tensions in Madagascar: Still possible?; *L'Express* (10/10/97): "The ethnic question is a false problem but castes are a real one"

The role of democratic intermediaries: political parties catch the ball on the bounce

In 1997, MADIO grafted onto the employment survey some socio-political modules, one aspect of which focused on the role of political parties and politicians. The analysis derived from it revealed the deep disillusionment of Antananarivo residents about the benefits of democracy. This reversal, which contrasted strongly with the popular enthusiasm for transition to democracy and multi-party politics in the early 1990s, could be largely explained by the almost unanimous rejection of the politicians. Ninety-five percent of them stated that the elected representatives defended only their personal interests (Roubaud 2000b). The study's conclusions suggested a few avenues to remedy the situation, including: changing the conditions governing the formation of representative political parties; mode of financing and electoral campaigning, and; requiring elected officials to declare their assets and fortune before taking office to detect illicit enrichment in office. (Pierre-Bernard et al. 1998).

The dissemination of these results led politicians to react. Most of MADIO's recommendations were incorporated in the final document of the "Consultations on Political Ethics" Round Table held during the first quarter of 1999, at the instigation of LEADER-FANILO, the second most important political party in Madagascar. For two days, this party invited the representatives of the major political parties to take stock of current political practices and to develop a strategy for "raising the moral standards of political activities". Unfortunately, despite the good intentions and a thorough diagnosis, the resolutions adopted at that consultative meeting have gone unheeded till now. This is evidence that self-regulation is not an effective tool. Even firm voluntary adhesion to democratic principles among politicians is not enough; state intervention to legislate and ensure compliance with established codes appears the only recourse.

madagascar
TRIBUNE
QUOTIDIEN NATIONAL D'INFORMATION - N° 2831 JEUDI 23 AVRIL 1998 - 1000 FMG

6/3/99 Express -

EN APPUI À LA "CONCERTATION SUR L'ÉTHIQUE"

QUAND "MADIO" SCRUTAIT LES ÉLECTEURS SUR LES CAUSES DU DISCRÉDIT DE LA CLASSE POLITIQUE

Selon une enquête de "Madio"

Les attentes des Tananariviens vis-à-vis de la classe politique

— Nation

La classe politique discréditée

From left to right - *L'Express* (6/3/99): "When MADIO surveys voters on the reasons the political class has been discredited"; *Madagascar Tribune* (23/4/98): "According to a MADIO inquiry - The expectations of Tananariveans of the political class"; *Lettre mensuelle de Jureco* (*Nation:* 4/96): "The political class discredited"

CONCLUSIONS

The new democratic order in much of sub-Saharan Africa offers economists—whether they are researchers or executives in charge of economic analyses—new and largely unexplored horizons. Their mission should no longer be limited to supplying the authorities alone with economic information or publishing in reviews destined to a limited audience, the impact of which has historically proven to be very limited on a country's economy. The empowerment of the all the actors in a society (households and businesses) is necessary for the smooth functioning of a market economy. This means ensuring the population's access to reliable information that enables them to fully exercise their citizenship. It also requires researchers (economists, statisticians, etc.) to make it their priority to provide civil society with a

How Economic Analyses Can Favour Democratic Debate

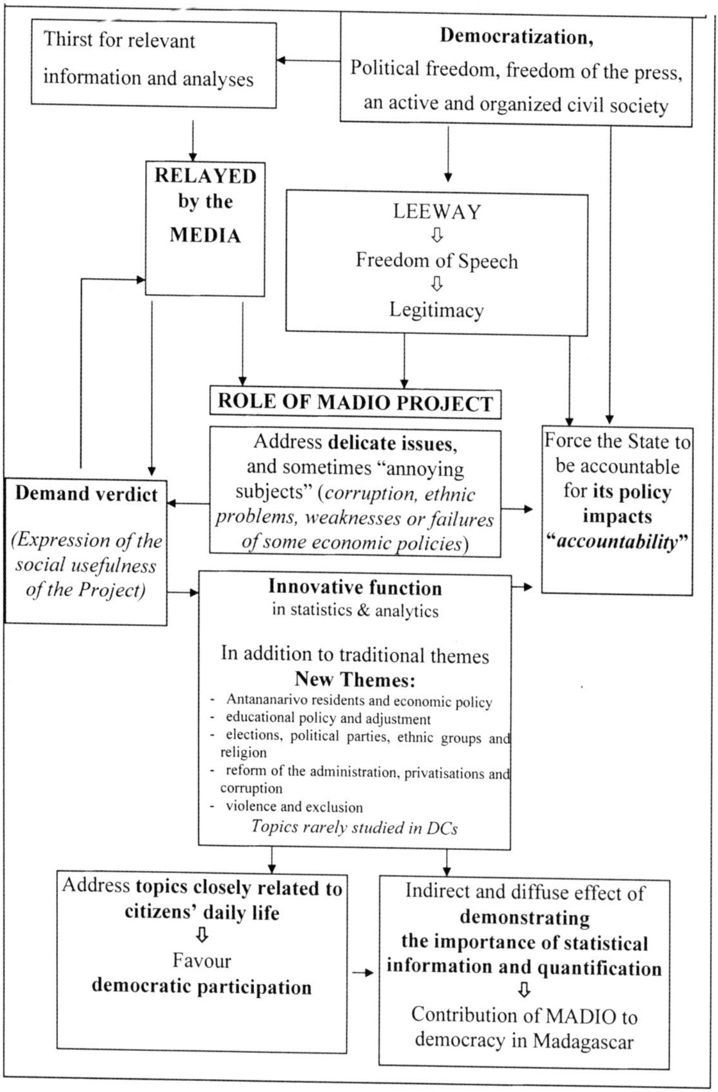

continuous supply of data on and analysis of the major problems confronting that society.

This reinforces and promotes public debate (also see the chart) that is a prerequisite of all development research activities—and of democracy. By fulfilling this mission, researchers can thus recover their lost credibility on the continent. The experience of the MADIO Project in Madagascar proves that such a research and dissemination strategy is not only possible but also highly practical and useful. Based on the lessons drawn from the Malagascan experiment, it is worth extending this method to other African countries where the analysis based on statistical data has not yet attained its rightful place in society. Where authoritarian regimes persist, as they do on many countries, this may not be an easy task for economists and statisticians. In such cases, international pressure should be applied to authoritarian regimes either directly or through civil society to "liberate" public information—which is a democratic imperative and also a right.

Notes

1. For concrete examples of the very poor quality of statistical surveys, see Razafindrakoto and Roubaud (2003).
2. For all those who are sceptical, let them compare the publications based on the generation of surveys undertaken in the post-independence era during the 1960s (in French-speaking Africa, among others), which include a large component of technical support, with those available today. This paper also demonstrates that current deficiencies are not linked to any structural problem that would be responsible for the insurmountable difficulties making it impossible to grasp household activities, consumption patterns and behaviours in Africa. It shows that they are rather the direct consequence of several decades of budgetary adjustment and institutional weakening of African public administrations. Deaton (1995) synthesized and described issues relating to data quality in developing countries.
3. For example, Deininger and Squire (1996) put together, from survey reports, a series of 2600 observations on inequality measures in 112 countries over the 1947–1974 period. Only 700 of them were rated "of very good quality", including a very few from Africa. This labelling, however, did not prevent a countless number of economists to embark on the production in series of growth equations on inequalities, without the slightest precautions before use. This practice was denounced notably by Srinivasan (2001), Fields (1994), and for OECD countries: Atkinson

and Brandolini (1999). More generally, the criticism applies both to Summers' and Heston's databases on GDP in *Purchasing Power Parity* (Summers and Heston 1991) or to those of the World Bank and IMF on GDP series and the main aggregates of national accounts.

4. For example, can the consequences of alternative measures be measured? (With a limited budget, is it more advisable to build rural lanes or improve the quality of primary education?)
5. This analysis is partly based on a document presented at the IAOS (International Association of Official Statistics) conference in Montreux (on "Statistics and Human Rights") published in English in the *Interstat* journal (Razafindrakoto and Roubaud 2003). This text has since been updated and supplemented.
6. At the behest of INSTAT, MADIO Project donors agreed to renew the experience for an additional three years (1999–2001). During the second phase, the work was carried out by a team made up exclusively of Madagascan researchers, with the occasional technical support from DIAL researchers. We shall not discuss the results achieved under the second phase since their assessment process has not yet been completed. For various reasons, including the unstable political context, in-fighting between team members and the dispersion of human resources, the outcome was more mixed. However, a number of achievements (such as periodic surveys on employment in both urban and rural areas to monitor living conditions of the population, as well as the principles of systematic diffusion of analysis outcomes) were maintained.
7. For a detailed assessment of MADIO, see Roubaud 2000a and 2003a.
8. For a general analysis of the project and factors contributing to its success, see Roubaud 2000a and 2003a.
9. See the institutionalization of the *Afrobarometer Survey (for information on the network, see www.Afrobarometer.org),* the surveys on corruption carried out by the local chapters of Transparency International (TI) in many countries, the peer review process within the framework of the New Partnership for African Development (NEPAD), etc.
10. Bureau Veritas was supposed to control and improve efficiency of the customs services. Their contract was denounced and the official reason was their inefficiency, but it seems that it was also linked to problems of corruption.
11. See Razafindrakoto and Roubaud 2005.
12. Refer to the example of the crisis in Ivory Coast as described by Roubaud (2003b).

References

Atkinson AB and Brandolini A. 1999. Promise and pitfalls in the use of "secondary" data sets: income inequality in OECD countries. Mimeograph, Oxford: Nuffield College.

Cling J-P, Razafindrakoto M and Roubaud F. (eds). 2003. *New International Poverty Reduction Strategies*. London/ New York: Routledge.

Deaton A. 1995. Data and econometric tools for development analysis, *IN:* Behrman J and Srinivasan TN (eds). *Handbook of development economics* Vol. 3A. North Holland: Elsevier, pp 1785–1882.

Deininger K and Squire L. 1996. A new data set measuring income inequality. *The World Bank Economic Review* 10(3), pp. 565–91 .

Easterly W. and Levine R. 1997. Africa's growth strategy: policies and ethnic divisions. *Quarterly Journal of Economics*, 112(4): 1203–1250 .

Fields G. 1994. Data for measuring poverty and inequality changes in the developing countries. *Journal of Development Economics*, 44 (1): 87–102.

INSTAT, Madagascar Central Bank (CBM). 1998. Perspectives macroéconomiques et politiques publiques: la question fiscale. *Economie de Madagascar Review* (3).

International Monetary Fund, Poverty Reduction Strategy Papers: http://www.imf.org/external/np/prsp/prsp.asp .

Naudet J-D. 2000. Les "guignols" de l'info: réflexions sur la fragilité de l'information statistique. *IN:* Jacob J-P (ed). *Sciences sociales en Afrique: les rendez-vous manqués*, PUF, Collection Enjeux, Nouveaux Cahiers de l'IUED (10), Paris/Geneva, pp. 31–55.

Pierre-Bernard A, Ramarosaona F, Razafindrakoto M, and Roubaud F. 1998. Partis et classe politique: les intermédiaires démocratiques jouent-ils leur rôle?. *Working Document MADIO* n°9736/E. Madagascar.

Razafindrakoto M and Roubaud F. 1996. Ce qu'attendent les Tananariviens de la réforme de l'Etat et de l'économie. *Politique Africaine* 61, Karthala : 54–72.

______. 1997. Les entreprises franches à Madagascar: économie d'enclave ou promesse d'une nouvelle prospérité? *Economie de Madagascar Review* (2).

______. 2003. The existing systems for monitoring poverty: weaknesses of the usual household surveys . *IN:* Cling J-P, Razafindrakoto M and Roubaud F. (eds.), *op.cit.* 265–294.

______. 2003. Statistics at the service of the democratic debate in Africa: the example of the MADIO project in Madagascar. *InterStat* 26 (April), , pp. 33–50.

______. 2005. How far can we trust the experts' opinion on corruption? An experiment based on surveys in francophone Africa. *IN: Global Corrup-*

- to analyse 50 summary cases studies as part of Phase I of the GDN Bridging Research and Policy Project (Court and Young 2003), and
- in workshops and seminars with researchers, practitioners and policy-makers in Botswana, Morocco, India, Moldova, Kenya, UK and USA.

The political context

The research–policy link is shaped by the political context. The extent of civil and political freedoms in a country clearly makes a difference for bridging research and policy. The policy process and the production of research are in themselves political processes, from the initial agenda-setting exercise through to the final negotiation involved in implementation. Political contestation, institutional pressures and vested interests matter greatly. So too, the attitudes and incentives among officials, their room for manoeuvre, local history, and power relations greatly influence policy implementation (Kingdon 1984; Clay and Schaffer 1984). In some cases the political strategies and power relations are obvious, and are tied to specific institutional pressures. The majority of staff in an organization may discard ideas circulating if those ideas elicit disapproval from the leadership.

Evidence

Experience suggests that the quality of the research is clearly important for policy uptake. Policy influence is affected by topical relevance and, as importantly, the operational usefulness of an idea; it helps if a new approach has been piloted and the document can clearly demonstrate the value of a new option (Court and Young 2003). A critical issue affecting uptake is whether research has provided a solution to a problem. The other key set of issues here concern communication. The sources and conveyors of information, the way new messages are packaged (especially if they are couched in familiar terms) and targeted can all make a big difference in how the policy document is perceived and used. For example, marketing is based on the insight that people's reaction to a new product or idea is often determined by the packaging rather than the content in and of itself (Williamson 1996). The key message is that communication is a very demanding process and it is best to take an interactive approach (Mattelart and Mattelart 1998). Continuous interaction leads to greater chances of successful communication than a simple or linear approach.

Links

Third, the framework emphasizes the importance of links; of communities, networks and intermediaries (e.g. the media and campaigning groups) in affecting policy change. Some of the current literature focuses explicitly on various types of networks, such as policy communities (Pross 1986), epistemic communities (Haas 1991), and advocacy coalitions (Sabatier and Jenkins-Smith 1999). While understanding remains limited, issues of trust, legitimacy, openness and formalization of networks have emerged as important. Existing theory stresses the role of translators and communicators (Gladwell 2000). It seems that there is often an under-appreciation of the extent and ways that intermediary organizations and networks impact on formal policy-guidance documents, which in turn influence officials.

External influences

Fourth, the framework emphasizes the impact of external forces and donors' actions on research–policy interactions. While many questions remain, key issues here include the impact of international politics and processes, as well as the impact of general donor policies and specific research-funding instruments. Broad incentives, such as European Union Accession or the PRSP process, can have a substantial impact on the demand for research by policy-makers (Court and Young, 2003). Trends towards democratization and liberalization and donor support for civil society are also having an impact. Much of the research on development issues is undertaken in the North, raising issues of access and perceived relevance and legitimacy. International donors fund a substantial amount of research in the poorest countries, which also raises a range of issues around ownership, whose priorities, use of external consultants and perceived legitimacy. As policy processes become increasingly global, this arena will increase in importance.

ANIMAL HEALTH POLICY IN KENYA–AN ANALYTICAL FRAMEWORK

One of the ODI case studies (Young et al 2003) examined the complete failure of animal health policy development in Kenya where,

A traditional animal healer in Kenya (photo by John Young)

despite good evidence of the value of local community-based animal health services accumulated over a 20-year period, and their development on the ground across much of northern Kenya, such services remain illegal. Why has the government not changed its policies and practice to accommodate and promote them, especially in the more remote regions of the country?

Prior to Kenya's independence in 1963, clinical veterinary services there were provided by private veterinarians on the white-owned farms, and by Veterinary Scouts–local farmers with a bit of on-the-job training who lived in the villages and were employed by local councils–in the African smallholder areas. Veterinary services were controlled by the Veterinary Surgeons Act, borrowed more or less unchanged from the UK, which made it illegal for non-veterinarians to treat animals other than their own. After independence many of the private vets left the country. In the early post-colonial period, the government made great efforts to Africanize and professionalize the service, setting up a veterinary school for vets and technical training colleges for diploma-level animal health assistants. These staff were deployed throughout the country in the major centres, often many miles from livestock-keeping areas. Even these clinical services to livestock-keepers more or less vanished due to lack of funds under the Structural Adjustment Programs of the early 1980s.

It was in this context that a few NGOs began to experiment with "paravet" projects. These are community-level services based on the Chinese barefoot-doctor model. Although illegal, the approach spread rapidly, especially in the more arid northern part of the country, largely invisible to the veterinary department. At about the same time, international donors were encouraging the veterinary department to set up veterinary privatization schemes in which government vets would be encouraged to establish private practices with an interest-free loan. While initially unpopular, Kenyan vets gradually realized that privatization schemes offered the only job opportunities for veterinary graduates, no longer being employed by the government, and they regarded the burgeoning community-based services as a threat to both their professional prestige and their ability to make a living by charging for their services. The situation boiled over in January 1998 when the Kenyan Vet Board published a letter in the national press denouncing community-based services as illegal and threatening legal action against anyone involved in them.

The government realized they had to do something to resolve the situation. It was clearly not realistic to establish private veterinary services in the arid northern areas. And although a multi-stakeholder process developed a new policy framework and draft legislation encompassing private vets in the high potential areas and community-based services elsewhere, the veterinary profession has continued to block its progress and the legislation has not yet been passed.

The case study used the RAPID Framework to examine how factors in the political context, evidence and links have evolved over the last 20 years, and why the evidence was somehow never sufficient to convince veterinary policy-makers to change the law to legalize the community-based services.

How the political context shapes vet services in Kenya

The political context for veterinary services, and in particular, the "climate" for establishing policies to allow community-based services, has fluctuated dramatically over the last 30 years. The move towards professionalization not only removed the vet scouts from the villages where they were providing a useful service but also encouraged veterinary staff to regard themselves as the only people who could treat sick animals. Structural Adjustment Programs then constrained veterinary department budgets to such an extent that they could pay staff fees only, with very little left for services. The Director of Veterinary Services at the time recognized this, and was becoming convinced by the early results of some of the paravet projects of the need for policy reform. Then the realization that their only realistic long-term future lay in privatized services, made the veterinary profession regard community-based services as a threat, rather than a potential ally. A new Director of Veterinary Services appointed at this time, previously head of the vet school and never actually in practice, was very concerned to ensure the ethical integrity of the profession, and opposed the idea of community-based, or para-professional services. Nevertheless, community-based services continued to expand in the more arid parts of the country, and eventually into marginal areas where newly trained vets were trying to set up private practices. Their growing concern at what they perceived to be a threat to their livelihoods led to the Kenya Vet Board letter in the press. The multi-stakeholder process to develop new policies and legislation that included input from the veterinary profession, vet school, government and NGOs involved in community-based services, was very successful and resulted in draft policies and legislation agreed by all parties. But leadership in Kenyan veterinary bodies changes annually, and the new leadership no longer supports the new policies, so has blocked adoption of the new legislation that would put them into practice.

Evidence . . . to no avail

Evidence from formal research seems to have played a relatively minor role in the evolution of animal health policies in Kenya. International research and discourse about service provision (the Chinese barefoot-vet model), participation and indigenous technology inspired NGOs such as the Intermediate Technology Development Group (ITDG) to test community-based services in Kenya in the mid-1980s. It also stimulated much interest at the World Bank, which undertook some research into paravet programs around the same time. The ITDG projects were established as an action-research program to develop and test the approach, and if they proved the case, to use the results to promote a climate in which they could be replicated more widely.

ITDG gathered much systematic information, both about the need for livestock services in rural areas, and about the value and impact of the new community-based services that were established. Some was published, but much more was shared informally through workshops and seminars and very little reached the government. The only formal research into alternative forms of animal health services in Kenya was commissioned as part of the multi-stakeholder process. The Hubl study was undertaken by a team including members from the Department of Veterinary Medicine at the University of Nairobi, the Ministry of Livestock, and a well-respected international consultant after which the study was named (Hubl, Gathuma, & Kajume 1998) The project involved a series of studies and multi-stakeholder workshops in various parts of the country, and provided convincing evidence of the need and value of community-based services.

Links . . . with lapses

Shortly after setting up its first decentralized animal health projects, ITDG organized the first of what were to become annual "vets' workshops", which became the focus of a network of people involved in paravet projects. A conscious effort was made at the start to invite senior government veterinary staff to participate, to convince them of the value of the approach. Many NGO and bilateral project staff who were already involved in, or who wanted to start decentralized animal health projects, were keen to join the network, and it increasingly focused on practical issues. While this contributed to the rapid spread of the approach across northern Kenya, it neglected to involve senior government policymakers. Dr Julius Kajume then Provincial Head of Veterinary Services, heard about one of these workshops by accident. He checked with the national Director of Veterinary Services in Nairobi, and was instructed to attend the workshop, tell the participants it was illegal, and close it down. Instead, he became convinced of the value of the approach and persuaded the Director to allow the projects to continue. So paravet projects continued to spread across northern Kenya, deliberately ignored by the Director of Veterinary Services, until the publication of the Kenya Vet Board (KVB) letter brought matters to a head, and he was forced to do something about it. At that point, Dr Kajume, now Deputy Director of Veterinary Services, persuaded the Director to support the process of multi-stakeholder workshops and commission the Hubl study that led to the development of a new policy framework.

When does evidence influence policy?

It seems in the case of animal health policy in Kenya, the political context was more important then anything else, fluctuating between moderately supportive to downright hostile. While convincing for people directly involved in the projects, the practical evidence of the value of the new services became increasingly invisible to policy-makers as the ITDG paravet network lost its policy edge and ITDG's workshops and publications were aimed at practitioners rather than policy-makers. Professional sensitivities, personalities and personal relationships were at least as important as any formal relationships and structures. The Director of Veterinary Services in Kenya more or less controls policy development and implementation, and successive directors through most of the period were more influenced by donors promoting privatization and by disgruntled veterinarians, than by people supporting decentralized services. The crisis caused by the KVB letter in 1998 clearly provided a tipping point, or policy window when something had to happen. Dr Kajume, the movement's key champion in government, was discovered only by accident. When he attended the workshop on paravet, he had instructions from his superior to close it down. But livestock keepers and field vet staff demonstrated the system's value and he became a strong proponent of community-based vet services. The final multi-stakeholder process, which included collaborative policy research by a team credible to all sides and wide-ranging discussions, generated the new policy framework, which may soon be adopted.

Results from this and the other studies seem to indicate that research-based and other forms of evidence are more likely to contribute to evidence-based policy only if:

1. the evidence fits within the political and institutional limits and pressures of policy-makers and resonates with their assumptions, or if sufficient pressure is exerted to challenge them
2. the evidence is credible and convincing, providing practical solutions to current policy problems, and is packaged to attract policy-makers' interest

3. researchers and policy-makers share common networks, trust each other, communicate honestly, and represent the interests of all stakeholders and communicate effectively.

These three conditions are rarely met in practice. Although researchers and practitioners can control the credibility of their evidence and ensure they interact with and communicate well with policy-makers, they often have limited capacity to influence the political context within which they work. Resources are also limited, and researchers and practitioners need to make difficult choices about what they can–and cannot–realistically achieve. By making more informed, strategic choices, researchers can maximize their chances of policy influence.

A PRACTICAL FRAMEWORK

An interesting thing about the RAPID framework is how well it maps onto real-life activities. As shown in Figure 2, the political context sphere maps onto politics and policy-making, evidence onto the processes of research, learning and thinking, and links maps onto networking, the media and advocacy. Even the overlapping areas map onto recognizable activities. The intersection of the political context and evidence represents the process of policy analysis–the study of how to implement, and the likely impact of specific policies. The overlap between evidence and links is the process of academic discourse through publications and conferences; the area between links and political context is the world of campaigning and lobbying. The area in the middle–the bulls-eye–is where there is a convergence of convincing evidence providing a practical solution to a current policy problem, which is supported by and brought to the attention of policy-makers by actors in all three areas. And it is here that there is likely to be the most immediate link between evidence and policy.

So, if you are a researcher, policy-maker or development practitioner with the desire to promote a particular policy you need to know about:

- the external environment that might influence how people think or behave: who are the key external actors? what is their agenda? and how do they influence the political context?

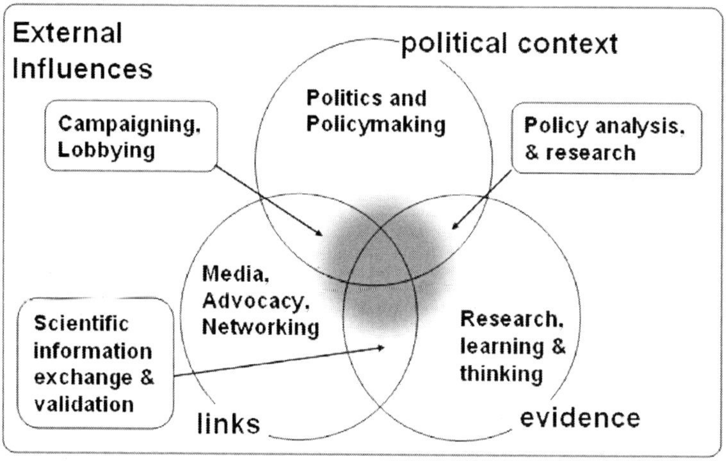

Figure 2: A Practical Framework

- the political context you are working in: is there political interest in change? is there room for manoeuvre? how do policy-makers perceive the problem?
- the evidence you have, or could get: is there enough of it? is it convincing? is it relevant? is it practically useful? are the concepts familiar or new? does it need re-packaging?
- and the links that exist to bring the evidence to the attention of policy makers: who are the key organizations and individuals? are there existing networks to use? what's the best way to transfer the information: face-to-face or through the media or campaigns?

But understanding the context, evidence and links is just the first part of the process. Our case studies also identify a number of practical things that researchers need to do to influence policy and practice, and how to do them:

- In the political context arena you need to get to know the policy-makers, identify friends and foes, prepare for regular policy opportunities and look out for policy windows. One of the best ways is to work with policy-makers through commissions, and establish an approach that combines a strategic focus on current issues with the ability to respond rapidly to unexpected opportunities.
- Make sure your evidence is credible. This has much more to do with your long-term reputation than the scientific credibility of an indi-

vidual piece of research. Provide practical solutions to policy problems in familiar language and concepts. Action-research using pilot projects to generate legitimacy seems to be particularly powerful.

- Make the most of the existing links by getting to know the other actors, working through existing networks and building coalitions and partnerships. Identify the key individuals who can help. You need people who can network with others, mavens to absorb and process information, and good salespeople who can convince the sceptics. You may also need to use informal "shadow networks" as well as more formal channels.

With the benefit of hindsight, distance and the results of this study, it is possible to suggest some changes in what might have been done to accelerate the process of animal health reform in Kenya. ITDG should have made more effort to understand the political context–the legal and policy framework, the key actors, their attitudes and influences, and other reform processes. The project should have involved policy-makers from the start, especially non-veterinary staff, and parliamentarians, and encouraged government staff, especially those opposed to the idea, to visit Community Animal Health Workers schemes and learn about them at first-hand. More empirical data to counter the fears of critics and convince policy-makers, and greater efforts to get to know the key players–the Director and Deputy Directors of Veterinary Services in Nairobi–and figure out how best to influence them, might have been more effective than working with like-minded organizations. Work to convince the bilateral and multilateral donors–who were promoting the privatization schemes–might also have helped convince them to support, and encourage Kenyan policy-makers to support, the decentralized service approach for more arid parts of the country.The RAPID approach to maximize the policy influence of research is summarized in Table 1.

Table 1: How to influence policy and practice[3] (Young and Court 2005)

What you need to know	What you need to do	How to do it
Political Context: • Who are the policy-makers? • Is there policy-maker demand for new ideas? • What are the sources / strengths of resistance? • What is the policy-making process? • What are the opportunities and timing for input into formal processes?	• Get to know the policy-makers, their agendas and their constraints. • Identify potential supporters and opponents. • Prepare for opportunities in regular policy processes. • Look out for unexpected policy windows.	• Work with the policy-makers. • Seek commissions. • Line up research programs with high-profile policy events. • Reserve resources to be able to move quickly to respond to policy windows. • Allow sufficient time & resources.
Evidence: • What is the current theory? • What are the prevailing narratives? • How divergent is the new evidence? • What sort of evidence will convince policy-makers?	• Establish credibility over the long term. • Provide practical solutions to problems. • Establish legitimacy. • Build a convincing case and present clear policy options. • Package new ideas in familiar theory or narratives. • Communicate effectively.	• Build up programmes of high-quality work. • Action-research and pilot projects to demonstrate benefits of new approaches. • Use participatory approaches to help with legitimacy & implementation. • Clear strategy for communication from start. • Face-to-face communication.
Links: • Who are the key stakeholders in the policy discourse? • What links and networks exist between them? • Who are the intermediaries and what influence do they have? • Whose side are they on?	• Get to know the other stakeholders. • Establish a presence in existing networks. • Build coalitions with like-minded stakeholders. • Build new policy networks.	• Partnerships between researchers, policy-makers and communities. • Identify key networkers and salespeople. • Use informal contacts.

External Influences:		
• Who are main international actors in the policy process? • What influence do they have? • What are their aid priorities? • What are their research priorities and mechanisms?	• Get to know the donors, their priorities and constraints. • Identify potential supporters, key individuals and networks. • Establish credibility. • Keep an eye on donor policy and look out for policy windows.	• Develop extensive background on donor policies. • Orient communications to suit donor priorities and language. • Try to work with the donors and seek commissions. • Contact (regularly) key individuals.

PUTTING RAPID INTO PRACTICE

In early 2004, ODI ran a workshop for stakeholders in a project aiming to improve access to groundwater for poor farmers in India. Groundwater management falls within the remit of three sectoral policies in India–water, watersheds and forestry. The three sectors have a historical legacy of poor coordination that results in poor implementation on the ground. Many of the policy measures are based on narratives with no science base, including the strong belief among policy-makers that planting trees protects water resources. Political considerations and vested interests create resistance to improved management of land and water conservation measures in watershed projects. The project faced the dual challenge of developing new policy recommendations, and overcoming this resistance to new approaches.

A wide range of researchers, policy-makers and practitioners were invited to the workshop. They used the RAPID framework to develop a new strategy for the final phase of the project. Rather than recommend further research, this strategy emphasized the evidence they had already generated from pilot project sites and used existing links and networks to convince key policy-makers of the need to change their policies.

Specific activities included:

- engaging with the key policy-makers and determining how best to convince them
- capitalizing on political opportunities offered by the new government and bilateral projects
- taking policy-makers to visit the research/demonstration project sites

Groundwater in India Project Workshop participants (photo by John Young)

- collaborating more closely with national programmes
- arranging workshops, seminars and meetings with key stakeholders
- generating appropriate communication materials.

But doing all of these things requires a wide range of skills beyond those required for the research itself. Researchers who want to be good policy entrepreneurs also need to be:

- Storytellers: Practitioners, bureaucrats and policy-makers often articulate and make sense of complex realities through simple stories. Though sometimes profoundly misleading, there is no doubt that narratives are incredibly powerful.
- Networkers: Policy-making usually takes place within communities of people who know each other and interact. If you want to influence policy-makers, you need to join their networks.
- Engineers: There is often a huge gap between what politicians and policy-makers say they are doing and what actually happens on the ground. Researchers need to work not just with the senior level policy-makers, but also with the "street-level bureaucrats".
- Fixers: Policy-making is essentially a political process. Although you don't need to be a Rasputin or Machiavelli, successful policy

Figure 3: Policy Entrepreneurs

entrepreneurs need to know how to operate in a political environment–when to make your pitch, to whom and how.

There are a wide range of well known and often straightforward tools that can provide powerful insights and help to maximize your chances of impact on policy which are summarized in *Tools for Policy Impact: A Handbook for Researchers* (Start 2004). These include ODI's RAPID framework that can help you to understand the context you are working in and the Policy Entrepreneur Questionnaire (Table 1) to figure out what you are good at. Other useful tools to help to understand the policy context include Stakeholder Analysis, Forcefield Analysis, Write-shops, Policy-Mapping and Political Context Mapping. There is a wide set of research tools–from case studies to action research–that can help generate new or better evidence to support your case. The key communications questions are: Whom do I want to convince? What do I want them to do? What will convince them? What relevant material do I have? A Strength Weaknesses, Opportunities and Threats (SWOT) analysis can help focus a communications strategy on the key messages and targets, and using the media can help you to reach a wide audience. Many tools have also been developed by organizations involved in lobbying, advocacy and campaigning for change that will benefit the poor.

CONCLUSIONS

While policy processes remain complex and context specific, an improved understanding of the role of evidence in policy-making and the application of some simple well-known communication and policy advocacy tools can greatly increase the impact of development research on policy and practice. This is demonstrated dramatically in the Tanzania case where household disease surveys in rural areas led to health service reforms and an enormous reduction in infant mortality.

The RAPID Framework provides both an analytical tool and a practical framework to help researchers, policy-makers and practitioners decide what to do to maximize the chance that research or the results of pilot projects do influence policy and practice, and that policies are evidence-based.

There is a growing body of experience in this area, which provides much useful information and advice to researchers wishing to improve the policy impact of their work. Of particular note are the recent Policy Impact Study by IDRC (IDRC 2004) and the work by the International Food Policy Research Institute (IFPRI) on the impact of agricultural research on poverty (IFPRI 1996).

Much more information about ODI's research and practical work in this area, and links to related work by other organizations is available on the RAPID website as www.odi.org.uk/rapid.

Notes

1. For information on RAPID research and practical projects, see: www.odi.org.uk/rapid
2. This was based on and remains similar to the OECD definition: "creative work undertaken on a systematic basis in order to increase the stock of knowledge, including knowledge of man, culture and society, and the use of this stock of knowledge to devise new applications" (OECD 1981).
3. Policy Entrepreneur Questionnaire

References

Clay EJ and Schaffer BB. 1984. *Room for manoeuvre: an exploration of public policy in agricultural and rural development.* London: Heinemann Educational Books. p.192.

Court J and Young J. 2003. Bridging research and policy: insights from 50 case studies, ODI Working Paper 213.

______. 2004. Bridging research and policy in international development: context, evidence and links. *IN:* Stone D and Maxwell S (eds). *Bridges across boundaries: global knowledge networks and international development.* London: Routledge. PP 18-36.

Crewe E and Young J. 2002 Bridging research and policy: context, evidence and links. ODI Working Paper No 173, Available at www.odi.org. .

de Vibe M, Hovland I and Young J. 2002. Bridging research and policy: an annotated bibliography. ODI Working Paper 174.

Garret JL and Islam Y. 1998. Policy research and the policy process: do the twain ever meet? *Gatekeeper Services* no 74. International Institute for Environment and Development.

Gladwell M. 2000. *The tipping point: how little things can make a big difference.* London: Little, Brown & Company.

Haas EB. 1991. *When knowledge is power: three models of change in international organizations* Berkeley, California: University of California Press .

Hubl Dr K., Gathuma, Prof J.M. and Kajume, Dr J.K. (1998) *Improved Delivery of Animal Health Services in Kenya, Volume 1*, Ministry of Agriculture and Rural Development, Nairobi, Kenya.

IDRC. 2004. IDRC in the public policy process: a strategic evaluation of the influence of research on public policy. http://web.idrc.ca/en/ev-26606-201-1-DO_TOPIC.html.

IFPRI. 1996. Research theme on the impact of agricultural research on poverty (IARP). http://www.ifpri.org/themes/iarp.htm.

Keeley J and Scoones I. 2003. Understanding environmental policy processes in Africa: cases from Ethiopia, Mali and Zimbabwe. London: Earthscan Publications.

Kingdon JW. 1984. Agendas, alternatives, and public policies. New York: HarperCollins.

Lindquist Evert A. 2003. Discerning policy influence: framework for a strategic evaluation of IDRC-supported research. International Development Research Centre (IDRC), Canada. http://www.idrc.ca.

Mattelart A and Mattelart M. 1998. Theories of communication: a short introduction. London: Sage.

Neilson S. 2001. Knowledge utilisation and public policy processes: a literature review. Evaluation Unit, IDRC, Ottawa, Canada.

Neilson S and Smutylo T. 2004. The TEHIP "Spark": planning and managing health resources at the district level. A Report on TEHIP and its Influence on Public Policy, Final Report, Evaluation Unit, IDRC, Canada.

OECD. 1981. The measurement of scientific and technical activities: proposed standard practice for surveys of research and experimental development (Frascati Manual). Paris: OECD.

Pross P. 1986. Group politics and public policy. Toronto: Oxford University Press.

RAWOO. 2001. Utilization of research for development cooperation: linking knowledge production to development policy and practice, Publication no. 21.

Sabatier P and Jenkins-Smith HC. 1999. The advocacy coalition framework: an assessment. *IN:* Sabatier P (ed). *Theories of the policy process.* Boulder, Colorado: Westview Press.

Start H and Hovland I. 2004. *Tools for policy impact: a handbook for researchers.* London: ODI.

Stone D, Maxwell S and Keating M. 2001. Bridging Research and Policy: an international workshop. Warwick, UK, July 2001.

Sutton R. 1999. The policy process: an overview. ODI Working Paper 118.

Weiss CH. 1977. Research for policy's sake: the enlightenment function of social research. *Policy Analysis* 3 (4): pp 531–545.

Williamson J. 1996. Decoding advertisements. *IN:* Marris P and Thornham S (eds). *Media studies: a reader.* Edinburgh: Edinburgh University Press.

Young J, Kajume J and Wanyama J. 2003. Animal health care in Kenya: the road to community-based animal health service delivery. ODI Working Paper 214.

Young J and Court C. 2005. Bridging research and policy in international development: an analytical and practical framework. RAPID Briefing Paper No 1.

Chapter Four

CONTEXT MATTERS—THE INFLUENCE OF IDRC-SUPPORTED RESEARCH ON POLICY PROCESSES[1]

Fred Carden

ABSTRACT

The strengthening of research centres is crucial to the sustainability of research. Researchers are important, but without a "home" and support base, it is very hard for an individual researcher to make a significant contribution. Context is important and an analysis of 22 IDRC-supported projects reveals that policy windows range from being wide open (where there is clear demand for the research in government and among policy-makers) to fully closed (where there is government disinterest or even hostility) to the ideas behind the research. However, there is also room to manoeuvre, and over time projects may find ways to open previously closed policy windows in the context of the decision process. Evidence from the case studies examined here suggests that the relationship between research and decision processes are complex and dynamic and should be factored into project planning, monitoring and evaluation.

INTRODUCTION

The idea of creating a direct link between research and policy influence is still controversial to many researchers, who feel quite strongly that research should not be limited to and directed by the demands of a society, but that more is accomplished when research is unfettered and free to follow its own directions. This is a valid position, and free research should be an important part of research in any field.

At the same time, research guided by and focused on the development needs of a society is equally legitimate. As the then Minister of

Environment in Indonesia put it, "Here, we have to build the boat and sail it at the same time." (personal communication 1989). This situation is further compounded by the fact that social science comes up with contradictory findings and of course, findings do not necessarily hold over time and space. Carol Weiss noted many years ago, ". . . since social scientists acknowledge the fragility and time-and situation-bound character of most research, there are serious questions about what it is that we expect government officials to plug into their decisions." (Weiss 1982).

Several questions arise from this. How does research influence the policy process? How is knowledge used? How do researchers bring ideas to decision-makers? And how do decision-makers get access to ideas?

ASSESSING THE INFLUENCE OF IDRC-SPONSORED RESEARCH ON POLICY

Recognizing that the set of questions outlined above is a complex and multi-faceted set of questions, this paper focuses on one important aspect, that of the contexts in which policy influence takes place. But first, it is useful to look at the background and rationale for that study.

The strategic program document of the International Development Research Centre states that, "IDRC will foster and support the production, dissemination and application of research results leading to policies and technologies that enhance the lives of people in developing countries." (IDRC 2000).

This means that the Centre sees the influence of research on policy processes as an important contribution to development. Because of the diverse nature of IDRC programming—from trade policy research with senior researchers and government decision-makers, to farm-level decision-making in research about community-based natural resources management, and including a variety of other approaches, it has not developed a common language for thinking about influencing policy. So, when we talked about policy influence, we were talking about many different things. We wanted to find out what the Centre meant by policy influence, where the research it has supported has had influence, and what are the key factors in that influence.

The study began with an extensive literature review (Neilson 2001), which, while completed several years ago now, remains an important documentation of the literature in this domain as it pertains to development work.[2] A key point noted in the review is that there were no examples of research on this topic in the developing world until fairly recently. This is the first study initiated with a set of case studies and a primary focus on the use of research for policy influence in the South. There are now several other studies underway, notably at the Overseas Development Institute (ODI)[3] in the United Kingdom and also through a project of the Global Development Network (GDN)[4].

It is important to clarify that this study focused on policy *influence,* not policy *impact.* In our view, while external agents such as a donor may have an influence, only those who work and live within a system create impact. By the time impact occurs, anything IDRC may have done is so mixed in with so many other things that it is impossible to tease out the Centre's impact—nor is it desirable that IDRC see itself as having an impact. Its role is to support the research process, to challenge and introduce new ideas. The IDRC role does not include the uptake of those ideas nor does IDRC have to live with the results. In terms of measurement, it is impossible to measure impact. Rather, IDRC is interested on the influence of its programs by examining what has happened in the projects it supports, which may have changed how the researchers behave or what they do, so that over time they may have an impact within their own systems.[5]

The intention then, was to find out what had happened in IDRC around policy influence. To do this, we developed a framework of what we thought policy influence was, in very general terms (Lindquist 2001). This framework, developed in consultation with IDRC staff, identified three different types of influence that were explored in the project. The three types were:

1. expanding policy capacities
2. broadening policy horizons
3. affecting policy regimes

These indicate that policy *influence* of research goes far beyond changing policies themselves. It includes building the capacities of those involved—both researchers and decision-makers—in using research in the decision process. It also includes expanding what we look at in the policy and research processes; knowing that policy is not usually made within a narrow domain of study, researchers need to have a much broader understanding of society and must bring other factors to bear on the findings they are putting forward.

We used a case-study approach, developing a set of guidelines and a common framework that was used to develop 25 rich case studies of IDRC-supported activities that were thought to have had an influence on policy, delimited here as public policy only (Carden 2004). Of these 25 case studies, 22 were completed in time to include in the cross-case analysis.

The case studies were selected from a sample of projects suggested by staff. They were projects where the staff asserted that there had been an influence on policy of some sort. This positive sample was chosen because we wanted to understand the nature of influence; we did not want to find out overall how successful IDRC has been in obtaining influence. The case studies covered the regions in which the Centre works and the domains of work it supports. In many cases, they were projects with a significant history, either from more than a decade ago or else projects that had been supported through several phases of activity.

The first step was for staff and researchers supported by the Centre to analyse these case studies collectively in a series of workshops[6]. Out of these initial consultations, the project team then developed a set of key issues of most importance to IDRC and its partners, and used those to conduct an in-depth, cross-case analysis. It is this that forms the basis for the discussion below.

The findings

The categories for analysis that emerged from the workshops with staff and researchers were defined around how the Centre supports research and how that research is delivered when policy influence is at issue. Three main categories emerged where findings were explored:

1. what we do
2. where we work
3. how we work[7]

What we do refers to the guiding values and principles behind IDRC support. Concretely, that is reflected in the nature of IDRC inputs, the intent of the research and the role that IDRC assumed in the relationship (as funding agency, technical adviser, levelling the playing field, and so on). These issues were important because they reflect the values that guide IDRC work as a central factor in understanding the nature of successes and failures.

Where we work refers to the environment in which the research was undertaken. As is often noted, context is key. Without understanding the environment, it is difficult to influence it. One can look at environment and its effects in many different ways. Here we took a look at the environment particularly from the perspective of how the policy and knowledge processes intersect. Where we work is the central theme of the discussion in this chapter.

How we work is the final category of analysis. By this, we refer to what happens in the projects themselves. By making use of the network modality for example, IDRC achieves certain types of successes.

General conclusions drawn from the analysis

First, there are no "best practices" when it comes to research influencing public policy. Rather, it is about the confluence of factors that interact in a variety of ways leading towards—or away from—influence. These factors, outlined later, work together. Each of them is dynamic and the relationships among them are dynamic. What this suggests is that policy influence requires an on-going awareness of how the factors evolve, an assessment of their relative importance over time, and changes in strategies according to how the situation is unfolding. This is small comfort to those who seek a simple planning tool, but it is reflective of the reality of policy influence. As Jantsch (1981) put it so succinctly, "Reality *is* complex and evolution manifests in the increase of this complexity. Greater complexity (which is not the same as greater complicatedness), therefore means a more realistic attitude taken to planning."

The second general conclusion is that depending on when and from what perspective they are viewed, projects can be both successes and failures. The purpose of the strategic evaluation was not to assess the overall success or failure of each project but to look at them through the lens of whether and how they had an influence on public policy.

The third important point is that policy influence is a means, not an end. This may seem obvious, but it is easy enough to forget to look upon success at influencing policy as the end. As soon as we do this we lose sight of our objectives and begin to build what we do around the intent to influence policy rather than at using influence as a tool to support development. The objective towards which the IDRC-supported research projects are working is an improvement in the lives and living conditions of people in developing countries. Influencing public policy is one of the practices in which these projects and researchers engage in order to enhance their contributions.

The fourth point is that relationships are critical. No matter what systems are in place or how well or poorly governance systems function, the relationships that the researchers have with decision-makers play a key role in their opportunities to influence. These are more than personal relationships. They are built on professional reputation, quality of work, the experience of past efforts to provide policy advice, and the work of the researchers or research groups over time.

A final overall comment on the analysis is that the findings need to be understood in the context of the nature of relationships between IDRC and its projects. The Centre operates on the philosophy that local ownership of research processes and research findings is critical. Therefore the support the Centre offers is intended to provide the impetus for locally driven research and locally generated use of the research. The findings we present emerge from these conditions. As noted in another analysis of these case studies, " . . . providing support to the research community to engage with policy does not always assume specific linkages; but rather over time, builds ... capacity to engage." (Carden and Neilson 2005).

CONTEXT: WHERE WE WORK

Context matters. This is not surprising and is an important element of consideration in most of what is done in development and development research. The functioning of systems and the development of relationships are central. The nature of the economy, the nature of society—including its political processes of continuity and change—and the nature of change, all play critical roles. Here, we will look at context from two perspectives.

The first is a deeper understanding of the relationship between context and the policy influence undertakings. That is, there are elements of context that are seen as manageable—elements that the project can understand and to which it can respond; elements that can be tracked and mapped over time so that the project uses the conditions as part of building its capacity for influence. This leads us to a discussion of five different contexts that emerged in the 22 case studies. These contexts show how the research project functions, the nature of the research process to be followed and the supporting elements that need to be considered.

The second important aspect of context that remains important is an ability to understand and grasp the situation at play in any policy context. These additional factors do not appear to be consistently related to any of the policy contexts we describe but can play a role in any of them.

Not addressed here is a most obvious factor in any process of change—the severe and sudden change brought on by political, economic, environmental or social turmoil, processes over which IDRC and the researchers it supports, have little or no control and for which they cannot simply adjust what they do. This occurred in very few of our case studies (one example is the Guatemala case), and we recognize of course that this is a factor in the context that cannot be ignored.

Our 22 case studies presented us with five different settings in which policy influence occurred to a greater or lesser degree. These five contexts reflect the level of receptivity of the policy process to the use of research findings, or the integration of researchers into the decision process. More than a simple description of the policy context, the different settings provide insights into what the researchers need to consider as part of their interest in having an influence. The particular context informs the research process about the nature of communication of research findings; it informs about the nature and level of advocacy that is required, about the nature of leadership required of the research team; and finally it informs about what needs to be done to ensure that the policy process has a home in the decision system, or the nature of institutionalization required for this to occur. We will review the key aspects of these features of the research-to-policy process before we describe the characteristics of the five settings in which policy influence occurred.

Research-to-policy process: project advocacy, communication, leadership and institutional structures for implementing policy proposals

The analysis of contextual factors revealed that for IDRC-sponsored research to have some impact on policy-making there should exist either a strong desire among decision-makers for such research, or there should be effective advocacy by project staff for the relevance of the research to policy. If there is weak desire for research among decision-makers, there needs to be strong project advocacy; a strong interest in the research by decision-makers reduces the need for strong promotion of the research. In either of these situations, institutional structures need to be available to implement recommended policies. The level of interest among decision-makers affects the nature of communication. Where there is a high degree of openness to influence, communication is straightforward and requires limited thought by the researchers: they need only to provide the findings and the data for the decision-makers to use. Where there is less openness, more thought needs to be given to the nature and format of communication, as well as to the audiences—indeed, sometimes influence is through other interest groups, not directly with decision-makers. Finally, where there is a high degree of openness to influence, there is generally a home for the policy in the decision system; that is, the decision to be taken about the policy is largely ready to be taken, a group has been designated the responsibility for the decision (and presumably its implementation). However, where the decision-makers are not completely prepared to take a decision, it may well be that there is nowhere in the system where responsibility to take action has been granted. As a consequence, in presenting findings, the research team needs to think about the necessary processes of institutionalization as part of how they present the research; it is not simply a knowledge question but also a question of how to use it that is important. Characterizing these relationships is useful in helping to answer the following questions:

- Should the project focus primarily on knowledge generation to aid a decision process of policy-makers or can it be less constrained in its choice of research areas?
- What type of leadership is demanded of the project?
- What is the nature of the advocacy connected with the research and affecting its potential to influence?

- What is the nature of communications connected with the research and affecting its potential to influence?
- To what extent does the project have to address the implementation of research findings as part of its policy influence objective?

Five contexts—types of relationships between decision-makers' desire for research *and* research project advocacy—are discussed below. In all of these, the factors above each play a slightly different role and take on a different importance. It is also noteworthy that these are dynamic types. With the exception of the first category, projects seldom stay in only one of the categories, but move over time as they achieve more or less success in their efforts to influence. This evolution of cases over the course of project implementation will be discussed later.

1. Clear demand for research from policy-makers

Open window of policy influence. Policy-makers want research results for decision-making purposes and are ready to act on them.

In this context, there is a government desire for knowledge in a decision process. To make an effective contribution, the researchers generally need to have built a relationship of trust with the decision-makers and have a reputation for high-quality research and timeliness. The researchers or research group needs credibility but not necessarily an agenda of their own. Policy-friendly presentation of findings may be less important here, given the policy-makers' intention to act.

There is little or no need to consider institutionalization of the issue as the decision-makers are determined to proceed and are considering how to do so. This is illustrated by the case of the MIMAP (Micro Impact of Macroeconomic and Adjustment Policies) program in Senegal[8]. There, the research group was asked by the government to play a central role in the development of the Poverty Reduction Strategy Paper (PRSP). The research team was brought in because of its reputation and government relationships with the lead researcher, and thus was able to make a significant contribution to a government decision process.

Policy influence was also achieved in the Acacia projects to apply adapted information and communications technologies (ICT) in Africa, and in the information technology (IT) policy development project in Nepal, where IDRC initiatives were responsive to the governments' search for ways to use IT to promote economic growth. Similarly, in Viet Nam, IDRC-funded economic research projects were started at the request of the head of one of the central economic research institutions in the country and they produced results that appeared to serve as a basis for many economic policy decisions in the country[9]. In sum, in cases where decision-makers want the type of research offered by IDRC projects to make policy decisions, the likelihood of impact on policy is high. In this welcoming context, project staff may not need to exert their own efforts on dissemination of research recommendations, nor on advocacy around their findings.

2. Government interest but leadership gap

Partially open window of influence. Policy-makers consider the issue important but do not have the necessary structures or activities in place, through which research recommendations can be implemented.

In this context, the issue is well known to the government, and it is clear that there are public policy implications. But there is no clear decision process in play. Government is not yet taking the lead in determining what to do. In this situation, there is a need—and an opportunity—for the project to play a leadership role. The research team needs to think carefully about its communication strategies with decision-makers. It should also consider the institutional structures that are available to implement the recommendations (or implications) of its research. If there is no system in place to implement the proposed recommendations, the research findings may never be acted upon. The case study of the Tanzania Essential Health Interventions Project (TEHIP) is instructive. The challenge was how, and at what point, to institutionalize the TEHIP tools within the central Ministry of Health. A lack of coordination among the various players in the health sector led to a slowdown of the project after its pilot phase. In the Philippines, the need to increase poverty monitoring in order to address the poverty gap was articulated by the MIMAP researchers; and their work resonated with policy-makers. However, as with TEHIP, the challenge here appeared to be moving beyond the local level contribution and institutionalizing the poverty-monitoring system at the national level. MIMAP-Bangladesh, on the other hand, is an example of successful institutionalization of research activities within government institutions. The project staff worked from the very beginning to train officials in the Bureau of Statistics and in the National Planning Commission in the use of the economic analysis tools, thus placing the weight of the project implementation on the officials' shoulders. Since the staff at one of these institutions in Bangladesh were also involved in designing a national economic development plan as well as the PRSP for the country, they drew on the MIMAP research in formulating these documents.

These and other cases suggest that government interest in research is not a guarantee of its influence on policy. It seems crucial that decision-makers have a plan for implementing the lessons from the research within government structures or current activities. When such a plan is missing the project team may need to demonstrate leadership by working with relevant decision-makers to develop it; for example, they may decide to train government staff, as in the MIMAP-Bangladesh project.

3. *Government interest, resources gap*

Partially open window of policy influence. The government has been working on the issue before and acknowledges the need for such research, but has more pressing priorities and/or a shortage of resources to engage with it.

In this context, the issue addressed by the research is generally well known and is not disputed as a topic of concern. However, leadership clearly resides within the research project, not within the decision-making systems. The government is interested in addressing the issue in the future, or would like to address it now but does not have the resources or has more important priorities to take care of. The links to decision processes are generally weak. In this context the project staff should first of all be concerned with research capacities and especially with *moving the issue up on priority list* of the policy-makers, before thinking about undertaking the research in a resource-scarce policy environment.

An example of a project doing well in such a context is the Environmental Management Development in the Ukraine (EMDU) program. Local researchers had carried out research on water quality long before the IDRC project was initiated. However, the work was under-funded and technologies were out of date. The IDRC project strongly advocated the use of new water-testing technologies and bringing data and evidence to policy formulation on water management. The staff also worked on creating popular support for the project, which helped reinforce policy makers' attention to the research. To make its work practical and advance its implementation, the project offered cheaper technology solutions for environmental testing and trained government officials in maintaining and updating the databases on water quality. In this context, the project played a strong role in advocating the importance of using data and evidence in policy formulation and decision-making, and in bringing forward issues the government saw as important, but for which it did not have the resources.

4. Government neutral, research interest

Partially open window of policy influence. Policy-makers are not interested in the research program but there is a strong research agenda.

In this context, there is no government involvement or interest in the issue, and so a strong research agenda and advocacy are needed to obtain influence. While individuals in the government may know of the issue, it may be controversial or not yet have affected a key political constituency. The research group has to promote the agenda in the policy and public domains and draw attention to the issue. Here, advocacy is central. Further, it is important to communicate and disseminate information about the issue to diverse audiences. It is also important to note that the audiences are diverse; it is not simply a matter of communication to decision-makers but also to those with a range of interests in the issue, groups and individuals who may influence decision-makers in their own ways. The project team has to work on creating even an initial interest in the issue. As in earlier cases, they might also establish the structures to move the issue forward. The potential for failure is high in this environment. A high number of IDRC projects fall into this category. It is worth noting that none of the 22 case studies stayed in this category; they were either somewhat successful in creating the change they sought, thus opening the policy window, or they failed and the policy window closed (see the Table later in this chapter). The high risk is not a reason not to operate in this environment: the issue is recognition of the nature of the environment and the risks that accompany it.

In the case of financing education reform in Guatemala, it was not the government's priority to focus on ethnic and gender differences in educational spending. The country was undergoing political and economic turmoil at the time, recovering from a lengthy and divisive civil conflict and so the priority of the government was to create unity rather than recognize diversity and special needs. This was an essential condition for the research team to address. Without it, however strong their advocacy work, however careful they were with timing of release of their findings, however careful they were in reaching the right people, the message was not in sync with the government's view of its necessary message of the day.

Successful examples of strong advocacy by a project in the face of the lack of government interest are Society for Research and Initiatives for Sustainable Technologies and Institutions (SRISTI) and the Peru Copper Mining project. SRISTI created awareness among policy-makers of the importance of its work and was able to institutionalize its activities through government structures. It accumulated convincing evidence, tailored its appeals to specific decision-makers, and proactively created networking opportunities for government officials and project staff. Similarly, the Peru Copper Mining project was able to influence government and private industry by gathering evidence, building relationships with officials as well as members of the community, and by generating wide publicity. These and other cases indicate that in the context of little or no government interest in the issue, the project should not only produce but also engage in advocacy for implementation.

5. *Research interest, government disinterest*

Closed window of policy influence. Policy-makers are explicitly pursuing other priorities and there is no public interest to change their views.

In this environment, the public policy system is actively disinterested and may be hostile to the issue (while we saw no cases of outright hostility, one can anticipate that strong disinterest leads to hostility over time). The research team must therefore have a strong sense of purpose and a clear recognition that the project is risky from a policy influence point of view. Here, the research team may be ahead of the game, either in terms of the research it is carrying out or in attempting to use research to influence policy in a decision-making system that is closed to external inputs. Where innovation is valued as it is in the research process, it is highly likely that at least some projects will fall into this category. Over time, one could envisage an issue, heretofore ignored or hidden, finding its way to the fore.

A good example of this situation is found in the High Altitude Mining case in Peru. Here, researchers found that mining at high altitudes in Peru adversely affected the health of miners and their families. However, the national Ministry of Health was not receptive to these results, as they challenged the traditional belief that people adapt to living and working at high altitudes. Shortly after the project was completed, the Peruvian government underwent political and economic reforms. This resulted in a new policy agenda and further hampered any kind of influence the research might have had. In addition to decision-makers, the population shared this traditional belief about adaptation to high altitude so there was little opportunity, at least in the short term, to rally public interest that might advocate for change.

Summary

The above analysis suggests that the ideal condition for policy influence is policy-makers' strong interest in research for the purposes of policy creation. However, interest alone is not enough; policy-makers should have structures and procedures to implement research recommendations. Future IDRC-sponsored and other projects may benefit from the analysis of these contextual factors before engaging in action. The project teams should ask: How much interest is there in this type of research among policy-makers? Are there structures and procedures in place that enable policy-makers to implement policy recommendations of the research?

The answers to these questions will inform the project staff about 1) how seriously they should engage in advocacy work for their project, and 2) how much effort they should make to work with policy-makers on implementing policy proposals that stem from research.

THE CASES AND THE CONTEXTS: EVOLUTION OVER TIME

Table 1 below presents the analysis of our 22 case studies that looked at them from the perspective of the environment at the beginning of the project and the environment at the end of the project.

Table 1: Analysis of 22 case studies of IDRC-funded projects by context and over time

Context	At beginning of project	At end of project
1. Clear demand	MIMAP[10]-Senegal Nepal ICTs[11] MIMAP-Viet Nam Acacia[12]-South Africa Acacia-Mozambique Acacia-Uganda	MIMAP-Senegal Nepal ICTs MIMAP-Viet Nam Acacia-South Africa Acacia-Mozambique Acacia-Uganda AFSSRN[13] SRISTI[14]
2. Govt interest, leadership gap	TEHIP[15], Tanzania MIMAP-Bangladesh MIMAP-Philippines LATN[16] G-24[17]	TEHIP, Tanzania MIMAP-Bangladesh MIMAP-Philippines LATN G-24 Copper mining, Peru Greywater re-use, Jordan
3. Govt interest, resources gap	Environmental management, Ukraine (EMDU)	Environmental management, Ukraine (EMDU) Arsaal, Lebanon[18] (local)
4. Govt neutral, research interest	High-altitude mining, Peru ECAPAPA[19] Arsaal, Lebanon AFSSRN SRISTI Greywater re-use, Jordan Copper-mining, Peru Financing Education Reform Water Demand Management, Tunisia	
5. Research interest, government disinterest	Brackish water irrigation, Syria	Brackish water irrigation, Syria Arsaal, Lebanon (national) Financing Education Reform Water Demand Management, Tunisia ECAPAPA High-altitude mining, Peru

Because we started by looking for cases of successful influence in order to better understand processes of influence, not surprisingly, a significant number of the cases (half) fall in the top two categories at the beginning of the research. Again, for the same reason, there was significant movement over time, with four more cases (AFSSRN, SRISTI, Copper-mining in Peru and Greywater re-use in Jordan) moving up into these two categories. What is particularly striking is that no research stayed at the level of an emergent issue (Government neutral, research interest). While this would not hold for pure research, the projects analysed here suggest that where there is intent to influence policy, when you start from a relatively risky position in terms of weak relationships with the decision process, the researchers either find a way to make it more relevant or it falls away from the decision process. Again, this does not reflect the validity of the research enterprise, nor does it reflect on the quality of the research itself. Rather, it reflects the ability of the research team to bring the research idea and issue to the decision table.

One case appears twice in the table, the Arsaal case. This case study looks at a project in the Arsaal region of Lebanon that lies on the eastern side of the Beka'a Valley. The project focussed on local land-use conflicts (e.g., between herders and fruit producers). While the action research was successful in terms of local policy change, as the case notes, the Ministry of Agriculture remains relatively "impervious" to the findings of the research on local land-use issues and focuses its attention on commercial farming issues almost exclusively. This will have some long-terms effects on the permanence of local influence.

Additional contextual factors relevant to policy influence

In addition to these five contexts that can influence decision processes, there are some common factors that cut across all of these, which were found to be important in our case studies. These are factors that neither facilitate nor impede policy influence in themselves, but that do inform the process of influence. These factors are external to the project, relating to the situation in the country and in its decision-making bodies. Therefore, not much can usually be done about these factors, except perhaps to focus work on those countries where fewer external barriers exist and where external facilitating factors are present. These are not dealt with at any length here, but they should still be mentioned as factors that merit further exploration.

1. Stability of relevant decision-making institutions

In several of the case studies, minimal policy influence appears to have been a result of instability in the policy-making structures involved. In most cases this instability became apparent only after research had already been carried out and it was time to implement the recommendations. For example, in the case of the High Altitude Mining project in Peru, budget cuts led to the elimination of the government institute dealing with occupational health risks, which could have lent support to policy proposals based on the project research. While research on health hazards of working in the mountains had been produced, lack of a relevant government agency impeded use of the results.

In another case, in Guatemala, the government went through drastic structural changes, with decision-making powers moving from the executive to the legislative branch. The project staff were not ready for these changes and thus were not able to lobby the new structures. Instability in the national policy-making structures was also a challenge for the research activities of the Latin American Trade Network (LATN), as well as for the Environmental Management Program in Ukraine. However, in the latter case, the project staff were able to overcome these challenges to some extent by addressing their research-based messages to a much wider audience (through TV programs, for example), as well as to more stable governmental structures, including the president of the country. LATN dealt with instability in decision-making structures by working at the third level of the bureaucracy, which was more stable than higher or lower levels of the civil service and where continuity across regimes was assured. These first and second levels of the bureaucracy usually change with each regime change but the third level tends to stay in place and serves as the institutional memory from regime to regime. In some cases, less fluid decision-making structures may be found at regional or local levels. Relying on provincial decision-making structures that appeared to be quite stable was one of the factors in the success of institutionalizing the Poverty Monitoring System in the province of Palawan in MIMAP-Philippines project.

The instability of relevant decision-making structures may be detrimental to policy influence of the IDRC-funded projects. Fortunately, project efforts suggest that it is possible to identify the decision-making structures that are more stable and to focus energies on collaborating with these structures.

2. Capacity of policy-makers to use research

In several cases, and especially in the LATN and G-24 Technical Service Support projects, the policy-makers who were the recipients of the IDRC-funded research had low capacity for research utilization. In the case of LATN, government officials appeared to be unfamiliar with basic concepts of trade negotiations. In the G-24 projects, the finance ministers of the developing countries were initially sceptical of the econometric models generated by the research group. In both cases, the research staff had to devote more attention to basic education of government officials than it had initially planned. In addition, the government officials from developing countries in the case of G-24 were frequently in a position of dependency on IMF/WB funding, and thus tended to be timid and conservative in using research findings to propose changes in international financial policy-making. These examples suggest that in the cases where policy-makers either need basic training before they can benefit from research findings or are torn by competing interests, policy influence may be less pronounced or slower. These factors may need to be considered by project designers. For example, additional time may be allocated early in the project to educate government officials about the basic ideas behind specific research and its relevance to policy. Partnership and collaboration with others may be an essential ingredient for success in working in such a situation.

3. Decentralization versus tight government control

Whether the country has a centralized or decentralized government does not seem to be unequivocally associated with particular policy outcomes. Whether decentralization is a help or a hindrance to policy influence depends on the nature of the project, specifically on whether the project aims to have an effect at the same level at which the decisions on the issue are made. For example, the MIMAP-Philippines project was aimed at institutionalizing poverty-monitoring tools throughout the country. However, this project was conducted under conditions of decentralized responsibility for poverty monitoring and poverty eradication. MIMAP systems of poverty monitoring were successfully instituted in one of the provinces of the Philippines, but project staff encountered difficulties in trying to institutionalize such systems nationwide, since the relevant national institutions did not feel they had the authority to dictate to the provinces. In the TEHIP project, for example, the government was interested in promoting decentralized decision-making by health workers at the district and local levels. The pilot project carried out through IDRC was valuable for learning how to do so. Similarly, in the case of the Acacia projects, the governments were interested in using IT to facilitate the decentralization of decision-making and the projects were quite successful in helping them. The projects provided tools that could support the process. Over all, it appears that when the projects were trying to exert policy influence in line with the government decision-making structure, they were able to have greater policy impact.

Tight central government control over the country and over research priorities can be either beneficial or detrimental for policy influence, depending on the nature of the project. It appears to be beneficial for national level policy effects when the research is aligned with country national interests as perceived by the central authority. Thus, economic studies carried out by IDRC-trained researchers in Viet Nam were of great interest to the government as it strove to re-orient itself from a central to a market-based economy and needed well-researched economic reform proposals to attract donor funding. As a result, major research centres in the country supported IDRC-funded research. The results of the studies were already in the air in the policy-making arena. On the other hand, in Syria, with its equally strong central control of decision-making, the focus of the IDRC-funded project to explore the possibility of supplementing irrigation schemes with brackish water was not a priority for the government. Even though an internationally renowned research institution carried out the project, the research results were never utilized for policy purposes.

In sum, it appears that IDRC-funded projects have a chance at policy influence when the intended level of influence corresponds to the decision-making structure in the country. If the project aims to have a national effect while the decisions are made locally, policy effect is less likely. Instead of pre-planning the level of policy influence in IDRC projects, it may be useful to conduct some initial investigations into what level of policy influence is actually possible in a given case.

4. Special opportunities in countries in transition

Two research projects were in countries whose institutions were in transition from communism. The projects on environmental management in Ukraine and on economic restructuring in Viet Nam were effective not only in generating policy-relevant research and affecting policy, but also in teaching local researchers and policy-makers new approaches to inter-institutional collaboration and decision-making. These countries were undergoing transition to more liberal approaches to governance (Ukraine) and economy (Viet Nam), and thus were attuned to new ways of functioning. For example, IDRC partners in Ukraine observed that IDRC staff had brought with them a new culture of management characterized by open information sharing, consultation with all relevant stakeholders before decision-making, and basing decisions on research evidence. It appears that in countries that are undergoing transitions, IDRC-funded research has a potential to affect not only *what* policies are made but also *the way* they are made and the way research is utilized.

5. Economic pressures on the government

In most of the cases where the government expressed a clear need for and an interest in the project, it was responding to economic pressure. For example, MIMAP projects appeared to be successful largely because there was pressure on the governments to produce Poverty Reduction Strategy Papers in order to receive donor funding, and the data generated by the projects could be used for the PRSPs. Similarly, in Viet Nam the politicians needed to attract donor funding and thus were interested in producing feasible economic proposals. Finally, in Acacia projects and in the Nepal ICT policy development case, the governments felt the need to develop their economy and saw ICT development as an effective strategy. These examples suggest that the likelihood of project influence is higher if it is linked to the economic needs of the country. When this is not the case, the project has to be able to undertake advocacy work to prove its worth and significance to policy-makers. SRISTI is a good example of such a process, as described in the section on relationships.

CONCLUDING REMARKS

This study of research and its relationship to decision-making and context is a mere snapshot of a key part of a very complex—and changing—process that is a crucial component in all research-to-policy processes. How a research team deals with the various relationships with those involved in this process will be affected by their values and operating principles, but they will have to deal with the decision environment in some way. The purpose here was to outline a way to think strategically about change and how to maximize opportunities for influence.

What is made clear by this examination of 22 cases of efforts to influence policy is that policy influence itself is a complex and changing process. There is no single factor that is key; there is no single condition that is essential. Rather, there is interplay of capacities, contexts and conditions that we must map and monitor on an on-going basis if we are to understand how to use knowledge to inform policy. As policy windows open and close, we need to be aware of these changes in order to seize opportunities.

Obviously, all is not chance and circumstance. This investigation looks at ways researchers can start looking at efforts to influence public policy then try to situate their work and assess what should be done if they are to increase the potential of their results reaching the policy process. Of course, the findings of this investigation come from just 22 specific cases, which means they are not automatically universally applicable.

What this study offers is a framework for considering the influence of research on policy and decision processes for planning, monitoring and evaluation. It is a tool that we think can be used throughout the process of trying to influence policy processes. But it also needs to be tested, refined, revised and strengthened, through use in a variety of settings.

Notes

1. The views expressed are those of the author and do not necessarily reflect the views of IDRC.
2. This and other documents related to the study are available at www.idrc.ca/evaluation/policy.
3. See the website of the RAPID project at: www.odi.org.uk

4. See the website of the Bridging Research and Policy project of GDN at: www.gdnet.org
5. For a more detailed discussion see: Earl, Carden and Smutylo. 2000. *Outcome mapping*. Ottawa: IDRC. Chapter 1.
6. Odilia Maessen, Influence of research on public policy, Workshop #1, Johannesburg 8–9 November 2002; Odilia Maessen, Influence of research on public policy, Workshop #2, Montevideo, 5–6 December 2002; Odilia Maessen, Influence of research on public policy, Workshop #3, Bangkok, 13–14 January 2003; and Evaluation Unit, Cases, Concepts and Connections: the influence of research on public policy, Ottawa, 24–25 March 2003. All reports are available at www.idrc.ca/evaluation/policy.
7. I would like to acknowledge the important contribution to the design of the analytical approach by Professor Carol H Weiss, and to the analysis by Professor Weiss and her researchers at the Harvard Graduate School of Education: Svetlana Karuskina-Drivdale and Shahram Paksima.
8. This, and all other cases, can be found on the Policy Study page of our website at: www.idrc.ca/evaluation/policy. The full set of case studies is listed at the end of this paper.
9. It is difficult to trace with certainty the effect of specific projects on policy decisions in Viet Nam, since political decision-making is an opaque and secretive process.
10. MIMAP: Micro Impacts of Macro Adjustment Policies (more on MIMAP-Senegal can be found in Chapter Ten of this book).
11. ICT: Information and Communication Technologies.
12. Acacia: A series of Information and Communication Technology for Development programs.
13. AFSSRN: Asian Fisheries Social Science Research Network.
14. SRISTI: Society for Research and Initiatives for Sustainable Technologies and Institutions.
15. TEHIP: Tanzania Essential Health Interventions Program.
16. LATN: Latin American Trade Network.
17. G-24: The Group of 24 developing countries designated by the larger Group of 77 developing countries to represent them on international financial reform issues.
18. Arsaal: Project for sustainable improvement of marginal land in Arsaal, Lebanon.
19. ECAPAPA: Eastern and Central Africa Program for Agricultural Policy Analysis.

References

Carden F. 2004. Issues in assessing the policy influence of research, *International Social Science Journal* No. 179 (March):135–151.

______ and Neilson S. 2005. Confluence and influence: building policy capacities in research networks. *IN:* Stone, D and Simon M (eds). *Bridges across boundaries: global knowledge networks and international development.* Milton Park: Routledge.

Earl Sarah, Carden Fred and Smutylo Terry. 2000. *Outcome mapping: building learning and reflection into development programs.* Ottawa: IDRC.

Global Development Network (GDN). Bridging research and policy project. www.gdnet.org.

International Development Research Centre. 2000. Corporate strategy and program framework 2000–2005. Ottawa: IDRC.

Jantsch Erich. 1981. *The self-organizing universe.* NY: Pergamon.

Overseas Development Institute. Research and policy in development (RAPID) website. www.odi.org.uk.

Lindquist E. 2001. Discerning policy influence: framework for a strategic evaluation of IDRC-supported research. Ottawa: IDRC. Available at www.idrc.ca/evaluation/policy.

Neilson S. 2001. IDRC-supported Research and its Influence on Public Policy. Knowledge utilization and public policy processes: a literature review. Ottawa: IDRC. Available at www.idrc.ca/evaluation/policy.

Weiss CH, Karuskina-Drivdale S and Paksima S. 2004. IDRC-supported research and its influence on public policy: preliminary results from a cross-case analysis. Harvard Graduate School of Education. Report to the Evaluation Unit, IDRC, Canada.

Weiss CH. 1982. Knowledge utilization in decision-making: reflections on the terms of the discussion. *Research in Sociology of Education and Socialization* Vol. 3: 21 and 17–41.

Case studies

All case studies are available on-line at http://www.idrc.ca/evaluation/policy.

Ackello-Ogutu Chris. 2003. *ECAPAPA Case Study.*

Argueta B. 2003. *Financing education reforms in Guatemala.*

Brooks D. 2002. *Case study of sustainable improvement of marginal land in Arsaal, Lebanon: Phases I and II.*

Burton L. 2003. *The development of Nepal's IT policy: a case study.*

______. 2003. *Society for Research and Initiatives for Sustainable Technologies and Institutions (SRISTI): A case study.*

Gillespie B. 2004. *Water demand management in Syria: the case of brackish water.*

Loayza F. 2003. *The cases of high altitude and mining, and the impact of copper mining on water resources in southern Peru.*

Lyzogub I. 2002. *Environmental management development in Ukraine.*

Macadar L. 2003. *Latin American Trade Network (LATN).*

Neilson S and Smutylo T. 2004. *The TEHIP "spark": planning and managing health resources at the district level.*

Ofir Z. 2002. *Acacia: The Case of Uganda.*

______. 2002. *Acacia: The Case of South Africa.*

______. 2002. *Acacia: The Case of Mozambique.*

Pomeroy R. 2002. *A case study analysis of the Asian Fisheries Social Science Research Network (AFSSRN).*

Riggirrozzi MP. 2004. *The Influence of research on policy: MIMAP Philippines.*

______. 2004. *Bridging policy and poverty: MIMAP Bangladesh.*

Saumier A. 2003. *The impact of research on public policy: the case of MIMAP Viet Nam.*

Sene K and Thioune R. 2003. *Acacia: The Case of Senegal.*

Surani E. 2003. *Greywater Re-use - Jordan.*

Tuplin T. 2004. *The case of water demand management in Tunisia.*

______. 2004. *The influence of research on policy: the case of MIMAP Senegal.*

Tussie D. 2003. *A study of policy influence: the G-24 technical support services.*

Chapter Five

FROM MYTH TO REALITY— BUILDING CAPACITY FOR ECONOMIC POLICY RESEARCH IN AFRICA[1]

Elias T. Ayuk and Basil Jones

ABSTRACT

If Africa's own economic research institutions (ERI) are to play an effective role in the policy-making process, they will need to grow and increase their capacity. In this chapter, we describe how the Secretariat for Institutional Support for Economic Research in Africa (SISERA) has worked to develop research capacity and we also summarize the lessons learned in providing support to the ERI. Drawing on seven years of continuous interaction with the centres, we show that ERI have a long way to go before taking their rightful place at the policy-making table and contributing their expertise to developing and applying sound economic policies in their respective countries and regions. More efforts are needed in the areas of institutional leadership, solidifying the resource base, staff retention, increasing the policy relevance of research, developing a communication strategy and developing good internal management practices. This chapter also suggests that recent developments on the continent provide numerous opportunities for economic research centres to play a more important role in both formulating and implementing economic policies — in, by and *for* Africa.

INTRODUCTION

Over the past seven years, the Secretariat for Institutional Support for Economic Research in Africa (SISERA) has supported economic research institutions (ERI) in Africa. The support, mainly in the form of technical and financial assistance, aims to strengthen and build capacities of these institutions, enabling them to position themselves as active players in the policy-making process in their respective countries and regions. Much of the impetus for SISERA's efforts to increase ERI capacities came from the observation that reform programs in Africa were failing, and that one reason for this was that reform policies were shaped without an adequate understanding of the local conditions on the continent, something African research institutions could and should be able to provide. Consider, for instance, that a third of all structural adjustment programs (SAP) were reported to have failed not because of their economic rationale but because of the poor policy environment in which they were implemented (Dollar and Svensson 2000; Burnside and Dollar 1997; Svensson 1999). In recent years, development assistance has shifted from investment financing to policy reform (Dollar and Svensson 2000), largely because of the growing recognition that a precondition of economic growth is a good policy environment. An FAO study examined 11 success stories in food security and concluded that an appropriate policy environment was a key to their success (FAO 1996).

The equation is straightforward: a good policy environment in any region or country can be created only if there are institutions there with the capacity to develop sound economic policies. In Africa, ministries of finance and central banks do play an important role in developing adequate policies. However, they are often short-staffed, and there is also the need for independent advice, which ERI are better placed to provide. For this reason, over the past decade, efforts have been made to build capacity of the ERI, so they can provide governments with economic policy analysis. But as the ERI emerged, it became clear that they lacked well-trained economists, and that an umbrella organization was needed to support them by developing a critical mass of economists within the research centres with the expertise to spearhead economic research that would feed the policy-making process.

In this chapter, we assess and summarize SISERA's experience in dealing with ERI in Africa, offering a birds-eye view of the challenges and opportunities these institutions face in influencing policies in their respective countries[2]. Our aim is to provide insight into the actual circumstances in which African ERI operate, to characterize their *modus operandi* and identify concrete measures that they must take if they are to become more effective in meeting their mandates. We begin with a review of the conceptual framework that focuses on the potential role economists can play in the policy-making process. That is followed by a summary of the various ways that SISERA has worked over the past seven years to build and strengthen capacities at ERI to assist them in the policy debate. Next we examine the lessons learned from the Secretariat's interaction with ERI, which lead to the concluding comments in the final section.

CONSTRUCTING THE FRAMEWORK FOR AFRICAN ERI

At the onset of political independence in the 1960s, African governments saw development problems as a high priority and experimented with a wide range of policy regimes. By the 1970s however, many African countries were suffering from economic stagnation (Ghai 1999) and it was obvious that there was a need to re-visit prevailing economic policies. Structural adjustment programs (SAP) emerged as the remedy for Africa's economic woes, even as poverty continued to grow. More recently, Poverty Reduction Strategy Papers (PRSP) became the talk of the day.

As mentioned earlier, one of the main criticisms of the SAPs was that they lacked local input and appreciation of the context in which reforms were being made. Lessons learned during the hey-day of the SAPs included the realization that without a critical mass of highly trained and qualified African economists, there was little hope that lasting home-grown solutions to Sub-Saharan Africa's economic problems would be developed. It became abundantly clear that SSA countries could not continue to rely on foreign experts and institutions to provide guidance on macroeconomic policy development issues, at least not if these were to benefit Africa first and foremost.

Several initiatives emerged to respond to the insufficient *indigenous* capacity for economic analyses in Africa. The African Capacity Building Foundation (ACBF) developed programs that have been instrumental in establishing economic units within government administrations. The foundation also provides training. The African Economic Research Consortium (AERC) has focused its interventions on strengthening the capacity of individual researchers and in providing training for MSc and PhD degrees in Economics. The *Programme de Troisième Cycle Inter-Universitaire* (PTCI) provides post-graduate training in Economics for francophone West Africa. The United Nations African Institute for Economic Development and Planning

(IDEP) based in Dakar provides training on economic development and policy. Economic research is an important component of the agenda of the Council for the Development of Social Science Research in Africa (CODESRIA).

When SISERA was founded in 1997, its primary objective was to provide African economic research centres with institutional support. The driving force behind the establishment of SISERA was the observation that there was no corps of elite economists whose research output could inform and influence the economic policy-making process, nor was there any institutional support geared specifically towards economic research institutions. Consequently, African economic research centres have not played a major role in influencing policies, which in turn further isolates them from policy-making circles, perpetuating their plight on the periphery.

Figure 1 shows a framework of the *potential* role that economic research institutions could play in policy development, as dynamic intermediaries between on one hand public and private sectors and civil society organizations (CSOs), and the policy process on the other. But the ability of the ERI to play an effective role depends on their ability to identify burning issues, rigorously investigate them, develop policy options and discuss their implications. Any effort to build the capacity of these institutions should therefore emphasize these three focal areas: problem identification; conducting research; and dissemination of research results.

SISERA STRATEGIES AND MECHANISMS FOR INSTITUTIONAL CAPACITY BUILDING

SISERA has channelled its capacity-building support into six main areas, following the solid track record of comparable organizations such as ACBF, AERC, CODESRIA and IDEP.

First, SISERA provides financial support in the form of core and seed grants. Core grants of up to 300,000 Canadian dollars (CAD) over a two-year period are made to partner institutions that qualify and submit an acceptable grant proposal. Seed grants do not exceed 50,000 CAD and are made to emerging centres. It should be noted that partner institutions are those centres that are considered to be well established, whereas emerging centres are the younger, newly created

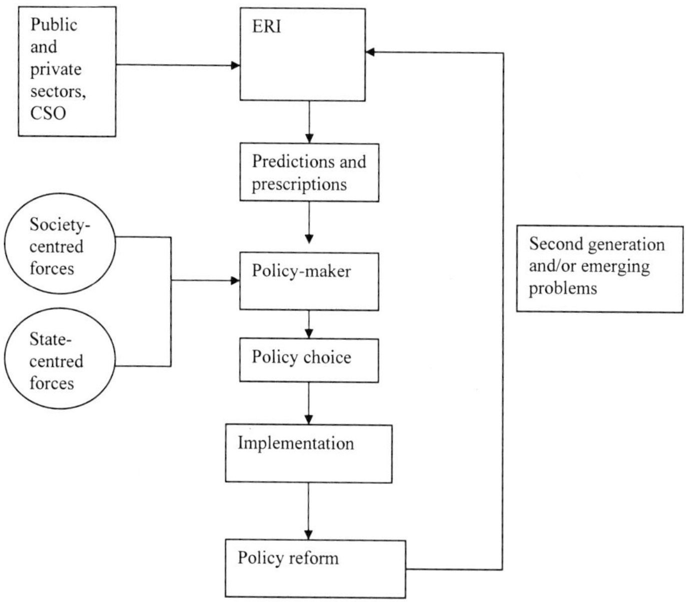

Figure 1: Framework for economic research institutions (adapted from G. Meier, 1991)

ones. These institutional grants are often used to acquire research tools such as books, specialized journals, databases, computers and software, and they enable recipient institutions to undertake individual research projects, train staff, organize seminars and publish research results. The ultimate goal of this form of support is to improve the working conditions within these institutions and to strengthen their internal capacity to conduct relevant economic policy research (SISERA, 2004).

Second, SISERA program officers provide technical support to the collaborating centres through regular visits to the institutions. During these visits, the program officers interact with centre directors and staff to provide advice on issues such as governance structures and administrative procedures, developing monitoring instruments, designing strategic plans for the ERI, implementing projects and on finalizing grant applications and reports. These exchanges permit program officers to monitor project progress and to be intimately involved with the centres' activities.

A third area of support is training that is offered in specialized subjects such as modeling and poverty analysis. The purpose of the training is to equip researchers with tools for analysing, formulating and implementing policies to address current economic problems.

A fourth important channel in institutional capacity-building is the enhancement of the managerial capacity of the research centres. To do this, SISERA organizes bi-annual meetings involving the directors of the collaborating centres. These meetings provide a platform for centre directors to share ideas on a variety of issues, including best management practices. The Secretariat also uses these meetings as fora for experts it has commissioned to deliver skills- enhancement training on a number of topics related to institutional development.

Fifth, SISERA has been instrumental in creating two research networks that bring together researchers from ERI throughout regions and sub-regions in Africa: one for Southern and Eastern Africa (SEAPREN) and another for West and Central Africa (WECAPREN). Such networks afford individual research institutions the opportunity to work across institutional and national boundaries. This is particularly valuable as thematic issues relevant to entire regions become increasingly important. Through the networks, individual research institutions end their isolation and strengthen their capacities for research that extends across national boundaries.

Finally, SISERA ensures that researchers forge links with end-users of their research results. To achieve this, the Secretariat encourages grant recipients to include dissemination activities in their grant requests so that they can bring their research results to the attention of key policy stakeholders. Thus, critical mechanisms for economic research institutions now include organizing policy dialogues, preparing and widely distributing policy briefs, and participating in inter-ministerial committees.

LESSONS LEARNED: CHALLENGES AND OPPORTUNITIES

Challenges

Seven years of regular interaction between SISERA and ERI have illuminated a number of issues that relate to the potential role these institutions can play to influence policies in their respective countries and regions. These issues range from the administrative and managerial to aspects of research.

Absorption capacity of grants

Although the lack of financial resources could be considered an important constraint for most ERI, SISERA's experience indicates that the capacity of the centres to absorb the financial resources at their disposal remains weak. Partner institutions that received core grants all requested an extension of the duration of the grant. In some cases, the project was closed and funds returned to the Secretariat because the centre did not have the human resources to put the funds to good use.

High turnover of professional staff

There is a high demand for scarce, skilled African economic researchers. As a result, there is a very significant turnover of skilled researchers at African economic research centres. The dilemma is that the skill-enhancing training acquired by researchers at ERI has made them more competitive and attractive internationally, and the meagre salaries offered at university-based centres in Africa are small incentive for skilled researchers to remain where they are. There has also been a high turnover in the leadership of the centres. The consequence is a lack of continuity in the research agenda of the institutions and in centre leadership. Clearly, more needs to be done to improve the professional working conditions in African research institutions.

Lack of strategic direction and inadequate internal managerial procedures

Strategic planning has been poor or non-existent in the ERI, meaning that most activities have been done on an *ad hoc* basis. Internal managerial procedures were found to be inadequate within several centres. Over the past seven years, the Secretariat has invested much of its time assisting these centres to develop strategic plans and to articulate the managerial practices within the institutions to ensure transparency and proper management of available resources. The good news is that a good deal of progress has been made in recent years in developing strategic directions for the institutions and ensuring that procedure manuals are developed.

Need to increase policy relevance

ERIs can influence policy-making only when their work is policy *relevant.* The centres have not been proactive in exploring the demand side for policy research. Soliciting the views of policy stakeholders will lead to policy-relevant research that produces results that are useful input in policy-making dialogue. However, there is a dilemma for researchers — trying to reconcile the conflicting interests of staff to advance their careers through academic research with the policy-makers' need for policy-oriented research. This conflict is often exacerbated by the limited exposure that most centre staff have to the reality of policy-making. Furthermore, very few of the ERIs have established a mechanism for regular interaction between their staff and policy-makers: internships, policy sabbaticals, and permanent fora with policy-makers, all of which would help resolve the dilemma.

Increasing research relevance to policy also requires a time-consuming commitment to approaching public and private officials, and cultivating relationships with them that are based on trust and reliability in the delivery of quality output that is both timely and easily comprehensible to the layperson. Indeed, researchers are often criticized for producing lengthy reports in a language that is inaccessible to decision-makers. At the same time however, even when they do produce digestible and relevant input for policy-makers, researchers may find themselves stifled by their government's institutional culture of secrecy and politically-motivated distrust of any nationals who may be active in politics or whose political leanings are not evident. As a result, policy-makers may unwittingly deprive themselves of the services of experienced researchers when dealing with critical yet sensitive issues that they are ill prepared to tackle alone.

Our impression at the Secretariat was that sometimes researchers and policy-makers seem to live in separate worlds. Researchers cannot understand why there is a resistance to policy change, despite clear and convincing evidence that it is needed. Policy-makers bemoan the inability of many researchers to make their findings accessible and digestible in time for policy decisions.

Several factors determine whether research will contribute to evidence-based policy. It must fit within the political context and the institutional limits and pressures of policy-makers, or researchers must exert sufficient pressure to challenge those limits. Research must also resonate with policy-makers' ideological assumptions, provide evidence that is credible and convincing, and offer practical solutions to current policy problems. It must be packaged so that it attracts the interest of policy-makers. Researchers and policy-makers should also share common networks, trust each other, honestly and openly represent the interests of all stakeholders, and learn to communicate effectively with each other.

Need to enhance scientific credibility

It can be argued that four factors constitute the main hurdles standing in the way of ERIs to increase scientific excellence, as follows.

1. Reduce academic isolation

Most research centres in SSA suffer from acute isolation from the international scientific community. They interact very little with prominent foreign researchers and have few opportunities to travel to meet their peers at scientific meetings. For this reason, they have enormous difficulty staying abreast of new developments in their fields of specialization or even in mainstream economics.

2. Eliminate the language barrier (francophone centres)

Most staff in francophone centres in Africa work almost only in French, with very limited proficiency in English. Thus they cannot access the most authoritative economic journals that are published almost exclusively in English; they often have to wait for French translations of reference materials and textbooks before updating their knowledge base. In recent years, there has been a trend for world-renowned economists from international financial institutions or universities in the West to work with African researchers on issues of policy-making. However, the majority of these experts do not speak French and cannot have a meaningful exchange with African francophone researchers.

3. Reduce the effects of a Malthusian process of staff promotion

Most governments in francophone Africa are members of the academic council, *Conseil Africain et Malgache pour l'Enseignement Supérieur* (CAMES). The role of CAMES is to screen candidates for promotion through the ranks of lecturers in law, economics and business management, and to ensure scientific rigour in the selection process. However, its decisions regarding the number of successful candidates from a given country are predicated by the number of academic positions budgeted for by the candidates' national governments, and not necessarily academic merit. Its historical record has been not to promote a larger number of candidates than the government is willing to accept, meaning that numbers promoted may not have anything to do with the number of qualified candidates there are or even how many a country requires.

4. Strengthen the culture of research

The French academic legacy has strongly marked teaching in francophone African universities, with research considered less important than lecturing, although this is gradually changing now. Research centres were established to compensate for this de-emphasis on research in universities, but the research culture remains considerably weaker than the culture of lecturing. As a result, universities continue to commit far more resources to teaching than they do to research, a trend that persists given the increasing enrolments in African universities and the prohibitive cost to Africans of studying abroad. University staff have so many teaching responsibilities that they have little time or resources for research endeavours, which would strengthen a home-grown scientific community. In addition, francophone universities tend to be very hierarchical, with little tolerance for scientific dissent by junior staff. So the academic forum where intellectual confrontation is meant to stimulate debate and new ideas are meant to flourish cannot fulfil its promise, and its scientific excellence is compromised.

Variation in size and structure of research institutions

Economic research institutions in Africa vary considerably in their size and structure, budgets, policy areas of specialization or competence, institutional independence and research output. Financial constraints push some centres to engage more in commercial work rather than in research into issues of public goods. Naturally, this impinges on their capacity to engage in the public policy debate.

Sustainability of research centres

For an African research centre to be sustainable, clearly it requires stable funding and a reputation for credibility. But most African economic research institutions do not have an institutional plan for monitoring progress and engaging in resource expansion drives. The result is high staff turnover and diminished effectiveness, which in turn threaten sustainability.

Opportunities

In spite of the daunting challenges listed above, the situation is perhaps not as bleak as it may initially appear for African ERIs. Indeed, there are also a number of opportunities that have emerged in recent years, which economic research institutions can and should take advantage of. The need for independent economic research institutions on the continent is even greater today than it has been in the past.

First, the impetus for domestic, home-grown solutions in and for Africa is growing in importance. The New Partnership for African Development (NEPAD) and several other similar initiatives show the growing interest in and need for finding solutions to Africa's myriad problems, solutions that are grounded in the realities of the continent. NEPAD emphasizes the need to develop and harness Africa's abundant human resources, including capacity-building initiatives in the form of training and research on the continent in the areas of political and economic governance, public sector reform and regional integration among others. The NEPAD initiative also calls for innovative approaches to redressing the brain drain, while harnessing African expertise to respond to current challenges in the continent.

Second, if PSRPs are to begin to reduce poverty in Africa, the strategies they use must be developed and owned nationally. Success of the PRSPs requires local research capacity to provide input for policy formulation and monitoring their implementation. This process cannot be sustained if there is no accompanying development in institutional capacity for economic research. It is therefore imperative that viable economic research institutions be created and then further strengthened so that a critical mass of economists is readily available to sustain the entire research–policy process.

Finally, from a global perspective, if there is to be success in reaching the targets laid out by the millennium development goals, sound economic policies must be developed and a prerequisite for these is sound economic research capacity both within nations and for Africa as a whole. Africa needs to raise the level of economic literacy not just among its researchers but also its policy-makers, if the millennium development goals are not to remain impossible dreams and become instead reality. Global initiatives such as the WTO meeting in Doha, Monterrey Consensus, annual G8 summits, the African Growth and Opportunities Act (AGOA), and the 2002 Johannesburg World

Summit on Sustainable Development are all laudable and full of encouraging promises, but for those to be fulfilled, there is a need to develop and strengthen capacity in economic research — *in, by and for* Africa.

CONCLUSION

Sound economic policies are the cornerstone of and prerequisite for economic growth in Africa. This is why initiatives have multiplied on the continent, which aim to build and strengthen the capacity of economic research institutions to enable them play an effective role in policy development.

SISERA's experience in building institutional capacity for policy research in Africa highlights the challenges that these institutions still face. While a number of institutions have had considerable success in influencing the policy debate, a majority of the institutions still need to make significant improvements in a number of areas, including strategic leadership, staff retention, policy relevance of their research, communication strategy, and best management practices.

Recent trends and developments on the continent indicate that the role to be played by ERIs in policy-making will only increase. Home-grown solutions are increasing in popularity; regional institutions are gaining in importance, and meeting the targets of the millennium development goals and the development of PRSPs all require strong local capacity.

Notes

1. The views expressed herein are those of the authors and do not represent in any form or shape the views of the Secretariat or IDRC. The authors wish to acknowledge the several donors that have provided support to SISERA to enable it undertake it activities over the years. They include the European Union, the French Ministry of Foreign Affairs, the Canadian International Development Agency (CIDA), IDRC, The Dutch Ministry of Foreign Affairs, the United States Agency for International Development (USAID) and the World Bank Institute.
2. More detail can be found in SISERA's Annual Report 2003–04 (SISERA 2004).

References

Burnside C and Dollar D. 1997. Aid, policies and growth. World Bank Policy Research Working Paper no. 1777.

Dollar D and Svensson J. 2000. What explains the success or failure of structural adjustment programmes? *The Economic Journal* 110: 894–917.

FAO. 1996. Success stories in food security. FAO Technical Background Document No. 2. Rome: FAO, World Food Summit.

Ghai D. 2000. African development in retrospect and prospect, *IN:* Ghai Dharam (ed). *Renewing social and economic progress in Africa: essays in memory of Philip Ndegwa.* London: Palgrave.

Meier G. 1991. Policy lessons and policy formulation, *IN:* Meier G (ed). *Politics and policy making in developing countries.* San Francisco: International Center for Economic Growth Press. 3–12.

SISERA 2004. Annual Report 2003–2004 of the Secretariat of Institutional Support for Economic Research in Africa.

Svensson J. 1999. Why conditional aid doesn't work and what can be done about it? World Bank mimeo.

Chapter Six

JOINING FORCES IN POLICY RESEARCH NETWORKS FOR POLICY-MAKING IN AFRICA—THE *SEAPREN* EXPERIENCE[1]

Dirk Hansohm and Erwin Naimhwaka

ABSTRACT

In this era of globalization of markets and the flow of goods and services, policy-making too is increasingly extending beyond the borders of nation states and shifting to regional and international levels and institutions. This means there is an increasing need for research on the regional level. Parallel to this, a number of research networks have been set up to connect researchers and research institutes regionally. Recognizing that a network approach of existing research institutes is preferable to the formation of new regional institutes, six national institutes in Southern and Eastern Africa joined forces to create the Southern and Eastern Africa Policy Research Network (SEAPREN) in 2000. This chapter examines the policy-making process on the regional level and the role policy research networks play. Following a general overview of the situation in sub-Saharan Africa, it presents and examines SEAPREN and reviews its approach to influence policy. The final section concludes with some lessons for researchers.

INTRODUCTION

Regional integration is finally gaining momentum in Africa. The Organization for African Unity (OAU) has been replaced by the African Union (AU), taking into account experiences of the European Union (EU). The New Partnership for African Development (NEPAD) has been founded. The Southern African Customs Union (SACU), the oldest customs union and arguably the only effective body of regional integration on the continent, is turning into an international organization. The Southern African Development Community (SADC) is striving to become more effective through restructuring and streamlining. The Eastern African Community (EAC) is experiencing a renaissance. In short, the idea of regionalism, long cherished by African policy-makers, is being transformed from abstract ideal to reality.

In this era of globalization, the realm of policy-making is increasingly extending beyond the borders of nation states and shifting to regional and international levels and institutions, there is an increasing need for research on the regional level. Underlying this development in the political sphere and in parallel, several regional research networks have emerged. This paper makes a first assessment of their experience in Africa by examining the experience of a specific network: the Southern and Eastern African Policy Research Network (SEAPREN).

The first part of this discussion considers the role of research networks in general and specifically in Africa; the second offers a review of SEAPREN and in a final section we draw some conclusions.

THE ROLE OF RESEARCH NETWORKS

Partly because of globalization and also as a result of technological progress, cooperation in networks has become an increasingly important feature of the interface between research and policy. This trend is also apparent in sub-Saharan Africa (SSA). However, Africa lags behind much of the world in both the number and size of networks, and also in the quality, output and impact of existing ones. This slow start in Africa can be attributed to the relatively small number of economic policy researchers on the continent and to the fact that a culture of scientific policy advice is only now emerging.

In general, African countries have a limited capacity for economic management and policy research. Economic policy interventions are based only to a small degree on the results of economic policy research (EPR). However, if African nations are to achieve social and economic goals, they require a well-developed capacity for economic management, both within the public sector and beyond, to effectively employ oftentimes limited human, financial, and material resources.

As Stolper (1964) reported just after many African countries achieved their independence, a major obstacle to economic development was the lack of knowledge or economic facts. Sadly, forty years later, this is still the case. In sub-Saharan Africa, there are still systemic problems that hinder the results of economic policy research from feeding into the policy process. These include data scarcity, unreliability of data, little relevance of EPR, social segregation of policy researchers from policy-makers, insufficient communication to the public, and lack of awareness of researchers that they need to sell their ideas to policy-makers (e.g. Gitu 2001). Research systems in SSA are generally characterized by weak institutions for economic research (e.g. Degefe and Pakkiri 1994, Goldsmith 2001, Hansohm 2002 and 2003, Obadan and Ugu 2000, Seck 2000, Wohlmuth 1998).

However, in the course of economic reform that has taken place in recent decades in SSA, the policy environment has been changing and there is now a growing demand for economic research. Both internal and external factors are contributing to this. Most African political systems are in a process of liberalization. This is putting an end to the public monopoly of policy analysis and to an increased domestic "public scrutiny of policy action" (Ndulu 1997). In many countries there are efforts to develop a more inclusive approach to policy discussion and development. In general there is a trend towards greater openness (Hoffmann 1995). Thus, the reality of policy-making is more positive than is often portrayed by a sceptical press.

On the external front, donors are also increasingly interested in using and promoting local economic research capacity. More importantly, in the context of globalization of economic activities, there is an increasing need for economic policy analysis, as matters become more sophisticated and more rapidly changing.

Policy research networks differ widely in Africa, in terms of age, size, finance, membership, target group, output and quality. African researchers are increasingly part of international networks; there are Africa-wide networks as well as sub-regional and national networks. With such diversity, generalizations about economic policy research networks in Africa remain thus problematic. Nevertheless, the following general observations can be made:[2]

- Networks concerned with economic policy-making generally group together researchers, while they include policy-makers to only a limited degree. Although some of the networks have communication and dialogue with policy-makers on their agenda, there is very little information available about the extent, nature and success of this communication between policy-makers and researchers.

- Most networks in Africa are at an emerging stage and distinguish themselves in a key way from networks in advanced economies, which tend to be driven by the interests of the individual or institutional members and to be self-financed. In Africa, this self-interest still needs to grow to the level where networks can be financed by institutions in the partnership.
- The evidence suggests that communication between policy researchers and policy-makers in Africa remains one-way. That is, researchers attempt to disseminate knowledge to policy-makers but there is seldom genuine communication between the two groups.
- Another type of network is concerned with policy advocacy. These networks are as well unidirectional, targeting rather than trying to engage the policy-makers in true dialogue.
- Evaluation and monitoring of the success of networks in particular, and economic policy research more generally, are almost absent. One reason for this is systematic—it remains very difficult if not impossible to track the influence of research and the knowledge it generates on policy, as the latter is subject to a multitude of influences. Thus, the push for measurability of development assistance for economic policy research networks may be important, but it may also be partly misleading and reductionist.
- Donors often have unrealistic expectations, a belief in the illusion of planning, of the singular importance of information, and of information as the most important or immediate constraint to improving policy. These are all unproven assumptions.
- Networks are generally supply-driven by external donors. There is nothing inherently wrong with this, but it still means there is a risk that the work of networks will miss focussing on the most relevant issues to them and to the people in their region. Sometimes they succeed by providing relevant and sought-after knowledge; sometimes they don't.
- As a result of globalization and the IT revolution, knowledge is readily available; this includes knowledge on economic policy-making. The bottleneck may not be the provision of information

and access to information, rather the transmission to and the ability to absorb knowledge of the policy-makers.

- However, there is a dichotomy of countries on the continent that are more globally connected (generally in Southern and Eastern Africa), and others that still appear to be rather disconnected from global data sources.
- There is a lot of emphasis, also by networks, on "best practices", on "blueprints"[3] and on standards. However, the critical issues are not the recognition and copying of available knowledge. Rather it is the ability to absorb this knowledge, in combination with local specific knowledge. This sets limits on the application of internationally available knowledge and determines its usefulness—or lack thereof.
- There is a proliferation of networks but not necessarily a parallel increase in communication among them. A key reason for this is competition among donors for the establishment and control of networks. The quality and impact of networks varies highly. There are relatively old, very established networks—the African Economic Research Consortium (AERC) is one—that exist side-by-side with growing, young networks and also stagnating, fading ones. The regularity of website updates gives an indication of the level of activity of a network or institution.
- Donors, as financiers, have determining influence on networks. There is insufficient communication among donors, policy-makers, and researchers. This contributes to the "blueprint" character of most networks. They and their success are evaluated on the basis of the latest donor fads. Any "good" network has to deal with issues that are currently in vogue with donors—gender, poverty, ownership, for example.
- There is a general underlying assumption that more knowledge is better, that good use can be made of this available knowledge.
- Inadequate attention is given by both donors and policy researchers to the constraints under which policy-makers operate.

THE EXPERIENCE OF *SEAPREN*

The set-up

In 1999, management members of six economic policy research institutes in Southern and Eastern Africa were invited to a workshop in Gaborone, Botswana, by the Secretariat for Institutional Support to Economic Research in Africa (SISERA). The institutes were:

- Botswana Institute for Development Policy Analysis (BIDPA), Botswana
- Development Policy Research Unit (DPRU), South Africa
- Economic Policy Research Centre (EPRC), Uganda
- Economic and Social Research Foundation (ESRF), Tanzania
- Institute of Economic and Social Research (INESOR), Zambia
- Namibian Economic Policy Research Unit (NEPRU) – Namibia

The aim of the workshop was to discuss the feasibility of forming a research network. There was a realization that with the increasing importance of regional bodies and regional policy-making, the demand for policy research with a regional perspective would rise. National and even regional research institutes on the continent had only a limited capacity to respond to such a challenge, and this meant that foreign clients seeking economic knowledge about an area usually engaged international consultants from donor countries rather than local expertise. At best, domestic researchers and research institutes were not cooperating with each other; at worst they were actually competing with each. The idea that emerged in Gaborone was that rather than try to establish a new regional research institute, the best way to use available research capacity in Africa would be through networking, linking and combining local and specialized knowledge bases and giving indigenous research a comparative advantage.

Following these discussions, the Southern and Eastern Africa Policy Research Network (SEAPREN) was launched with the signing of a Memorandum of Understanding (MoU) in February 2000 in Cape Town, South Africa. Its overall objective was to advance sound economic policy among Southern and Eastern African countries through informed collaboration by regional research establishments that would result in the adopting of best practices in research development, implementation and administration.

The network has worked to achieve this objective by executing joint research projects that lent themselves to comparisons across the member countries. These joint efforts are expected to enhance capacity-building in policy analysis and evaluation in the region through collaboration in research, exchange of best practices in management, learning from each other, and optimizing existing human resources within the network. The participating institutes complement each other not only through their local knowledge in different countries but also because of their specific areas of competence.

The idea was also that the stronger institutes in the network would strengthen weaker institutions that could benefit from their resources and know-how.

Focus areas for research were identified at the Gaborone workshop. These included regional and international trade, an economic inventory of poverty and its alleviation, governance and development, and also economic growth and industry. Individual institutes were charged with developing project proposals in these areas.

The activities of the network were to be coordinated by a rotating lead institution that had to appoint a project coordinator. A network meeting was planned for every year. BIDPA was selected as the first lead institution and its director was himself the project coordinator. Two years later NEPRU took over this position.

The MoU states that the objectives of SEAPREN are to:

- collaborate in the development and administration of joint national and regional research projects
- exchange best practices in research project development and implementation, as well as institutional management
- exchange information and knowledge regarding advances in the area of policy analysis
- exchange research and other personnel
- inform potential clients at the national, regional and international levels about SEAPREN, its capacity and resources
- exchange experience in information technology and libraries
- promote library exchange and exchange of library databases

- commit to the use of information technology to its full extent to create links among the member institutions and their staff through the facilitation of listservers/bulletin boards for discussions, a network website, extranet, video conferencing, etc.
- develop a close relationship between SEAPREN members and national and regional policy-makers.

Experiences to date

At the workshop in Gaborone in November 1999 and then at the launch of the network in February 2000, expectations and enthusiasm ran high. Donors such as IDRC through SISERA appeared ready to finance the endeavour, and others to co-finance it. Nevertheless, it took almost three years for the network to start operations. There were several meetings, but incomplete project proposals delayed proceedings; nor did the secretariat take the initiative that had been expected.

Because of pressure to complete existing research activities and the need to raise resources, research institutes tended not to regard as a priority the development of research proposals for the network, at least not while the financing of these remained uncertain. In the absence of a budget, the secretariat too did not feel it was in a position to devote the considerable time resources required to manage the network.

It was only in January 2003 that the SEAPREN project coordinator signed a grant agreement with IDRC. At the same time, the Norwegian development agency, NORAD, provided a second grant to finance the network's cooperation with the Christian Michelsen Institute (CMI) in Bergen. Several meetings had taken place and NEPRU had taken over project coordination from BIDPA. The only substantive issue at the meetings was the development of the project document that was the basis for the grant agreement. In between, a seventh research institution joined the network—the Institute for Policy Analysis and Research (IPAR) in Nairobi, Kenya.

The project document developed for the financing (SEAPREN 2003) was more explicit about project management than the MoU had been. The secretariat, the website, SEAPREN meetings and meetings of a project committee were now budgeted as coordination structure. The document also includes an element of capacity-building in institute management, which, however, is not budgeted for. Altogether, the seed funds provide 29 percent of funds that are planned to be spent; the rest remains to be co-financed.

Tasks of the secretariat include establishing and maintaining a communication system, identifying and sourcing additional funding, managing network and project committee meetings, pre-screening project proposals, liaising with donors, informing about the network through a newsletter, meetings, and conference presentations.

A fund for collaborative research was created, to spare individual members the responsibility for seeking financing. Any member institute is entitled to apply for funds from this budget line according to an established set of conditions for research projects. That is, there must be one lead institute and at least two others participating, the research must be comparative, of regional interest and relevant for policy, and the research team must be qualified, and led by one institute with at least two others participating. A Project Committee was established that has both network and regional policy-making institution members. Its tasks are to screen project proposals, to rank them and to allocate funds to projects accordingly.

The Project Committee met twice and has communicated in between via email. At its first meeting, it considered two submitted proposals. Neither was approved, but the Committee gave direction for improvement to both. Only one was re-submitted, but two new proposals were also considered and accepted during the second round of selection. In the end, one of the approved projects could not be implemented because the project leader left the institution, so the seed research funds were allocated to two projects.

1. efficiency and effectiveness of capacity building in economic policy-making: a comparative study of Botswana, Namibia and South Africa
2. poverty alleviation in rural areas through improving the access to financial services in sub-Saharan Africa: a comparative study of Botswana, Kenya, Namibia and Tanzania.

The second source of funding from NORAD complements the seed funding. It builds on contacts between the SEAPREN institutes and the CMI that date back to the early 1990s. The primary aim of the SEAPREN/CMI programme is to build a strong regional policy research network through the production of policy relevant studies and institutional support, in cooperation with the CMI. The cooperation program comprises two key elements:

1. Joint research (two research projects)
2. Institutional co-operation, with the sub-categories:
   - improving network communication and IT
   - supporting and promoting SEAPREN Public Relations (PR) with donors and the international community
   - improving institutional efficiency in the SEAPREN member institutes
   - exchanging of personnel.

The projects in the collaboration program with CMI consist of all member institutes, in contrast to the seed research fund that is allocated on a competitive basis for project proposals.

The first research project in the collaborative program with CMI deals with "budgetary processes and economic governance in Southern and Eastern Africa" and compares practices from all seven countries. Based on a general literature review, the project compares the experiences of medium-term expenditure frameworks (all countries have or intend to implement them), revenue agencies (integrated versus independent), the role of parliament, an auditor general, and NGOs in the budget process. This project has progressed furthest, with nine published papers.

The second project compares poverty reduction strategies in the seven countries. In all countries, poverty reduction plays a key role in policy-making. However, most countries follow World Bank-led programmes, while only a few others have "home-grown" approaches.

Three projects under the NORAD-financed program cover the area of institute management in the areas of information technology, public relations and overall institute efficiency. The objective of these projects is to compare practices and problems, identify lessons, and come closer to "best practices". The projects include email discussions, workshops, production of discussion papers, and inputs of external expertise, and are expected to lead to improved practices of the institutes. A first joint workshop of the three projects was held in 2004 in Cape Town (Naimhwaka 2004).

The IT project recognized the problem that access to information is a problem for most of the network institutions. Lack of timely information about the latest advances in relevant policy research led to a comparative disadvantage in terms of research output for these African institutions. On average, the cost of internet access in the region is double what it is in Norway, and internet speed is 50 times slower. The project aims to narrow this rather alarming IT gap by providing, to a limited extent, the latest hardware and software, and mainly by advising on and assisting in setting up joint data bases and library catalogues.

The PR project recognizes that if they are to succeed, institutes must be able to provide information about their services and capabilities. However, few of the institutes have any specialized PR function. Although the work of these institutions is largely demand-driven—meaning there is not a great need for PR—if they are to expand their role and influence policies they will need to develop PR or public awareness expertise. This project works to assist individual projects in this area, as well as developing a greater public identity for the network.

The project on institute efficiency is based on the premise that member institutes face a number of fairly similar management problems. This suggests that there is a potential for them to learn from each other through the exchange of information. This assumption was confirmed at the Cape Town workshop, where participants also identified areas for further work.

- future financing—sources, strategies and diversification—both at the level of the individual institutes and possibly a common strategy for future financing of the network itself
- incentives, performance, performance evaluation
- governance, institute structures, internal communication.

To conclude, after an initial delay caused by a combination of factors, the network then engaged in a number of projects, producing tangible results. In the meantime, the underlying assumption that led to the foundation of SEAPREN—increasing the importance of regional actors in research and policy-making in Africa—was proved to be valid.

Lessons

At the time of writing, the SEAPREN network is now in its fourth year of existence old, but in "real" terms—that is, since financing was secured—it is really just two years old. Clearly, it would be premature to try to assess its success in influencing policy in the region, but it is not too early to look at some lessons learned.

- The assumption of rising demand for regional research has been confirmed. The challenge of the network is to prove itself by delivering.
- SEAPREN's early experience highlights the erroneous assumption that research institutes have funds to run the administrations of such networks. Most research institutions in Africa do not benefit from public funds despite the fact they produce—and are expected to produce—public goods.
- Although some finance for network coordination has been available for some time, due to unforeseen circumstances this was not extended beyond the initial phase. In addition, a full-time senior person is necessary for coordination if the network is to expand its activities, size and effectiveness.
- Further, the idea that a network should facilitate the transfer of capacity from stronger to weaker institutions in the network, not surprisingly, has not always gone over well with the stronger institutions. In fact, this places an extra burden on the "strong" (a relative term in Africa) institutions, which are already under pressure because of the lack of sufficient funding. This further impedes the speed and progress of the network's activities. Without the necessary support and incentives, it goes without saying that those relatively strong institutions will be reluctant to subsidize weaker ones.
- There is an inherent conflict between the intention to build capacity of weaker institutions and the principle of efficiency in the network itself, which obviously favours competition among network members and thus domination by the stronger institutions.
- A key constraint of the network is the underlying institutional weakness of the member institutes. Given this, the projects financed and undertaken by the network wind up competing with better remunerated consultancy projects.
- A related general problem is staff fluctuation that undermines the continuity necessary for longer-term research and for healthy communication.

- Institutional weakness also results in an inability of member institutes to deliver on agreed commitments. This also results in the danger of polarization between stronger and weaker institutes.

The key general lesson from the experience of the network is that the network, especially in its infancy, requires a lot of driving, hand-holding and adequate communication among them. The strength of participating institutes needs still to grow to the level where self-financing of the network would be realistic. While it is clear that there is a need for regional research networks rather than more regional institutions, donors who may champion the formation of networks may also neglect the need for the administrative support to make networks effective, and some networks are stillborn. Thus, donors who expect networks to produce should also offer financial support that is a prerequisite for such production. There is a demand for the research that networks produce, but this production is hampered by limited capacity on the ground. So those who set up networks—and those donors who champion them—should be realistic and sensible when setting expectations and making commitments.

The SEAPREN experience suggests that the issue of institutional capacity in Africa is extremely important. If research institutions are to function well individually and within networks, they must have the capacity to do so, or be accorded the support and recognition that will build their credibility and relevance to policy-makers. It is thus important to set up an entrance criterion to the network. SEAPREN confirms that networking is beneficial; partners learn from each other and from joint research endeavours. There are enormous potential benefits to be accrued from institutional collaboration and cooperation, as the experience of the Southern and Eastern Africa Policy Network shows.

Notes

1. The opinions expressed in this article are those of the authors and not necessarily of the network. The authors thank Jan Isaksen and Mohamed Ali Marouani for their constructive comments.
2. This is based on work for the preparation of Olofin, Hansohm and Plummer 2003.

3. "Blueprint" networks are those that tend to conform to a current donor demand, following prescribed guidelines rather than responding to any particular need or demand.

References

Degefe Befekadu and Logan Pakkiri. 1994. The demand for PhD training in economics in sub-Saharan Africa, *IN:* Fine Jeffrey C, Lyakurwa William and Gordon-Drabek Anne (eds), *PhD education in economics in sub-Saharan Africa: lessons and prospects.* Nairobi: East African Educational Publishers in association with African Economic Research Consortium.

Gitu KW. 2001. Strengthening the link between policy research and implementation, Nairobi: KIPPRA, Occasional paper 1.

Goldsmith, Arthur A. 2001. Risk, rule and reason: leadership in Africa.*Public Administration and Development* 21: 77–87.

Hansohm D. 2002. Economic policy research, governance, and economic development: the case of Namibia, *IN:* Olowu Dele and Sako Soumana (eds). *Better governance and public policy: Capacity building and democratic renewal in Africa.* Bloomfield, CT: Kumarian Press, 195–213.

Hansohm D. 2003. Economic policy research as an input to good governance in Africa, Windhoek, NEPRU Working Paper 91, December.

Naimhwaka E. 2004. Report on the SEAPREN workshop. Cape Town: 23–25 August.

Ndulu Benno J. 1997. Editorial: Capacity for economic research and the changing policy environment in Africa. *World Development* 25(5): 627—630 .

Obadan Mike I and Edu O Ugu. 2000. Think tanks in Nigeria, *IN:* McGann James and Weaver R Kent (eds). *Think tanks and civil societies. Catalysts for ideas and action.* New Brunswick and London: Transaction Publishers, 509–528.

Olofin S, Hansohm D and Plummer M. 2004. The African Economic and Policymakers' Network (EFNET): a knowledge sharing network for enhancing effectiveness in policy analysis and implementation, report for the African Capacity Building Foundation (ACBF), unpublished.

SEAPREN 2003. Funding proposal for the Southern and Eastern Africa Policy Research Network (SEAPREN).

Seck D. 2000. An analysis of francophone economic research centres in Côte d'Ivoire, Burkina Faso, and Senegal, *IN:* James McGann and R. Kent weaver (eds). *Think tanks and civil societies: catalysts for ideas and action.* New Brunswick and London: Transaction Publishers, 491–507.

Stolper WF. 1964. The contribution of economic research to African development, *IN:* Robinson EAG (ed). *Economic development for Africa south of the Sahara. Proceedings of a conference held by the IEA.* London: Macmillan: 712–733 .

Wohlmuth Karl. 1998. *Good governance and economic development. New foundations for growth in Africa.* Bremen: University of Bremen, Berichte aus dem Weltwirtschaftlichen Colloquium der Universität Bremen.

PART II

EVERY COUNTRY HAS A STORY TO TELL

ECONOMIC RESEARCH AND POLICY-MAKING THROUGH NATIONAL EXPERIENCES IN AFRICA

Chapter Seven

STRENGTHENING RESEARCH AND ANALYTICAL SUPPORT FOR TRADE POLICY-MAKING IN AFRICA: THE CASE OF NIGERIA[1]

Afeikhena Jerome

ABSTRACT

In recent years, trade policy has become far more complex, both in terms of the issues involved and the participation of new actors. This study appraises research and analytical support for trade policy-making in Nigeria, within the context of the Doha Development Agenda of the World Trade Organization (WTO). It argues that trade policy formulation and implementation in Nigeria, even though conditioned by the global context, is dominated by governmental and inter-governmental agencies whose responsibilities overlap and among which coordination is deficient. There is no identifiable source or structure of research and analytical support for trade policy-making in Nigeria. Specialized knowledge and skills should be obtained through longer term contractual arrangements with institutions and individuals in Nigerian academia, consulting firms and the private sector.

INTRODUCTION

At the United Nations (UN) Millennium Summit of September 2000, 189 nations adopted the "Millennium Declaration", out of which a set of eight goals emerged, 18 numerical targets and 48 quantifiable indicators, all to be achieved over the 25-year period from 1990–2015. As the world strives towards achieving the Millennium Development Goals (MDGs), Africa faces enormous challenges. It is glaringly obvious that most of Africa will miss the MDGs by a wide margin. According to the joint projections by the Organization for Economic Co-operation and Development (OECD) and the African

Development Bank in their Economic Outlook for Africa 2003–04, only six countries are on track in achieving the first goal of halving the proportion of people living with less than US$ 1 dollar per day by 2015[2]. Meanwhile, half of the continent is slipping back or is lagging far behind on the target of halving hunger, while the prospect of achieving the other targets is even worse. Because of the continent's disproportionate burden of poverty and many other impediments to development, achieving the millennium development targets will hinge on making substantial and sustained advances in trade.

Two major trading initiatives have profound implications for African trade. One of these is the Cotonou Agreement that came into effect in June 2000 between the European Union and African, Caribbean and Pacific (ACP) states, succeeding the Lomé Convention that did not address human rights and governance issues. The second is the World Trade Organization (WTO), as a successor to the General Agreement on Tariffs and Trade (GATT). The Cotonou Agreement retains the trade provisions of the Lomé Convention for a transition period that expires in 2008. At the end of this period, it is expected that economic partnership agreements will be signed to replace the preferential trading arrangements of the Lomé Convention. The WTO came into being on 1 January 1995 as a successor to the GATT, and as a result of the Uruguay Round of multilateral trade negotiations, which lasted from 1986 to 1994. The responsibilities of the newly founded organization included the administration and implementation of some 60 trade agreements on a variety of issues, ranging from trade in goods to trade-related aspects of intellectual property.

Developing countries participated with enthusiasm and high expectations in the historic Uruguay Round of Multilateral Trade Negotiations that ushered in the new rules-based, multilateral trading system (MTS) and the birth of the WTO. They had hoped that the new trading regime would improve their trade fortunes, facilitate their effective integration into the world economy, and arrest their marginalization from the global trading system. Unfortunately, the vast majority of developing countries, particularly in Africa, have so far been unable to reap many benefits from their membership of the WTO.

Since the Uruguay Round, trade policy has become far more complex, both in terms of the issues involved and the participation of new actors. It is thus extremely important to enhance an understanding of the actors and institutions that shape and constrain trade policy formulation at the national level. Building on Agbaje and Jerome (2004), this study appraises the process of trade policy-making in Nigeria, as it relates—or does not relate—to research and analytical support for trade policy-making. It focuses on the main negotiating issues embedded in the on-going multilateral trade negotiations in the context of the Doha Development Agenda of the WTO.

This chapter comprises five sections. Section one presents an analytical framework for research in the policy-making process, the process of trade policy-making is appraised in section two, trade negotiation is presented in section three, research and analytical support in section five, and section six concludes.

RESEARCH AND POLICY-MAKING: ANALYTICAL FRAMEWORK

Prior to the 1970s, there was the implicit assumption that policy-makers regularly used research results for decision-making. As discussed in Chapter One of this book, the link was viewed as a linear process, whereby a set of research findings is shifted directly from the "research sphere" over to the "policy sphere". Since then, there has been empirical validation of this premise that led to a reappraisal of this view. The findings indicate, overwhelmingly, that policy-makers seldom used knowledge gained through research (Neilson 2001).

Several hypotheses have been tested to explain the under- or non-utilization of knowledge or research by policy-makers for decision-making purposes. The dominant explanations are the "two communities" theory expounded by Caplan (1979) regarding the behavioural differences or "cultural gap" between researchers and policy-makers, and the "enlightenment "function" of research put forward by Weiss (1977). According to Caplan, the use—or non-use—of research is a symptom of the cultural, or behavioural gap between researchers and policy-makers. The limited use of research by policy-makers is in part due to the fact that researchers and policy-makers have different world-views. The differences make for wide divergences in expectations, in perceptions of mutual impact as well as difficulties in achieving satisfactory and constructive relationships (Booth 1988).

Although the notion of a cultural gap between researchers and policy-makers still prevails, the weakness of early explanations, such as the simple dichotomy between "use" versus "non-use", has been elaborately debated. Later explanations by Weiss (1977), Webber (1991) and Sabatier and Jenkins-Smith (1993) acknowledge that research is only one of many sources of information for policy-makers, and it is not a simple dichotomy between "use" and "non-use". Knowledge and research utilization are built on a gradual shift in conceptual thinking over time. Although research may not have direct and immediate influence on specific policies, the production of research may still exert a powerful indirect influence by introducing new terms and shaping the policy discourse. Weiss (1977) describes this as a process of "percolation", in which research findings and concepts circulate and are gradually filtered through various policy networks.

The literature on the research–policy link is now shifting towards a more dynamic and complex view that emphasizes a two-way process between research and policy, shaped by multiple relations and reservoirs of knowledge (Garrett and Islam 1998). There are two broad camps when it comes to the idea that research can influence or inform the policy process: "rationalist" and "political". The rationalist view posits that new research can directly prompt policy change. The political camp, on the other hand, assumes that various external factors play a key part both in defining the question that a research project tackles and in influencing the impact of the answers on policy (Philpott 1999).

How the research is conducted and for what purpose, will shape its relevance and usefulness to policy-makers. In other words, whether it is participatory, "research as data" for the purpose of generating knowledge or for problem-solving, or "research as ideas" to "enlighten" policy-makers by conducting "action research", will shape or determine whether or not and also how it informs policy. The reasons for the limited relevance of research findings include weaknesses in the research itself, conflicting demands on policy, and disjunctions between the knowledge needs of policy-makers and the research outputs of social scientists. On the research side, much of what goes by the name of social science knowledge is currently flawed, inconclusive, ambiguous, and contradicted by evidence from other studies. Many research conclusions are limited in scope or out of date. On the policy side, there are a host of competing claims for attention. The policy-making is political, with the basic aim of reconciling interests in order to negotiate a consensus, not implementing logic and truth (Weiss 1977).

However, much of the literature on research and policy processes reflects the perspective of developed countries and there is need to acknowledge the diversity of policy contexts throughout the world. Many of the frameworks are not consistent with an African setting. The models assume democracy; yet for many African countries, the democratization process is in its infancy. Many developing countries depend heavily on international financial institutions such as the IMF or World Bank that dominate their policy-making. Conducting case studies in these settings adds considerable knowledge and information about policy processes in developing countries.

THE PROCESS OF TRADE POLICY-MAKING IN NIGERIA

Until recently, trade policy formulation and implementation in Nigeria, although conditioned by the global context, was dominated by governmental and inter-governmental agencies and dispersed among several public sector agencies whose responsibilities overlap and among which coordination is deficient. Public sector institutions tend to be weak, which means the policy process is diffuse and lobbying and ad hoc interventions tend to be the preferred means of influencing policy. The involvement of civil society was hardly accorded high priority. The non-governmental or civil society sector was generally looked upon with suspicion, and invariably became the target of repressive measures by state administrative machinery intolerant of alternative viewpoints among the citizenry (Akindele 1988). Military dictatorship that has plagued Nigeria for most of the post-independence period compounded the situation.

Trade policy is within the realm of macroeconomic policy. In Nigeria, the Federal Ministry of Commerce is the principal government agency with the overall responsibility for trade policy formulation, including bilateral and multilateral agreements. Under the present political dispensation in the country, there are three principal organs responsible for decision-making. These are the Federal Executive Council, the National Council of State, and the Senate. Trade policy ratification ultimately rests with the Federal Executive Council. Within the government, policy may be initiated at the ministry level, mainly Nigeria's Federal Ministry of Commerce or the Federal Ministry of Industries. Other organizations that offer policy inputs include the Federal Ministry of Finance, the Nigeria Customs Service and the Central Bank of

Nigeria. New policies requiring legislative backing would, after passage by the National Assembly, be submitted to the Ministry of Justice for legal drafting. There is also the Tariff Review Committee/Board, which reviews all requests and issues relating to tariffs.

At the formal level, the organized private sector (OPS)[3] or business linkages in policy formulation are mainly through membership in advisory public committees, direct lobbying through formal bilateral consultations and voluntary submissions, ad hoc opinion feedback, policy advice and pre-budget memoranda, which have become a traditional hallmark of the OPS. Although the contemporary trend of economic liberalization has altered the balance of power between the state and the OPS in favour of the latter, their role in policy formulation is still minimal and mainly reactive.

Effective formulation and implementation of trade policy requires collaboration among the relevant government ministries and agencies, as well as continuous dialogue and consultation with major stakeholders. As the expanding mandate of the WTO has drawn more domestic institutions into the process of designing and implementing trade and trade-related policies, coordination within and among ministries and other governmental agencies and stakeholders has become a major problem in Nigeria.

Consultation is still limited. The mechanism of coordination within the government is usually through inter-ministerial meetings or committees coordinated by the Federal Ministry of Commerce. Inter-Ministerial meetings may be held on a case-by-case basis to coordinate policies of various ministries. In addition, the National Council on Trade meets once a year to coordinate policies at federal, state and local government levels. There are also: the National Focal Point on Multilateral Trading Matters; the Export Strategy Committee; and the Committee on Export, Import, Free Trade Zone, Freeport and Procurement Policies; all of which meet on an ad hoc basis.

Policy decisions of non-state actors such as the Manufacturers Association of Nigeria (MAN), the Nigerian Association of Small-Scale Industry (NASI) and National Association of Chambers of Commerce, Industry and Agriculture that are relevant in trade policy formulation are often taken in the National Council on Commerce—the highest body dealing with trade policy and issues in Nigeria. It is necessary to emphasize that dialogue for and the policy decisions taken at the National Council on Commerce are institutionalized and officially sanctioned. However, the feedback mechanisms on the decisions taken are reported back to the Council annually as "Reports of Implemented Trade Decisions".

There are several coordination problems arising from the split in responsibility between those who formulate trade policy in Abuja and those with the authority to negotiate and sign trade agreements in Geneva, and the staffing of the various ministries and other government agencies involved with trade-related policy-making. Problems that manifest themselves include inadequate capacity for monitoring and analysing the trade policies of key trading partners, and limited personnel with the requisite knowledge of international trade law. National consultation and coordination on WTO activities involve functions that are largely technical, requiring the specialized knowledge and skills of trade analysts, lawyers, economists, and so forth, as well as rigorous analysis, all beyond the capacity of members of the inter-ministerial and other committees. The recently formulated Enhanced National Focal Point needs to be strengthened to provide technical support to the Geneva-based negotiators as well as ensure that Nigeria's interests at the WTO are effectively promoted and protected within the framework of the country's rights and obligations in future negotiations.

TRADE NEGOTIATIONS

Nigeria aspires to take full advantage of the opportunities and concessions available in international trade relations at bilateral, multilateral, regional or continental levels. This is noticeable in Nigeria's active participation in the Economic Community of West African States (ECOWAS), the African Union (AU), the Cotonou Agreement, the EU-ACP Agreement, and the Africa Growth and Opportunity Act (AGOA).

On attaining political independence in 1960, Nigeria automatically became a member of the GATT, and subsequently participated in many multilateral trade negotiations under its auspices. When the World Trade Organization succeeded the GATT, Nigeria then became a signatory and foundation member of the WTO agreement, and agreed to comply with its trade rulings on agriculture, textiles and preshipment inspection procedures. Nigeria's positions at the WTO are aligned with those of other developing countries, which seek improved market access to developed countries' markets, and preferential treatment on account of non-market issues such as food security, poverty eradication, rural development and debt repayment.

In 1995, Nigeria established the Nigeria Trade Office, which operates under the auspices of the Nigerian Permanent Mission in Geneva. The Trade Office handles all trade-related activities in Geneva, such as the activities of the WTO, World Intellectual Property Organisation (WIPO), the United Nations Conference on Trade and Development (UNCTAD) and the International Trade Centre (ITC). The substantive head of the Nigeria Trade Office is an ambassador who is the Head of Delegation to the WTO, and as such directly accountable to the Nigerian Minister of Trade, who is regarded as the Chief Negotiator in this round of negotiations under the Doha Development Agenda. The ambassador doubles as the Alternate or Deputy to the Minister. The Minister of Commerce represents Nigeria at the Ministerial Conference, the highest decision-making body of the WTO, which convenes every two years. The Nigeria Trade Office liaises with the External Trade Department, which has oversight functions for external trade matters, and hence the Trade Office itself. Reports of the Trade Office are mainly channelled to the Ministry, oftentimes to the Director, External Trade. The Commerce Ministry coordinates all trade-related activities in Geneva.

The work of the WTO is carried out in the context of meetings, which take place in formal and informal ways at several levels—the Ministerial Conference, General Council and subsidiary bodies. Various bodies, undermining the capacity of small delegations from countries such as Nigeria to participate, hold formal and informal meetings simultaneously. According to the provision on voting in Article IX.1 of the Marrakech Agreement establishing the WTO, it is absolutely essential that the process leading to the point at which decisions are taken should be all-inclusive, with clear participation by all stakeholders. However, according to Nigerian negotiators, there is not much information flow between Abuja and Geneva. The flow of information has tended to be more in only one direction, from Geneva to Abuja, with little or no feedback from the Nigerian capital.

The paucity of Nigeria's human and material resources and its limited knowledge base for the issues being negotiated at the WTO means that the country's trade policy-makers are not always able to fully grasp or deal with the implications of the issues and proposals discussed by various negotiating groups in Geneva. This, in turn, limits their ability to fully participate across the board, and to identify and effectively promote Nigerian interests in the negotiations. These handicaps are exacerbated by the unfortunate practice of frequently re-assigning officials to and away from Geneva, which prevents them from acquiring the necessary competence and confidence they would through long-term interaction with officials from other countries, and weakens the link between officials in Geneva and Abuja.

It is becoming apparent that because of the complexity of the entire WTO system, Nigeria made commitments that exceed the capacity her administration and institutions have to implement them. Like other developing countries, Nigeria took on unprecedented obligations not only to reduce trade barriers but also to implement significant reforms in trade procedures and in many areas of regulation that impact on the business environment in the domestic economy. These include regulations concerning intellectual property law and technical, sanitary and phytosanitary standards. Some of these obligations reflect little awareness among the more powerful members of the WTO of the development problems of developing economies and little appreciation of the limited capacities of these countries to carry out the functions demanded by the provisions and rules of the WTO agreement. Implementation of WTO rules requires more than just removal of obstructive policies. It also requires creating infrastructure and institutions that facilitate economic activity. For example, implementing the Trade-related Aspects of Intellectual Property Rights (TRIPS) provision would require installation of equipment, establishment of procedures, and training of staff that are beyond the means of an indebted, developing country dealing with pressing health and education problems.

RESEARCH AND ANALYTICAL SUPPORT FOR TRADE POLICY AND TRADE NEGOTIATIONS IN NIGERIA

Research and analytical support is perhaps the weakest link in Nigeria's trade policy formulation and negotiation. There is no identifiable source or structure of research and analytical support for trade policy and trade negotiators within the Federal Ministry of Commerce. Occasionally, national seminars are organized that furnish policy-makers with some form of information support. However, these can hardly be regarded as a credible and official strategy of feeding knowledge to those formulating policy, and do nothing to ensure that policies are backed with solid research and analysis. To address the research–trade policy divide, there were proposals to establish a Foreign Trade Institute that could play the same role that the Nigerian Institute of International Affairs does in the area of foreign affairs. This proposal was approved by the regime of former Nigerian President Abdulsalami Abubakar, who took office in 1998 after the death of President Sani Abacha, and then handed over power in 1999 to the elected president, Olusegun Obasanjo. With the change of government, the proposal seems to have fallen off the agenda.

One important institutional framework that has emerged in recent years is the reconstitution of two vital national committees: the national focal point on WTO that in 2001 was transformed into the Enlarged National Focal Point; and the National Trade Policy Review Committee, which drafted Nigeria's trade policy document. The Enlarged National Focal Point was a deliberate effort of the Ministry of Commerce to involve *all* stakeholders, including civil society, in the formulation and harmonization of Nigeria's position for multilateral trade negotiations. The Enlarged National Focal Point serves as the standing Inter-Ministerial body, charged with the overall coordination of government positions on trade-related developments in Geneva. It is responsible for articulating Nigeria's position in trade negotiations. Its membership is drawn from all relevant Ministries and agencies, including academia and the representatives of the organized private sector, with the Federal Ministry of Commerce as the Secretariat.

The Focal Point is thus expected to consider the various issues emanating from Geneva, to make recommendations and advise government accordingly. Thereafter, decisions taken can be communicated through its Secretariat, the Federal Ministry of Commerce, to the Trade Office in Geneva, for advocacy or defence, as appropriate. Sadly however, the Enlarged National Focal Point hardly meets, ostensibly because the Secretariat lacks the necessary funding to keep the process going.

The marathon negotiations in the Uruguay Round[4] cover a wide variety of complex issues. An active and effective participation by any country requires the regular presence of officials with appropriate technical skills and knowledge of how the WTO works. Clearly, to function well in such negotiations, Nigerian officials should be regularly provided with updated, appropriate and adequate technical analysis, advice and directives from their country's capital (Oyejide 2000). Unfortunately, this is not the case, largely because of the following capacity constraints:

- limited knowledge base and the resultant absence of in-depth knowledge and understanding of trade rules, technical issues
- limited research, analysis and evaluation capacities
- lack of access to up-to-date information about global developments and their potential impact, including policy formulation by trading partners
- lack of attention to detail and coordination in national policy formulation
- lack of attention to strategic and tactical planning, especially long-term and far-reaching planning
- lack of attention to the anticipation of possible future developments and the consequent formulation of pre-emptive positions or appropriate policy alternatives.
- lack of forward thinking, which greatly restricts a rapid-response capacity.

These constraints negatively affect Nigeria's capacity to participate effectively in the WTO negotiations with sound preparation and detailed strategy formulation. As a result, Nigerian participants around the negotiating table find themselves on uneven footing, in a reactive and defensive position, unable to take a proactive and results-oriented approach.

There are several external initiatives intended to build capacity in the area of trade policy. One of these is the Joint Integrated Technical Assistance Program (JITAP), sponsored by the WTO, the ITC and UNCTAD, which provides assistance in the follow-up and implementation of the Uruguay Round agreements. Nigeria is not a beneficiary of JITAP, but the country has received various kinds of support in the area of trade policy, mostly from the United States and the WTO. At the time this study was done, the Overseas Development Institute (ODI) was implementing a program to provide technical assistance to Nigeria for its preparation for Cancun[5], assessing the requests made to Nigeria in the negotiations for the General Agreement on Trade in Services (GATS) and to investigate how Nigeria could respond.

All well and good, but an evaluation of these capacity-building efforts indicates a problem: they fail to take sufficient account of the institutional inadequacies and structural deficiencies in Nigeria, which prevent efficient deployment of financial assistance to support activities that could ensure that the research results and knowledge they impart are used creatively in developing trade policy. The efforts to help Nigeria prepare for international trade negotiations are sporadic and dispersed; very rarely do they result in a comprehensive approach to trade capacity building.

There *is* local capacity in Nigeria for research relevant to supporting trade policy and trade negotiations, especially in the universities and research institutes. Even more than many other African countries, Nigeria does have expert skills and knowledge on many issues bearing on trade policy, both in academia and the private sector. Unfortunately, a wide gulf exists between academics and practitioners. The linkages between research and policy are tenuous and weak, and the research institutes are isolated from the policy-making process. As shown here, trade policy-making and negotiations have benefited only minimally from existing studies outside the trade policy-making circles in Nigeria.

CONCLUSIONS AND RECOMMENDATIONS

This study set out to appraise research and analytical support for trade policy-making in Nigeria. A study of best practices of trade policy-making reveals that three elements are critical for the process to be efficient. These are government leadership, institutional capacity and the inclusion of all actors, including the relevant ministries, the business sector, trade promotion and regulatory bodies, think tanks and other civil-society organizations.

All three of those elements are deficient in Nigeria. At the policy level, a key constraint is the lack of resources at the Federal Ministry of Commerce, readily observable from the limited access of officials to telephones, computers, email, internet facilities and other communication technologies. Access to information on trade issues related to Nigeria is extremely limited, in part due to poor access to the internet in the nation's capital. The current architecture of trade policy-making in Nigeria requires intense consultations among several ministries and stakeholders if coherent positions are to be developed. Unfortunately, linkages among the ministries are very poor and there are no formal mechanisms for coordination among officials. The division of tasks among the ministries remains the subject of conflict. There are insufficient resources to communicate and coordinate work across ministries on multilateral and other trade issues, and to raise stakeholders' awareness and invite participation in the formulation and implementation of trade policy and commission research. On external representation, the Nigerian delegations in Geneva are too few and ill equipped to deal with the complex, interlocking negotiating agendas. They lack the professional skills needed to interpret notification obligations under WTO obligations and then respond by gathering the relevant information. There is neither a WTO reporting mechanism, nor any formal coordination mechanism among ministries for notifications, while the links between the Nigerian capital and WTO offices in Brussels and Geneva are tenuous, at best.

Closely related to resource deficiencies is the serious capacity deficit in the Federal Ministry of Commerce. Very few trade officials have had basic training in trade economics or the management of international trade. The few competent ones are usually deployed outside the Ministry as part of routine civil service transfers. The business sector still plays a limited role, in spite of the formal inclusion of public/private consultative processes in trade policy formulation and implementation. Moreover, private sector organizations have very limited capacity to assess independently the risks and opportunities associated with Nigeria's participation in the various multilateral negotiating fora.

The WTO and other negotiating commitments have outgrown decision-making and negotiating processes that were appropriate for the GATT regime. Nigeria needs to evolve a process with a high degree of internal transparency that ensures effective participation of all stakeholders. Capacity gaps need to be addressed in a wide range of areas, from policy-making and implementation to supply side responses. Stakeholders from the public and private sectors, as well as academia and civil society, need to be engaged. The record suggests that no country has been able to achieve substantial gains in trade without an effective trade policy framework. The collective efforts of all should be guided by a vision of a trade policy process and development strategy rooted in an overall national development and poverty reduction plan.

Specialized knowledge and skills, necessary for conducting longer-term research on key issues, should be obtained through longer-term contractual arrangements with institutions and individuals outside governments. It is necessary to determine what capacities are available—or should be available—in Nigerian academia, consulting firms and the private sector and, where appropriate, international sources. Procedures for contracting and using this expertise should be specified.

There are several economic research institutes in Nigeria, but two agencies in particular have demonstrated considerable potential in forging the link between research and trade policy. These are the Trade Policy Research and Policy Centre in Ibadan and the Institute for Public Analysis in Lagos. The former is a non-profit, non-governmental, and non-partisan international organization set up within the Department of Economics at the University of Ibadan. Its mandate is the analysis of international trade issues to promote the integration of African economies, both regionally and with the global economy. The Director of the Trade Policy Research and Policy Centre, Professor Ademola Oyejide, was an adviser to the erstwhile Director General of the WTO, Mike Moore. The Institute for Public Analysis in Lagos is a private, non-profit organization involved in research, education, and publication on economic issues. Its objective is to provide market-oriented analysis of current and emerging policy issues, with a view to influencing the public debate and the political decision-making process.

Perhaps some lessons could be learned from South Africa where the Trade and Industrial Policy Secretariat was established as an independent agency, enjoying close ties to the South African Department of Trade and Industry. The Trade and Industrial Policy Secretariat, financed by the International Development Research Centre, sponsors a public forum on trade and industrial policy, conducts focused studies on behalf of the South African Department of Trade and Industry, and runs short training programs on methods for analysing trade policy. And as discussed in Chapter Six, it has helped to establish the regional network, SEAPREN, which conducts trade policy research within the Southern African Development Community (SADC).

Notes

1. The comments of participants at the International Conference organized by the Secretariat for Institutional Support for Economic Research in Africa (SISERA), especially Mr. Olugbemi A Agbola, Director, National Planning Commission of Nigeria, are gratefully acknowledged. The usual caveat applies: the views expressed in this chapter are the author's and do not necessarily reflect on the Department of Economics at the University of Ibadan.
2. These countries are Algeria, Egypt, Libya, Morocco, Tunisia, and Mauritius. For details, see: Growth trends and outlook for Africa: time to unleash Africa's huge energy potential against poverty, OECD Development Centre/African Development Bank; 2003–04 African Economic Outlook. http://www.oecd.org/dataoecd/43/43/32285652.PDF
3. The evolution of the OPS in Nigeria reveals dynamism bereft of consistency or stability, just like the wider political and economic environment.
4. Most WTO agreements, indeed the WTO itself, are the result of the 1986–94 Uruguay Round of trade negotiations, the final act of which was signed at the GATT Ministerial meeting in Marrakech, Morocco. It comprises 60 agreements, totaling 550 pages.
5. Val Imber from Oxford Policy Management headed the three teams brought in by the Overseas Development Institute. One formed a general negotiating strategy, one dealt with services (with Ian Gillson as the international consultant), and one dealt with agriculture, along with local consultants.

References

Agbaje A and Jerome A. 2004. Institutional framework and the process of trade policy making in African countries: the case of Nigeria. Final Report Submitted to the African Economic Research Consortium, January.

Akindele RA. 1988. The formulation and implementation of Nigeria's external economic policy: institutional structure and processes, *IN:* Akindele RA and Ate BF (eds). *Nigeria's economic relations with the major developed market-economy countries 1960–1985.* Lagos, Nigeria Institute of International Affairs (NIIA)

Booth T. 1988. *Developing policy research.* Aldershot: Gower Publishing Company Limited

Caplan N. 1979. The two-communities theory and knowledge utilization. *American Behavioral Scientist* 22 (3): 459–470

Garrett JL and Islam Y. 1998. Policy research and the policy process: do the twain ever meet? Gatekeeper Series No74. International Institute for Environment and Development

Neilson S. 2001. Knowledge utilization and public policy processes: a literature review. Evaluation Unit, IDRC, Canada. Available at: www.idrc.ca/evaluation/litreview_e.html

Oyejide TA. 2000. Interests and options of developing countries in a new round of multilateral trade negotiations. G-24 Discussion Paper Series, United Nations Conference on Trade and Development and Center for International Development, Harvard University, United Nations

Philpott A. 1999. Twists in the Mwanza tale: did one HIV research study shift global policy? London: Institute of Development. Available at: http://nt1.ids.ac.uk

Sabatier P and Jenkins-Smith H (eds). 1993. *Policy change and learning: an advocacy coalition approach.* Boulder, Colorado: Westview Press

Stone D and Keating M. 2001. Bridging research and policy: an international workshop. Warwick, UK, July: 16–17

Sutton R. 1999. *The policy process: an overview.* London: Overseas Development Institute

Webber DJ. 1991. The distribution and use of policy knowledge in the policy process. *Knowledge & Policy* 4(4): 6–36

Weiss CH. 1977. Research for policy's sake: the enlightenment function of social science research. *Policy Analysis* 3(4): 531–545

World Trade Organization Legal texts. 2005. http://www.wto.org/english/docs_e/legal_e/legal_e.htm

World Trade Organization. 1998. Trade policy review. Nigeria, Geneva: World Trade Organization.

Chapter Eight

AN ANALYSIS OF THE RESEARCH–POLICY NEXUS IN NIGERIA

Professor Ade S. Olomola

ABSTRACT

Despite the existence and activities of policy-oriented research organizations in Nigeria, public policy decisions seem not to have benefited from relevant research input. This is generating considerable disenchantment among researchers. This chapter uses multiple case studies to examine the existing linkage between research and public policy in the country, and then to identify measures that can strengthen the influence of research on public policy decisions. This study conducted at the Nigerian Institute of Social and Economic Research (NISER) found major pitfalls in the research–policy nexus, including gaps in policy initiation, poor culture of policy development, policy confusion and uncertainties, and inadequate linkage mechanisms. In Nigeria, the research and policy communities seem to work at cross-purposes. This report shows that to remedy this, the government should make research funding a priority and eliminate unhealthy competition between "in-house" research in government departments and that of statutory research institutes. A network of public policy research organizations should be established, as should feedback mechanisms between researchers and policy-makers. Research organizations themselves should emphasize demand-driven research, while the government should provide adequate research infrastructure.

INTRODUCTION

In Nigeria, research for use in the public policy arena is done largely in social science and closely related disciplines. It is generally targeted towards policies in the macroeconomic, social, technology and agricultural sectors. Apart from the studies conducted by academic researchers in social science faculties and research centres in several Nigerian universities, voluminous research information also abounds in specialized research institutes, established directly by the federal government to conduct research into socio-economic problems in the country. Departments of planning research and statistics at both federal and state levels are also supposed to engage in policy research. The existence of such an extensive research outfit does not, however, imply that policy research needs of the Nigerian government are being fully satisfied, as seen already in the preceding chapter.

Despite the recognition that there is an important role for research in policy decision-making in Nigeria, research input into the policy process is rather limited. Thus, the research facilities and potentials are neither fully developed nor fully explored. Funding of policy-oriented research institutes, as for other research institutes, has no place on the list of government priorities. Unfortunately, even as funding is diminishing, research needs and policy-related problems proliferate. As a result, the country has not been able to take full advantage of existing research infrastructure to benefit policy. The critical element in policy research- and evidence-based decision-making is the existence and function of effective links among researchers, policy-developers and decision-makers. No one of these three communities has placed enough emphasis on such linkages. Several decisions are still taken without research input, and several research studies are being conducted without policy relevance. Perhaps even worse, there are policy-relevant studies done with considerable public investment that are not being utilized. There is also the problem of overlap–several similar studies are being conducted in the country in different places at different times and even in the same place at close intervals. This syndrome of re-inventing the wheel not only wastes precious resources but it is also symptomatic of the extent of the dissemination problem within the research community itself.

Moreover, there is no commitment by the government to situate existing policy-oriented research institutes into the mainstream of policy decision-making. The reliance on several parallel ad hoc channels has tended to create conflicts in the flow of ideas and has placed politics in the forefront of policy decisions. This tends to cause disenchantment among policy researchers, and in turn it has adverse consequences on the supply of research output.

The importance of research for policy purposes has been receiving considerable attention in the developed world and research–policy issues are still being actively articulated and investigated. By contrast, in Nigeria little is known about this important field of study. An understanding of the interactions between the research communities and policy-makers is desirable not only to ensure that researchers are encouraged to deal with challenging development issues but also to ensure the country derives maximum benefits from its indigenous research.

This chapter examines the linkage between public policy and research in Nigeria. Specifically, using a multiple case study approach, we seek to:

1. examine the existing policy research capacity and the relevance of research in public policy decisions in the country
2. determine the challenges and opportunities for research–policy linkages
3. suggest ways of strengthening the influence of research in the policy process.

The case studies presented here are drawn from four policy-oriented research organizations. They are the Nigerian Institute of Social and Economic Research (NISER) and the National Institute for Policy and Strategic Studies (NIPSS), which are owned by the Federal Government. The others, which are NGOs, are the Development Policy Centre (DPC) and the Centre for Advanced Social Studies (CASS).

CONCEPTUAL FRAMEWORK

In examining the use of research in policy and the linkage between research and policy it is important to stress that various types of research have the potential to influence public policy. Although the various types are interrelated, they are conventionally classified into four categories, namely: policy research; policy-relevant research; academic research; and policy- oriented research.

These categories have been clearly defined in the literature. According to Cross (1998), policy research refers to studies carried out as part of the policy process. Their purpose is to shed light on the policy process in the interest of effective policy development. Policy research may include feasibility studies, background reports and evaluation research. The critical determining criterion for policy research is that it is premised upon the definitions, perceptions and priorities of policy-makers. A significant proportion of this research is carried out in-house, that is, by research and development department, or statistical divisions of government agencies.

Like policy research, policy-relevant research may focus on policy issues but by contrast, it does not share the assumptions of the policy-maker. It is thus more wide-ranging, perhaps more critical and often longer-term. It is driven by a combination of academic logic coupled with one that is essentially moral or ethical.

Academic research differs from the above two not by the standards it seeks to attain but by the origins of the problem it explores. When this is derived exclusively from the scientific literature itself without any recourse to policy or political debate, then the research may be said to be academic.

Policy-oriented research is defined as based on a shared perception of the issues, where relevance and topicality are critical, and where the object is to improve the quality and effectiveness of public policy. This differs from policy research in that it is more independent and thus potentially more critical; it differs from policy-relevant research in that it is constrained by policy priorities and perceptions (Cross et al. 2000).

The modeling of the linkage between research and policy is undergoing continuing transformation. Despite the different arrangements of the critical elements, however, the critical building blocks remain relevant till today. The "two worlds" model propounded over two decades ago (Caplan et al. 1975), viewed the linkage from two angles: that of the customer (the policy-maker) and that of the supplier (the researcher). The questions of under- or non-utilization are explained in terms of the non-compatible characteristics of the worlds, communities, or systems of customer and supplier. The policy and research communities have different operational cultures and time frames, different approaches to problem definition and different constituencies in terms of roles and accountability. The motivation for forging appropriate linkages is to resolve these differences. Despite the simplistic nature of this model, it is still a reference point today. It has generated further conceptualizations by various scholars over the years (Weiss 1977; Weiss and Bucuvalas 1980; Bulmer 1986).

In her own conceptualization, Weiss described the linkage model in terms of the influences that the make-up of knowledge exchanged between the research and policy communities, and thus emphasized research, policy, their interaction and their context. This involves a description of the characteristics of the research, characteristics of the researchers, characteristics of potential user groups and characteristics of the modes of dissemination or linkage.

In a more recent work, Cross et al. (2000) provided a modification of the Weiss framework. They argued for a different ordering of the constituting elements of the basic two-community template of the Weiss framework and provided additional characteristics to make the model a better analytical instrument. Essentially, the refinement shifts the perspective from utilization to that of relationship between research and policy. This framework provides additional characteristics for the actors in the research–policy interaction, the issue arena, the research parameter. It dwells also on the transformation use of scientific knowledge to articulate a functionalist perspective in the analysis of the relationship between research and policy.

In applying this framework to the case study analysis, we focused attention on specific research studies carried out by the selected organizations with a view to influencing public policy. The key issues addressed include initiation, motivation and purpose of the research, the calibre of researchers, conduct of the research, linkage mechanisms, the role of policy makers, the findings, dissemination channels and use to which the research results are put. We also carried out in-depth interviews of key officials of the research organizations.

HOW RESEARCH RELATES TO POLICY–CASE STUDIES FROM NIGERIA

Nature and impact of research–policy linkages in NISER

The Nigerian Institute of Social and Economic Research (NISER) conducts research on various aspects of the Nigerian economy and society. However, for the purpose of this assessment of research-policy linkage, NISER's Review of Nigerian Development (see NISER 2000) is one of the most appropriate projects and meriting emphasis. The project started in 2000 with the following objectives:

1. regularly profile and review selected performance indicators in various sub-sectors
2. serve as a database and reference point for key policy issues
3. identify areas of policy concern from time to time
4. make strategic policy recommendations as input for development programs.

This review of Nigerian development covers areas such as agriculture and rural development, science and technology, economic development, education, physical development, social development and political development of the country. Several indicators were developed to monitor performance in each area.

The project was designed to have a regular component, which focuses on the analysis of development in various sectors of the economy using appropriate performance indicators, as well as a thematic component, which deals with a salient issue of general concern in the country. Since its inception, the project has addressed three themes, namely:

1. the state of Nigerian development
2. understanding poverty in Nigeria
3. public–private partnership in Nigerian development.

The linkage mechanism is assessed using the six linkage variables presented in Table 1, and in the subsequent case studies in this chapter. These are:

1. the source of the initiatives for the study
2. source of funding
3. research personnel
4. linkage mechanisms with policy makers and users
5. role of policy-makers in research initiation, implementation, monitoring and dissemination
6. impact on policy articulation, implementation, monitoring and evaluation

Table 1: Assessment of Research-Policy Linkages in NISER

	Linkage variables	Details of the NISER Review of National Development project
1	Source of initiatives for the study	Within the organization, based on experiences in developed and developing nations and on Nigeria's peculiarities
2	Source(s) of funding	Internal funds mainly. Dissemination is enhanced with support of collaborators.

3	Diversity of research personnel and conduct of research	Researchers are always drawn from universities across the country to join their counterparts in NISER. Such resource persons serve as researchers, reviewers and discussants at various stages of the project. Data for the research are obtained from secondary sources and surveys.
4	Mechanisms for interacting with policy-makers and users	Some policy advisers and other users are involved as reviewers of research reports and participants in methodology and dissemination workshops.
5	Role of policy-makers and users in research initiation, implementation, monitoring and dissemination	The various government agencies and ministries in which data are collected for the studies are invited to send representatives to the methodology and dissemination workshops, and to provide inputs into further research directions. They are to suggest issues and indicators to be included or excluded from future studies and share their views with researchers about the current findings.

A key feature of NISER's Review of Nigerian Development project is the high degree of participation of relevant interest groups and agencies. To enrich the knowledge base for the project and thus create an atmosphere conducive for achieving its objectives, it adopted a participatory approach. This allows for extensive cross-fertilization of ideas, an evolving and genuine ownership of the project, the creation of awareness among potential beneficiaries, mobilization of resources for effective implementation, and the assurance that the project is truly result-oriented. The main elements of this approach include involving key institutions from the outset and through subsequent stages of the project, and designing a review process that draws input from a broad spectrum of professionals and interest groups. It is important to stress that measuring the exact impact of research findings on policy decisions and results may be difficult to do. For any particular policy decision, it is possible to have inputs from many sources and a variety of interest groups. No particular individual or group can determine with certainty the weight placed by policy-makers on his or her own input.

In assessing the impact of the national development review, NISER analyses responses of the key organizations that receive the project's publications. Some responses are summarized in Table 2. By and large, key government agencies and other users found the publications very valuable and promised to make appropriate use of the contents. This is an indication that the research has a positive impact on the users.

Table 2: Useful feedback from policy partners on the project (2000–2002)

Organization	Remarks
Nigeria Ministry of Foreign Affairs	"You may be glad to know that we found the publication very useful indeed . . ."
	"I have taken time to read . . . the opening chapter . . . together with the chapter on conclusions and policy perspectives. This provides useful prescription which cannot be ignored."
	"I am confident that your exertions would enhance the Ministry's role in the implementation of the nation's development agenda . . ."
Nigerian Ministry of Environment	"I feel highly honoured and am grateful for the copy of the NISER Review of Nigerian Development. This publication will certainly be useful as a reference book to me."
World Bank Office, Abuja	"The findings and recommendations in this publication will be very valuable for the planning and implementation of our poverty reduction interventions in Nigeria."
Office of the Accountant General of the Federation, Nigerian Ministry of Finance	"The publication will assist a great deal in policy deliberations." "There is no doubt your publications over the years have been of immense benefit to policy formulators and this one will surely not be an exception. I assure you that this office will optimize the use of it."
UNICEF	"It will certainly be a good reference material for our programming."
Centre for Management Development (CMD)	"The donated material is of inestimable value to our organization. It would be much appreciated if four additional copies could be sent to us to enrich our Library collection . . ."

Office of the Head of Civil Service in Nigeria	"The various chapters of the book will certainly be most helpful in policy decisions and other deliberations."
International Labour Organization (ILO)	"In view of the importance and relevance of the issues treated in the book we wish to request for four additional copies of the publication . . ."
Central Bank of Nigeria (CBN)	"The book appears very rich with information. Please oblige me with an additional copy." "It is very thoughtful of you to send the publication to me and I quite appreciate the kind gesture. The book will no doubt make interesting reading and will be of immense benefit to us in the Bank."
United Nations Development Program (UNDP)	"We congratulate you for this outstanding output and would like you to please send additional copies for the UNDP."
National Assembly (Senate)	"I have gone through the areas of focus and I am highly impressed by the scope and exhaustive nature of the discussion . . . No doubt our country and indeed all policy makers will find this latest effort by NISER indispensable . . . Your publication is important in our quest for a proper understanding of our situation . . ."
National Assembly (House of Representatives)	"We are delighted to note the issues raised in the publication and sincerely hope to make use of the contents at all times and appropriately."
Nigerian Ministry of Finance	"The publication is not only invaluable to us but is of immense research value. We are therefore, requesting two (2) additional copies for use in the Ministry's Library . . ."
Nigerian Ministry of Information and National Orientation (Office of the Permanent Secretary)	"I am also to convey her sincere and deep appreciation for your kind gesture and assure you that the publication will certainly be put to good use."

Nature of research–policy linkages in NIPSS

The records of the National Institute for Policy and Strategic Studies (NIPSS) show that the research department had not carried out a departmental research activity for up to ten years. In 2003, the institute secured the support of the Office of the Vice President of Nigeria to conduct a study on foreign direct investment (FDI) in Nigeria. The project was to be finalized at the end of the year. The objective of the project was to establish and document the exact nature, trend and country of origin of foreign direct investment in Nigeria since May 1999. The fieldwork was completed and a mid-term report submitted. Table 3 presents a summary of the assessment of the linkage mechanisms in NIPSS in this study.

Table 3: Assessment of research–policy linkages in NIPSS

	Linkage variables	Details of the study on foreign direct investment
1	Source of initiatives for the study	NIPSS research department
2	Source(s) of funding	Funds secured from the Office of the Vice President of Nigeria
3	Diversity of research personnel and conduct of research	Survey, library research and workshops involving NIPSS researchers, Office of the Vice President and other relevant Ministries
4	Mechanisms for interacting with policy makers and users	Workshop for stakeholders
5	Role of policy-makers and users in research initiation, implementation, monitoring and dissemination	Personnel from the Office of the Vice President joined the research team.
6	Impact (use of results)	Results form the basis of suggestions to policy-makers on ways to enhance the flow of FDI in the country.

Nature of research–policy linkages in CASS

To examine the nature of research–policy linkages in Nigeria's Centre for Advanced Social Studies, we considered three recently concluded research projects undertaken between 2003 and 2004. These are: democracy and development in the Niger Delta (pilot survey); oil and gas exploitation, agriculture and environment in the Niger Delta Region; and women and development in the Niger Delta.

The aim was to unravel the linkage mechanisms associated with the motivation, execution, dissemination and utilization of the research. They were initiated by CASS with the aim of generating scientifically determined factors necessary and sufficient for aiding public policy formulation and management, focussing on the Niger Delta where there has been little appreciable development over the years. The findings are presented in Table 4.

Table 4: Assessment of research–policy linkages in CASS

	Linkage variables	Details of the case studies considered
1	Source of initiatives for the study	Only within the organization
2	Source(s) of funding	Funds mobilized by the organization
3	Diversity of research personnel and conduct of research	Researchers were assembled by the organization. There were no representatives from the side of users
4	Mechanisms for interacting with policy-makers and users	Workshops and seminars
5	Role of policy-makers and users in research initiation, implementation, monitoring and dissemination	Not explicit
6	Impact (use of results)	Results form the basis of suggestions to policy-makers on good governance

Nature of research–policy linkages in the DPC

The consideration of the research–policy linkages in the Development Policy Centre is based a project it undertook called, "Ijebu-Ode Research on City Consultations on Poverty Reduction". This project was implemented between 1999 and 2003, but follow-up activities are still on-going. The main impetus for the project arose from the observation that traditional institutions tend to be quite successful in providing community services such as schools, maternity centres and palaces for traditional leaders, whereas government has often failed to provide even basic amenities for the masses of the people.

The DPC worked with the Urban Management Program, which had already developed the city consultation tool for mobilizing all stakeholders in a city to identify problems and together find appropriate solutions through consensus. The DPC approached the Urban Management Program, which was favourably disposed to committing funds to the project. The objectives of the project were to:

1. conduct a city profile to establish the incidence of poverty in the city
2. identify the power groups and existing opportunities for poverty alleviation
3. mobilize the people through consultations among small groups of people within the city
4. conduct a city consultation for people to reason and reach a consensus on the problem of poverty and appropriate solutions
5. draw an action plan to combat poverty
6. disseminate the findings.

We applied the standard six linkages to assess the research–policy relationship in this DPC project, and to examine interaction with users. And we found that this study exhibits interesting characteristics that indeed commend it for consideration as "best practice", especially on the basis of the inherent innovations and utilization of the outcomes. The details are presented in Table 5.

Table 5: Assessment of research–policy linkages in DPC

	Linkage variables	Details in respect of the study considered
1	Source of initiatives for the study	The initiation came from within DPC, but the support of the Ijebu-Ode City authorities, National Planning Commission, Ogun State Government, Urban Management Programme Regional Office for Africa and UN-Habitat were later sought and secured.
2	Source(s) of funding	From the inception to the inauguration of the implementation committee, the Urban Management Programme Regional Office for Africa provided funding worth US $35,000. The implementation of the Action Plan for poverty reduction, which is the output of the research, has been financed by donations–Naira 15 million (120,000USD) from indigenes and a Naira 15 million loan from the National Poverty Eradication Program (NAPEP).

3	Diversity of research personnel and conduct of research	All the critical stakeholders–the traditional authorities and local government–were intimated by the research process. Besides, local consultants were commissioned to carry out the research and prepare a city profile. DPC mobilized all groups through mini-consultations at meetings of societies, trade groups, artisans, etc. A three-day city consultation was held where local experts presented papers on the Ijebu-Ode poverty situation, as well as the local resources available. After this, an Action Plan was developed and adopted. A committee made up of representatives of all stakeholders was put in place to implement the plan. The committee then mobilized funds from indigenes and implementation of the plan began.
4	Linkage mechanisms (and mode of interaction with policy-makers and users)	The project started with the Urban Management Program Regional Office for Africa, the DPC and the community. The state government, National Planning Commission and several development partners, including the United Nations Development Program (UNDP), International Labour Organization (ILO) and foreign embassies in Nigeria, became part of the process before the implementation committee was inaugurated and continued afterwards as well.
5	Role of policy-makers and users in research initiation, implementation, monitoring and dissemination	Policy-makers were involved in the initiation of the research and they provided funds for the implementation of the research. The local government, state government and the NAPEP provided funds for the implementation of the Action Plan. They were not involved in monitoring except that NAPEP came to inspect what was on the ground before advancing the loan it provided. Policy-makers were not involved in the dissemination.
6	Impact (use of results)	The outcome of the research was the Action Plan and it is still being implemented. Other cities in Ogun State and Ekiti State have gone to Ijebu-Ode to learn from their experiences. Over 3,000 people have been trained in various small-scale enterprises and book-keeping, and granted loans to get their businesses started. Experiences gained in the project are being tested in similar projects in Minna, Nigeria, as well as in the cities of Tema and Tamale, in Ghana.

Indeed, so impressive were the results of this DPC project to analyse and propose solutions for poverty in the city of Ijebu-Ode, that it won a "best practice" competition organized by the Urban Management Program Regional Office for Africa in 2002. At a global competition in Dubai in the same year, the project came eleventh. The main constraint is that funds have not come from donors to implement the Action Plan.

PITFALLS IN THE RESEARCH–POLICY NEXUS

Before any improvement can be made in the linkage between research and public policy in Nigeria, clearly it is necessary to identify the weak links, the proverbial pitfalls in the research–policy nexus that need to be strengthened. This section describes the major pitfalls.

Unhealthy competition between "in-house" research outfits and statutory research organizations

In-house research outfits refer to small units within government Ministries, Departments and Agencies (MDAs) that occasionally carry out evaluation studies relating to government policies, programs and projects using internal resources. The existence of an in-house policy research framework should not be confused with the essence of autonomous policy-oriented research outfits (think tanks) whose services should feed back into the policy process. There are clear reasons for the distinct existence and activities of "in-house" research in MDAs and independent research institutions. They include the following:

- Civil servants operating under the "in-house" research framework often suffer from limited skills.
- Civil servants may be unable to concentrate their efforts on research when they try to fulfil their service mandates, which distract in an undesirable way from research.
- The coverage that time and resources will allow is very narrow. Usually funding is very limited for the activities of in-house research units. Moreover, the level of expertise available is usually inadequate. Thus, the design of studies is at a very reduced scale.
- The bureaucratic principles and actions underlying in-house research by civil servants are apt to jeopardize the thoroughness and timeliness required of research output delivery.
- At best, civil service and research service should be seen as two sides of the same coin. Any attempt to merge responsibilities will lead to the destruction of the coin. In other words, if civil service

tries to play both sides, this will seriously diminish the quality of research input for policy-making.

- Research that is motivated and conducted in-house may well be afflicted with political discolouration and thus be seen by citizens as working to provide government with a pre-determined answer based on political expedients and not independent research.
- Results of studies that are designed and executed in-house may not be presented in a critical and useful manner to warrant meaningful application to the policy process.
- With excessive dogmatism, the in-house research framework will lose credibility leading to unpopularity of both the government and its policies.
- Total reliance on in-house research capacity will spell doom for engagement between government and international development partners. Without inputs from think tanks (such as the autonomous research institutions with statutory responsibilities) within the country, this key international engagement will be thoroughly weakened, exacerbating the vulnerability of the country's economy to external economic evasion and suppression. In this circumstance, the economy will be operating in the interest of external agents rather than that of the citizens. Clearly, the consequences on political stability will be adverse.
- Those supplying information to researchers in focus group discussions, surveys and interviews may be more receptive to and open with researchers from independent institutions than they are with civil servants. If the population considers the government performance and political actions unsavoury, which is unfortunately often the case, they are unlikely to trust or reply to questions from civil servants, who appear to represent government.
- Relying on research institutions that act as independent think tanks will reduce the dependence on foreign experts, who are not only expensive but may also represent self- or even subversive interests.
- Experiences the world over acknowledge the need, relevance and strategic roles of policy-oriented research institutions. In recent times, it has become clear that there is also a need to foster and strengthen the linkages between such institutions and policy-makers.

In Nigeria, however, the problem is that there is an unhealthy competition between the two research communities–government-based and independent. They compete for research funds, policy ideas and recognition in the corridors of power. In the absence of proper coordination, it has been difficult to ensure that the research findings from the autonomous research institutions form the basis of key policy decisions.

Policy initiation gap

When research projects are completed, the next logical step is to make policy recommendations. But what we find in Nigeria is that there is a gap–researchers make their suggestions but find no one designated to take the initiative for appropriate actions to articulate policies. This gap exists even when the research findings and policy recommendations are conveyed directly to policy-makers and advisers. There is simply no one with the responsibility of embarking on the implementation of research recommendations. One of the respondents in our study of the research-policy nexus has this to say about this policy initiation gap.

> I'll give you an example. Last year I sought audience with the Presidency to present the findings of some research on all aspects relating to water utilization in the country–such as water for drinking, irrigation, transportation, industrial use, use in the health sector and so forth. At the middle of the presentation we were asked to stop and to repeat the presentation the following week when the relevant Ministers and policy advisers would be invited to be in attendance. This was done. But up till now, none of the policy recommendations has been addressed despite the relevance and potential utility. This is because no one is ready to take responsibility to initiate necessary actions to implement the suggestions. This is frustrating.

This lack of follow-up is probably due to the misperception by the authorities concerned that the research itself is diversionary and not likely to yield immediate political benefits to policy actors.

Policy confusion and uncertainties

Government often claims that there is a shortage of funds, and that this accounts for long delays in the release of budgeted funds for and financial commitments to research institutions. But this does not give the whole picture. Sometimes delays or non-release of research funds are due mainly to what can be regarded as confusion in the policy arena. One of the respondents in this study put it this way:

> How can we agree on the implementation of a project with well thought-out procedures for funding, and suddenly funds are withheld even when the project is about 75 percent completed, simply on account of an observation raised by an individual?

The answer is that often the individual responsible for discharging the funds does not fully understand the considerations guiding the approval and implementation of the project. Invariably, funding of projects can be stalled on the basis of the flimsiest of excuses by egocentric commentators.

Poor culture of policy development

Political leaders often have a disjointed and nebulous perception of policy development and this leads to dysfunctional policy actions and a general lack of progress. There is no systematic follow-up of policy actions and reactions in Nigeria. Typically, policy changes are based on afterthoughts, uncoordinated inferences from developments in the policy arena and individual preferences. Policy initiators, monitors and evaluators work at cross-purposes. The knowledge base for meaningful policy articulation is discountenanced and continually destroyed. Many leaders prefer to keep genuine policy recommendations at the background, while actively investing huge amounts of resources in search of myriad policy ideas that will enable them to maximize personal gains in the course of implementing public programs. Needless to say that in the process, existing institutional arrangements are sidelined, while individuals who are likely to be easily manipulated are engaged as consultants. Invariably, the output is usually more of a reflection of individual idiosyncrasies and interests than it is genuine concern for the welfare of the people. This practice often leads to unending conflict between personal and public interests and it is therefore, a major source of policy instability in the country.

Inadequate linkage mechanisms

The only aspect of the linkage between research and policy that research organizations sometimes address in Nigeria is the dissemination of findings. But dissemination workshops seem not to have achieved the desired objectives of sensitizing policy-makers and inducing them to take appropriate actions. One partial explanation for this is that it is not possible at all times to involve the policy-makers in dissemination seminars and workshops because of resource limitations. But there are other reasons for this weak linkage. Usually, policy-makers view dissemination workshops as very low priority. So they either don't attend or they send as their representatives people without the calibre or clout to be effective participants and links to more powerful policy-makers. Without doubt, the policy-makers or their representatives treat the information they obtain at dissemination workshops with levity or ignore it completely. A more serious problem is that there is no rallying point for the crystallization of the research ideas in the policy process before the research starts. This is a major gap. In general, researchers behave as if they have a monopoly on problem identification, while policy-makers appear to claim monopoly of solutions. In the end, both parties lose, but the biggest loss is to the people who derive no benefits of research and policy actions.

HOW TO FIX THE RESEARCH–POLICY LINK IN NIGERIA

1. *Give priority to research funding.* Nigeria's Federal Government should increase research funding through the annual budgetary allocations. Think tanks should consider establishing a Research Trust Fund that they can invest in a very reliable manner. The proceeds of such investment can be used as the need arises to supplement annual budgetary releases from the government.

2. *Establish a network of public policy research organizations.* There should be a network of think tanks that can operate jointly to influence policy decision-making by offering useful contributions at the appropriate time. By pooling resources (human, financial and others) it should be possible for them to expand the coverage of their studies, operate rapidly as the situation may warrant, and provide formidable and dispassionate policy options that will be respected by policy-makers.

3. *Ensure that research is demand driven.* The National Planning Commission should collate research studies annually from different ministries, identify suitable research institutions and together with the relevant ministries, design mechanisms for joint implementation

that will help ensure research is driven by demand. The government should also demand a minimum annual contribution from each of the think tanks. This will ensure that each of them has something to show for the funds allocated to them. Rather than creating parallel research groups, the think tanks should be challenged from time to time and be required to make necessary inputs to vital policy questions that the government wants to resolve. Of course, their views that should be a product of in-depth research may pass through a caustic review process until the most appropriate option is found.

4. *Establish feed back mechanisms between research institutions and policy makers.* Abrupt and frequent reversal of policies can be avoided if the government provides a framework for involving the think tanks in the review and evaluation of policies. The results of such monitoring and evaluation should indicate the appropriate direction for a policy change, if one is contemplated by the government.

5. *Provide adequate research infrastructure.* Research organizations should operate in an environment that is conducive for meaningful intellectual engagement. They should have modern computer networks and full internet connectivity.

CONCLUSIONS

In Nigeria, research and policy communities work at cross-purposes, and the problem is growing. There is need to strengthen the linkage between research and public policy in order to minimize policy inconsistencies, confusion and instability which are the bane of development in the country. A proper linkage will accomplish three important things: (1) minimize the resources currently being incurred in seeking out policy ideas from numerous sources; (2) streamline and re-direct the focus of public policies from serving the whims and caprices of individuals and interest groups to satisfying the needs and welfare of the populace in general, and; (3) encourage the research institutes to fulfill their mandates and enhance their performance. To enhance the policy relevance and utilization of research findings, interactions between policy-makers and researchers should begin right at the start of the research and continue unabated through the review stage to finalization and dissemination.

References

Bulmer M. 1986. *Social science and social policy*. London: Allen & Unwin.

Caplan N, Morrison A, and Stambough R. 1975. *The use of social science knowledge in policy decisions at the national level.* Ann Arbor: University of Michigan.

Cross M. 1998. Research within metropolis: an agenda for action. Paper prepared for the 3rd International Metropolis Conference, Zichron Yaacov, Israel.

______, Henke R, Oberknezev P and Pouliasi K. 2000. Building bridges: towards effective means of linking scientific research and public policy–migrants in European cities. Research Papers/Netherlands School for Social and Economic Policy Research (AWSB). The Netherlands.

NISER 2000. NISER Review of Nigerian Development: the State in Nigerian Development, Nigerian Institute of Social and Economic Research (NISER), Ibadan, Nigeria .

Weiss CH. 1977. *Using social research in public policy making.* Mass: Lexington Heath.

______ and Bucuvalas M. 1980. *Social science research and decision-making.* NY: Columbia University Press.

Chapter Nine

THE NINE COMMANDMENTS—A SOUTH AFRICAN CASE STUDY IDENTIFIES ROLES FOR APPLIED RESEARCH INSTITUTIONS

Haroon Bhorat

BACKGROUND TO THE DPRU—LEAN AND MEAN

From its inception in 1990, South Africa's Development Policy Research Unit (DPRU) had strong linkages with the anti-apartheid mass democratic movement. In its initial phases, the central objective of the DPRU was to provide economic policy research to a movement that ostensibly was—and turned out to be—a future democratic government in waiting. Thus, from the beginning, the DPRU cultivated a strong relationship with policy-makers through its core activity, namely the production of academically credible policy research. This role became even more vital after 1994, with the advent of democracy.[1]

Since that time, in the post-apartheid decade, relationships between networks linking the policy-making and the research communities were strengthened and new ones forged. While the key mission and objectives of the DPRU were elaborated before 1994, the research orientation and focus have shifted and kept abreast of the most pressing policy concerns of the post-apartheid and democratic period.

Taking the current political and economic environment into account, the mission of the DPRU is to:

- undertake high-quality, policy-relevant research
- maintain and develop effective networks with government, civil society and the research community in southern Africa

- engage in training and teaching activities
- participate directly in the process of formulating, implementing and evaluating policy.

In carrying out its mission, the DPRU has always sought to concentrate on developing and strengthening its fields of research. In the past, these research activities included labour markets and poverty, regulatory reform and regional integration. The latter two have gradually been subsumed by the fields of poverty, inequality and labour markets. This is partly symptomatic of the key challenge posed by labour markets and poverty for the viability of South Africa's democracy. In addition, however, it has been a deliberate strategic decision of the DPRU to pursue research excellence in a specific area of economic policy research, rather than spreading itself too thinly across a range of issues. This is critical in a country that is fairly well populated, with a number of highly focused policy research institutes. But it also means that DPRU's research activities have shifted from the unit's original research themes and gravitated towards research activities that can be broadly demarcated into six new themes. These themes, deliberately broad in scope, that capture the on-going research agenda of the DPRU are:

- education and skills development
- employment in the formal and informal sectors
- the economics of labour market regulation
- poverty and access to public services
- poverty and labour market outcomes
- economic growth, trade and poverty.

At the same time, the Development Policy Research Unit continues to adhere to its well-entrenched operational mandate, which constitutes its goals and objectives:

- foster high quality, policy relevant research within the DPRU
- train a new generation of research economists within the DPRU
- disseminate knowledge (research and its implications for policy) to decision-makers in government, the private sector and civil society.

The DPRU has only eight staff members. Five comprise its research component, with four working under the director who undertakes and supervises research production. The operations division has three staff members: the office manager; the secretary and the publications manager. The management team consists of the director and the office manager. Those at the DRPU recognize the virtue of its being, as popular speech puts it, "lean and mean". This philosophy governs the unit's principles of financial responsibility and the consciously embedded imperative of economic sustainability.

The DPRU's *Modus Operandi*

The DPRU, in pursuing its mandate of producing academically credible policy research, has as its client base numerous national and provincial government departments[2]. These range from the National Treasury (typically the Ministry of Finance in a developing country) and the Presidency, to line ministries such as the Department of Labour, Department of Social Development and the Department of Trade and Industry. Given the solid track record of the institute, these departments often approach the DPRU directly to request an area of policy research be undertaken. However, in trying to ensure financial viability, the DPRU also—on a highly selective basis—competes for public tenders put out by the national and provincial departments.

In addition to delivering research products to our client base, the DPRU also pursues a program of capacity-building for public sector officials and members of the NGO network, union movement and civil society in general. This program is two-pronged. The first is to translate on-going policy-relevant, but technical research into more digestible material for a non-academic audience. For example, three times a year the DPRU runs an extension course called *Labour economics and labour market policy*, geared for a diverse audience composed of unionists, labour lawyers and public sector officials. The second aspect of the capacity-building program is to try, more formally, to build a sort of research–policy toolkit for technocrats within the bureaucracy. In this vein, we offer a training course called *The analysis and measurement of poverty and inequality,* which has as a key component the training of participants on a relevant statistical software package. This course is "harder" in that specific skills are taught, to sharpen the analytical tools at the disposal of the policy-maker.

While the first *modus operandi* of the DPRU is essentially knowledge production and the second capacity-building, the third of its operations is arguably the most important. That is the all-important task of disseminating and distilling knowledge. This is done through a variety of avenues, including regular workshops, an annual conference, a working paper series and a policy brief series. These are all governed by a regularly updated website. It is this particular function of the DPRU that provides numerous entry points for potential consumers of the unit's research output.

THE ROLE OF APPLIED POLICY RESEARCH INSTITUTIONS: THE NINE COMMANDMENTS

Given the unit's rich history and its location within one of the premier universities in South Africa, it has accumulated a significant quantum of knowledge and expertise in pursuing effective policy research. This can be expressed—for want of better labelling—as the "nine commandments" to which applied policy research institutes should adhere when trying to fulfill their mandates. While these truncated lessons apply directly to South Africa, there should be ideas here that resonate with similar institutes throughout the developing world.

1. Inform policy and policy-makers

One of the approaches to research, which distinguishes applied research institutions from consultancy firms, is that the former organizations undertake research principally to inform the policy process. This is distinct from undertaking research to influence the policy process. Hence, upon a policy issue being raised by a specific government agency, the task of the research group would then be to *inter alia:* sharpen the analytical parameters of the issue; provide exhaustive and value-added baseline information; close any obvious information gaps and question conventional wisdom on the issue. Using rigorous tools of economics, the research institution should attempt to provide a product that delivers information that complements and improves the quality and orientation of the decision-making process for the public sector institution.

For example, the DPRU has been engaged with the Department of Labour in a study on the incidence of atypical employment. The study was an attempt, through firm survey data, to both categorize and quantify the existence of atypical forms of employment in South Africa (see Lundall, Majeke and Poswell 2004). The Department of Labour is currently interested in seeing how it can legislate on this new development in the South African labour market. However, the information base from which the department was working was very poor. Hence the clear focus of the study was to improve on this information, with a view to sharpening the direction, and eventually the impact, of the intended policy interventions. Using local surveys, the study illustrated that there are numerous forms of atypical employment, ranging from part-time and shift work to out-sourcing, casual work and flexi-time workers. Such a nuanced definitional distinction around the particular policy issue—in this case atypical employment—had not even entered into the decision-making process of the relevant government department. So what the research managed to do was, in the first instance, suggest a direction for the policy intervention—namely ensure that the department would be focusing on what it viewed to be the most important subset of atypical forms of employment. Secondly, it improved on the quality of the policy-making process, in that the Department of Labour would have a much more nuanced assessment and appreciation of the incidence and typology of atypical employment, and indeed the particular factors that influence firms to engage in these forms of employment.

This is a very specific example, but it offers a general lesson. It may seem obvious, but it is still worth noting that the art of good policy research is really to inform rather than influence the policy process. In other words, policy research should complement policy decisions, and not be a reiteration or reformulation of these decisions. Once this is clear, the research institute needs to ensure that in the process of undertaking a piece of specific rigorous and credible research, it can help improve the quality of the policy decision and perhaps even the direction or nuance of the intended interventions.

2. Distil and disseminate knowledge

Research institutes, particularly those based at universities, often develop a poor reputation in policy circles for constantly delivering a high volume of unreadable or barely understandable reports to government ministries—the proverbial report that is read by no-one and simply occupies shelf-space. Herein lies the second lesson for policy institutes: the work only begins once the final report has been finished.

The final report is the version that lends credibility to and provides details for the activities that will follow. In sum, these activities involve distilling and disseminating—in as deliberate a manner as possible—the results emanating from the research report.

Dissemination involves a well-known set of activities, including the publication of a working paper series, regular policy briefs and a functioning website with generous dollops of downloadable material. While these elements are well known, it is less clear whether all applied policy research institutes dedicate sufficient resources to this activity. The pursuance of the research contract, without ancillary activities designed to disseminate and share this information with a wider client base (donors, other government ministries, multilateral institutions), is in effect an implicit dilution of the potential impact of one's research. A key lesson then for policy institutes would be to dedicate specific resources on a continuous basis to ensure efficient and effective dissemination of their products. Implicitly, this is about a research institute having a well-functioning and well-resourced marketing division.

What is often less appreciated, however, is the need to *distil* information in the process of dissemination—the art of writing the one-pager, if you will. The policy community could legitimately argue that any product they receive that cannot be reduced to three or four key messages of substance is of no use to them. An example of how a final research report can be distilled comes from the DRPU, and a paper commissioned by the Presidency for the 10-year Cabinet Review Process commissioned a paper (Bhorat 2003b). The DPRU produced a 40-page report, then reduced that to just half a page by boiling down the key results that would inform the policy process. If these distilled ideas are powerful and relevant enough, they will permeate through the policy community. And if they do that, your research is already at the early stages of having an impact on policy. If you fail to deliver a distilled product, you can count on failing to have a policy impact.

It is these "headline" results that policy-makers incorporate into their decision-making. Ultimately then, any research institute that explicitly sees itself as policy-oriented needs to accept the notion that it is not just the ideas that are important in formulating policy; even more crucial is how effectively these ideas are transmitted to policy-makers.

3. Develop human capital

Research institutes are often ideally placed to recruit graduate students based within academic departments with which the institutes are associated. If appropriately managed and mentored, these students can often be trained, in the long-run, into highly competent research economists. However, for a significant number of new graduates, the research institute acts as a half-way station—the time they spend completing dissertations while working on a number of internal projects[3]. They will often leave the institutions after a stay of 12 to 18 months, either to pursue their own careers or perhaps when short-term research funding dries up. If possible, research units should try to help manage these young graduates' exits, perhaps helping find them appropriate positions in the public sector.

The public sector environment and its reputation as an employer may vary a good deal from one country to another, but in a number of developing nations there is a shortage of well-trained, experienced technocrats. Research institutions can provide these technocrats by acting as the link between the educational institution where these individuals are enrolled and the final employer. The DPRU has placed a large number of such individuals over the years, and indeed the public sector continues to request from the DPRU potential applicants for specific posts. This is clearly a "public good" that is being offered to government ministries, but it also builds the reputation of an institute—so that it is viewed as a competent enterprise providing a very good supply of young, well-trained technocrats. In addition, should this process continue over time, the institute widens its nodes of interaction with government officials, where a significant number of its ex-employees will be well-represented in ministries. This is the case for the DPRU, where members of its staff have over the years moved into senior positions in government, cementing good relations between researchers and policy-makers.

Indeed, this process needs to be carefully managed to ensure that the research institution does not lose staff members to the (often) better-paying public sector jobs, in cases where it does not want employees to leave. This requires careful management of more senior and experienced staff who should be retained with appropriate incentives, a flexible work environment and opportunities to advance their careers—a critical set of issues. Ultimately, what does distinguish an applied policy institute from the private consulting firm is that it serves as a partner (although not an uncritical one) on research with government ministries and other policy bodies. As such, this partnership should also extend, within reason, to providing value-added human capital to these bodies that very often lack skilled staff.

4. Build public sector capacity

It follows from the above that an additional focus of any applied policy research unit should be to build capacity within government. Government ministries often lack the requisite suite of skilled personnel to shape effective policy interventions. This is not the same as arguing that ministries should have research capabilities—as research is precisely what ministries should *not* be doing. The comparative advantage of government departments is in formulating, implementing and monitoring policy. But the experience (at least in the case of South Africa) suggests that ministries are either over-stretched to meet these obligations or simply possess staff without the right skills to fulfill their mandate. And it is here that research institutes can and should assist. This assistance should come primarily in the form of training workshops and extension courses. The former is represented by a hands-on, intensive (usually computer-based) course on a particular set of policy issues. These may include for example, a course such as the one mentioned earlier in this chapter, on analyzing and understanding poverty and inequality, or a course on trade and trade agreements. Policy-makers are often very receptive to such training. Evaluations of DPRU courses show that participants often leave feeling they have a clearer analytical framework than before, and equally important, a better set of tools with which to undertake policy work.

For example, many of the participants on the DPRU's *Analysis and measurement of poverty and inequality* course were members of the Department of Social Development, which is responsible for disbursing state transfers such as old-age pensions and child support grants. Many had not been previously exposed to the extensive literature looking at the welfare impact of these grants, nor indeed to the software that would allow them to track the progress of the grants, identify their recipients, calculate the poverty-alleviating impact of the grants, and so on. This course thus offered an essential capacity-building exercise for technocrats, transferring knowledge from the research institute to the public sector.

Extension courses are a second form of capacity-building. These involve a set of lectures to an audience of policy-makers, which rapidly offers them insights into on-going relevant research—both local and international—in a particular area. The DPRU's *Labour economics and labour market policy* course [4], for example, highlights some of the unit's on-going research into labour market issues. Topics include: the notion of "jobless growth" for South Africa; new trends in internal migration; quality of public education, and so on. Such extension courses for policy-makers benefit both audience and trainer. They introduce the research institute's program, market its product, to an important audience, while allowing policy-makers to rapidly absorb a condensed review of new local and international research material on a particular theme, building capacity in the public sector.

5. Be an honest broker to advance national policy debates

Academically credible research institutes occupy a key place in civil society; although they produce research for policy bodies, they do not—or at least should not—lose their credibility as an objective source of policy-relevant information. In societies with strong interest groups—and South Africa is of course no exception here—the presence of an objective, credible voice in the policy process is an invaluable one. That means that policy research units can carve out a particular niche as intermediaries within policy processes. The DPRU for example, has been involved in a number of key policy debates about the labour market, debates in which the union movement, business and government obviously may take differing positions. So the research unit plays a key role in trying to provide objective research to inform these debates among the social partners. Often these policy debates move forward largely because of research that clarifies the issue at hand and provides rigorous supplemental evidence. In the best-case scenario, policy research can actually break a stalemate in a policy debate.

The danger of course is that over time the institute's research products could actually help to cement in place a particular view on an issue. This may lead to perceptions that the institute is unfairly sympathetic to the views of one interest group over another, especially if the research in the past—albeit objectively—delivered verdicts perceived to favour a particular interest group. This may be very difficult to avoid, and an applied policy institution should be aware that its role as the purely objective interlocutor among interest groups might be difficult to maintain over time.

But this is not the only concern for research institutes. As they develop their public profiles and their presence in the market for research, donors and/or governments may begin—with varying degrees of persuasion—to use the institute to try and "front" or legitimize their policy positions. A ministry may want, for example, the institute to deliver a report on the benefits of privatization or the positive employment effects of trade liberalization, where the expressed intent may be to produce research that supports the policy position of the ministry. This seriously threatens the institute's role as the intermediary or the objective voice. It is critical that the institute manage these relationships carefully, keeping in mind that these actors (government and donors) do offer significant financial support to the institutes[5].

6. Balance the benefits and costs of research networks

Research networks can operate both at the formal and informal level and each has its own challenges. Formal networks tend to be regional or sub-regional, and usually involve institutes doing a cross-section of policy research. Country networks are generally informal and develop through individual contacts and collaboration, without any strict form or cohesion.

Regional networks confront a number of difficulties. Member institutes may have no common thematic expertise, or have uneven levels and quality of expertise. They may be grouped because of their common region rather than shared research themes, and their work may also have varying degrees of policy relevance. All of these obstacles can make it very difficult to run and sustain an effective network. The absence of a champion or lead institute makes it more difficult to sustain a viable network.

Research units are also often organized and run on tight timelines, with deadlines for delivery and short-term funding. In such an environment, membership in a network can sap time, energy and human resources and become a burden for individual research institutes. On the other hand, networks do offer a rare opportunity to engage with peers and institutions outside one's own country and to learn from their experiences. They can offer useful cross-pollination of ideas in diverse areas, including: operational, financial and human resource management; dissemination activities; fund-raising protocols; and proposal writing. Perhaps the key role for an institution in a network—if it is a strong, well-functioning one—is to assist weaker partners in the network in a way that does not draw too heavily on its own internal time and resources. Ultimately though, networks are an important part of the research environment and institutes should try and involve themselves in these activities, taking care not to sacrifice their own internal activities.

A local network usually operates far more loosely and tends to provide a higher rate of return to its member institutions. They offer the obvious advantage of being able to spread information evenly among members, and without great cost. An institute may become aware of a donor's new area of research focus or a government ministry's pending call for tenders through an informal network that permits constant interaction with other domestic policy units. Such networks are also useful for institutes with different areas of expertise, allowing them to come together to collaborate on projects to which they can all contribute, and perhaps qualify for funding of a project that individually they would not obtain. In a slightly different vein, being part of an informal network offers the opportunity to outsource segments of a project to external qualified individuals or institutes. This offers significant long-term advantages, saving the institute costly up-front commitment to human resources they cannot afford, or which cannot be sustained if there is not a constant stream of projects or funding is not guaranteed, and it rarely is in the current funding environment. Finally, members of such informal networks can help control quality of each other's research. This may happen more formally, when, for example, the client requests a formal evaluation of a product. But as an internal member of the policy research community, units can and should ensure that the quality of work that is delivered to clients does justice to policy formulation and to the policy process in general.

7. Paint the "big picture" for policy-makers

Policy-makers need baseline information but they also require data that give them the "big picture". This means they need standard sets of indicators on a variety of macroeconomic, trade, labour market, financial and other themes. In some countries in Africa, the national statistical agency may not function well enough to distribute these data. Clearly, the research institute is ideally positioned to serve as the locus—for a national and international audience—for this type of data. Such "big picture" data can become a springboard for future, more intensive research and so can be viewed as a sort of market-entry strategy for a new institute. In countries where the statistical agency does function well, research institutes may also need to produce more value-added indicator data. For example, in the South African context, while Statistics South Africa does publish employment and unemployment data regularly, these data may not always fully serve the needs of policy bodies. So the DPRU often provides data on employment distributions by sector and occupation—data that can be garnered only through manipulation of the unit's records. SSA seldom publishes this type of data. These kinds of standard indicators can also include more obvious statistics that policy-makers often look for, such as the headcount index or the Gini coefficient, which are seldom found in a statistical agency's releases.

This broad-based and extensive indicator information should also be disseminated appropriately, preferably through an institute's web site where it is easily and freely accessed from anywhere and by anyone. Such information can be invaluable in attracting donors to an institute; newcomers in a country who want a quick overview will visit the web pages of a relevant institute, if it is appropriately marketed. These generalized "Economy by Numbers" data that draw the big picture as well as small ones, can provide newcomers to a country, foreign donors and government ministries with vital but straightforward information, thereby raising the profile and relevance of the research institute.

8. Collaborate wisely with international researchers

Research institutes are ideally placed to engage constantly with international researchers. This can be with researchers working in their particular field of interest, who may not have special knowledge of or interest in the country in which the institute is based but who have made significant contributions to the body of economic knowledge. Interaction can also be with international researchers who do have a special interest in the country, often individuals who have built their careers as renowned experts on a particular country or region.

Accessing and engaging with these researchers is a key role for applied policy research institutes. This can be done in two main ways. One is to attempt to fund projects that would formally draw these individuals into the given project as collaborators. Second is to provide these foreign experts with a platform for engaging with local government ministries and other senior members of civil society. For the former, the institute needs to ensure that it is getting an external individual who adds value to the project, and is not simply a substitute for a researcher who could be locally hired. That is, they should bring with them particular skills that are hard to find locally. The DPRU, for example, is working on a project on schooling that will engage a number of externally recruited researchers. They bring with them a very high level of experience, knowledge and specific expertise that would be difficult, if not impossible to find locally. An additional component of this collaboration would be to ensure that the international recruit transfers some skills to the institute. This skill transfer is always stipulated formally in contractual agreements, but such transfer rarely takes place. For this reason, the institute should organize formal sessions during which particular skills are transferred, and ensure that publications that emerge from the collaboration are jointly authored. There are cases when an international researcher may not offer a unique set of skills or perspective, and research institutes need to avoid this type of collaboration.

Apart from collaboration with international researchers *within* the institute, it is also important to facilitate their engagement with local policy-makers. This can take two forms. The first is to arrange training workshops for policy-makers at which international researchers are some of the key presenters. They bring with them a fresh perspective and new ideas for local audiences, and this sparks useful interaction. A note of caution here: the international researchers must be informed of the nature of the audience to ensure that the training is well-suited to their needs and interests.

The institute should also arrange a series of high-level dialogue sessions bringing together their foreign experts and local policy-makers who stand to benefit from their particular expertise. For example, an institute could invite an internationally renowned macroeconomist to have a dialogue with Treasury and Central Bank officials. This obviously builds the profile of the institute, but more importantly, it facilitates potentially fruitful engagement between a highly-skilled foreigner and local policy-makers.

9. Take advantage of useful new methodologies and approaches

An advantage to a research institute that is based at a university is that the institute has ready access to new techniques and advances in the economics literature, although this can also be the case for research units off-campus. This access comes in three forms. First is that universities tend to subscribe to relevant and recent international and local scientific journals. Second, universities permit engagement of researchers and academic staff. And third, research institute staff can lecture in graduate courses; individuals teaching graduate courses engage with the academic material in a way that they may not when they are conducting a research project. This builds technical capacity for researchers at all levels. For example, teaching a course on survey econometrics will build the capacity of the researcher, and introduce him or her to new methodologies in a far more efficient and effective manner than any given research project is able to do.

The secondary effect of keeping abreast of new methodologies in this way is a solid return to the research unit—and to the policy process. For example, the use of what were to the South African research community relatively new techniques in panel data estimation played a key role in informing policy-makers on income and job mobility in post-apartheid South Africa. Another example of the benefits of new techniques in South Africa are the approaches being developed to understand intra-household behaviour and activities. These new approaches will be instrumental in understanding the impact of government's social grants system, particularly the child support grant. Recent econometric advances—the mixed logit models that are in use in developed countries—will no doubt add more nuance to research in developing countries.

However, there is an art to adopting new methodologies. Namely, they should only be adopted if they offer two essential advantages: they add new or more nuanced policy information to the analysis; and they deliver a significantly more robust analysis, even if their contribution to policy is only marginal. Where the gains from new techniques are not substantial in either of these two ways, then their adoption should be approached with circumspection.

CONCLUSION

Obviously no listing of the key components of an effective policy research unit can be exhaustive. As stated at the outset, this overview is offered as a case study from South Africa and clearly, the emphasis on each of the prescribed roles for an applied policy research institute will vary for other countries, regions, research units with different areas of interest, and indeed the capacity and financial well-being of the institution. However, it is likely that for a medium-sized institute undertaking economic policy research in a developing country, these "nine commandments" do apply to some extent, and would contribute to an institute's strategy to deliver quality policy research in an efficient and effective manner.

Notes

1. For a more detailed and broader overview of the role of research in policy-making in late- and post-apartheid South Africa, see Bhorat 2003a.
2. South Africa has nine provinces, each with their own provincial line ministries. In theory, the national departments set out the broad frameworks for specific interventions, while the provincial departments' brief is to implement the policies within this broad nationally-crafted remit.
3. Ideal, of course, is to have the graduate student work on a project that eventually can be reformulated with minimal effort into a dissertation.
4. Details for this labour markets course can be found at http://www.commerce.uct.ac.za/dpru/MESP_Course/EXTENT2004.HTM; and for the poverty and inequality course, at http://www.commerce.uct.ac.za/DPRU/TechnicalAssistanceCourse2004.htm
5. For an excellent insight into some of these difficulties within a South African context, see Cassim (2004).

References

Bhorat H. 2003a. South Africa: policy-orientated research on labour markets and poverty, *IN:* Phillips LC and Seck Diery (eds). *Fixing African economies: policy research for development.* Colorado: Lynne Rienner Publishers.

______. 2003b. *Employment and unemployment trends in the post-apartheid South African labour market.* Paper commissioned by the Presidency for the 10-year Cabinet Review process. Cape Town: Development Policy Research Unit, University of Cape Town

Cassim R. 2004. Reconciling the mismatch between the producers and consumers of economic policy research: the case of trade and industrial policy strategies (TIPS) in South Africa. Johannesburg: Trade and Industrial Policy Secretariat. Unpublished mimeo.

Lundall P, Majeke A and Poswell L. 2004. Atypical employment and labour market flexibility: experiences of manufacturing firms in the Greater Cape Town Metropolitan Area. Report to Department of Labour, South Africa. Development Policy Research Unit, University of Cape Town.

Chapter Ten

WHERE LOCAL RESEARCH AND PUBLIC POLICY MEET: EXPERIENCES FROM SENEGAL

Gaye Daffé and Abdoulaye Diagne

ABSTRACT

In post-independence Senegal, as in much of Africa, the State had exclusive control of economic policy, and planning was its privileged instrument. Moribund economies, however, then led to structural adjustment programs, formulated externally and implemented with the collaboration of only a small circle of high-ranking officials. The lack of input from indigenous researchers, academics and other sections of civil society meant that these policies did not improve living conditions of the population. Poverty reduction strategy papers were intended to remedy this problem and this is where national research units such as the Centre for Applied Economic Research (CREA), based at the Cheikh Anta Diop University in Dakar, have an important role to play. In this chapter, we resume the experience of CREA in the economic and educational policy-making history of Senegal, looking at the factors and conditions that both favoured and hindered the influence of research on policy choices. These include institutional framework, resource availability and perhaps most important, the advantage of engaging local research to formulate appropriate and adapted policies for African countries.

INTRODUCTION

After more than 20 years of structural adjustment, applied economic research has become all the more crucial in Senegal; living conditions seem hardly to have improved despite the continuing economic growth since the devaluation of the CFA Franc in 1994. Successive governments over the past decade have understood that in the face of diverse and equally urgent social needs on the one hand, and limited resources on the other, they need to define ambitious policies and strategies that emphasize internal consistency, equity, as well as financial and political feasibility.

It is now generally accepted that weak endogenous policy analysis and weak local management capacities are largely responsible for the failures of policies applied within the framework of structural adjustment. For policies to succeed, they must take into account national economic structures, the behaviour of economic units and mechanisms, the interaction of which determines the economic and social development of the country. Research that contributes to policies which foster greater efficiency and equity in resource allocation in a context of resource scarcity will certainly have positive effects at all levels of social life.

For a long time, there has been a need for broadened knowledge about the Senegalese economy, knowledge that can provide a framework for cooperation between different players in public life–civil society, the private sector, the administration and the university–and shape policy reforms to make them effective and successful in invoking positive social and economic change. In this chapter, we examine how the *Centre de Recherches Economiques Appliquées* (CREA or the Centre for Applied Economic Research) in Senegal tried to fill this knowledge gap. We attempt to answer two main questions:

1. How and through what channels have CREA research results influenced decision-making in public policy?
2. What are the factors and conditions that have favoured or hindered the influence of CREA research on economic policy choices in Senegal?

Before responding to these questions through three examples, we will first review the institutional framework within which CREA carries out its research activities and examine the limitations to these activities.

THE INSTITUTIONAL CONTEXT

The government decree that originally established CREA in 1972 assigned to it an economic and social research mission designed to contribute to a better understanding of development issues and more enlightened decision-making. A parallel assignment was to provide young researchers with a framework that permits them to forge the analytical tools they need to carry out their own research. However, its work was severely limited for the first two decades, and it was only in 1995 that CREA drew up an overall institutional development strategy, which we detail here.

CREA–its history, how it works and what it does

The experience from more than ten years of activities suggests that the mission assigned to CREA is still highly relevant given the current unsatisfactory level of Senegal's social and economic development. However, the Centre's economic research agenda requires more resources and technical assistance than the scanty financial resources allocated to it by the Cheikh Anta Diop University, under the budget of the Economics and Management Faculty. By developing a research agenda answering to the needs of decision-makers, however, it is possible to meet both the demands for additional funds and policy-relevant research.

However, most research that is likely to address the concerns of decision-makers draws simultaneously from various branches of economics, management, statistical techniques and even sociology. Only a *team* of researchers can bring together these different skills. Besides, researchers' performance very much depends on interactions with the actors involved in economic and social activities, and on their relationship with their peers from other countries in the developed and developing world. Such inclusive research requires an appropriate framework for organizing and developing it.

In 1995, after a long period of lethargy, CREA drew up its overall institutional development strategy with three phases. The first spanned three years during which the Centre would resume its activities. That is, CREA needed to reactivate itself to demonstrate its usefulness as an institution, providing an adequate research setting, publicizing its research status, developing a strong partnership with public and private sector decision-makers and building researchers' scientific capacities.

In the next two phases, the achievements of phase one were to be consolidated by turning CREA into a "reference centre" for the sub-region. To accomplish this it was necessary to produce a strategic plan tracing the institutional development of the Centre, to improve human resources, to develop capacity to mobilize funds from external sources, to organize the research in order to produce maximum results with a minimum of resources, and last but not least, to plan and carry out high-quality research.

Key in the reactivation and consolidation of our Centre was institutional support from the Secretariat for Institutional Support for Economic Research in Africa (SISERA) of the International Development Research Centre (IDRC). This support first translated into individual capacity-building for researchers, both in economic analysis and management and quantitative techniques. It then led to the organization of workshops on the tools and methods of quantitative analysis, the exploitation and processing of survey data, etc. In addition to helping the Centre formulate a publication policy, the institutional support also enabled it to build its management capacity, with the support of a technical, financial, and administrative staff. Despite the lack of highly-qualified accounting staff, CREA honestly and efficiently managed the resources put at its disposal by relying on the advice provided by a firm hired to do an internal audit of the institution's accounts and to improve its administrative and financial procedures.

In its reactivation phase, CREA also entered into useful partnerships. These included: the *Direction de la Prévision et de la Statistique* (or Department of Statistical Forecast, DPS); the *Unité de Politiques Economiques* (or Economic Policy Unit, UPE currently known as CEPOD) at Senegal's Ministry of Economy, Finance and Planning; and the *Direction de la Planification et de la Réforme de l'Education* (Department of Planning and Educational Reform DPRE) at the Ministry of National Education. Experts from these departments and other segments of the economic administration were associated with the research programs of the Centre. This cooperation increased the Centre's access to important public sector information, and also helped diversify skills needed for the Centre to successfully complete all its activities. The Centre and the Economic Policy Unit jointly hosted two "Scientific Focus Days on the Senegalese Economy", which enhanced this cooperation and simultaneously increased the visibility of academic research.

CREA thus succeeded in immediately demonstrating its usefulness. It earned its legitimacy at the national and regional level by developing research programs that addressed current public concerns, publishing and disseminating reliable scientific information, opening itself to the public and private sectors, and by building researchers' scientific capacities.

Taking advantage of its budding reputation, CREA tried to broaden its financial autonomy by leading a series of studies, which significantly contributed to the development of the current Ten-Year Education and Training Program (known as PDEF), to be discussed later in this chapter. A number of the Centre's researchers bid for and won research contracts that provided them with additional financial resources.

The making of economic policies in Senegal[1]

In the first two decades after its political independence, the State of Senegal had almost exclusive control over economic policies–both their definition and implementation. It was with the advent of structural adjustment programs introduced by international financial institutions such as the International Monetary Fund (IMF) and the World Bank, that the State lost its control of economic policies, and then later was asked to re-enter the process by contributing to poverty reduction policies, as laid out in Poverty Reduction Strategy Papers (PRSPs).

In the post-independence era, development policies were in the hands of the government, part of an overall social and economic transformation project. They were characterized by a high degree of consistency between major options, objectives and resources; planning was the privileged instrument of the policy-makers. It is noteworthy that up to the late 1970s, these policies were supported, if not approved by the World Bank and other bilateral and multilateral cooperation agencies. The development model underlying these policies was founded on the control and development of natural resources, the modernization of agriculture as a procurement source for the industrial apparatus, the import-substituting industrialization, and the public control of the so-called strategic sectors.

However, this model quickly revealed its limitations. The building of the State translated into the development of a plethoric and budget-eating administration. The "bureaucratization" of production facilities, combined with the expansion of an urban middle class with a strong propensity to spend, resulted in a disequilibrium between public finance and external accounts. Instead of integrating the vast majority of subsistence farmers, the modernization of agriculture rather led to their exclusion from economic development. Government enterprises turned out to be the sources of both inefficiency and public indebtedness.

The resignation of President Léopold Senghor and his replacement by Abdou Diouf as head of state in 1980 also marked the end of an era of a type of economic regulation and management. Financial disequilibria reached such levels that development plans had to be put aside while short-term crises resulting from economic disequilibria were managed. Concurrently, the State's role in the definition of economic policy weakened.

Pressing financial constraints relegated the planning system to the back burner. There was an attempt at reforming the planning model in the middle of the 1980s, but the new system remained a simple project and was never pursued. It was the merger of the Economy and Planning Ministries, and the grouping of the departments responsible for planning and structural adjustment monitoring, that finally put an end to the planning system.

Structural adjustment programs, in fact, translated into stripping most of the State institutions of their economic policy-making power. The deep involvement of the IMF and World Bank in policy choices meant that only a small circle of high-ranking officials close to the President or to the Minister of Economy and Finance knew the exact content of the reforms. Many departments of the Economy and Finance Ministry thus saw their functions reduced to producing statistical information, seeking funds from external sources and monitoring the structural reform policies.

In fact, the processes of planning and implementing the reforms initiated from 1979 up to 1993 were hardly internalized by the institutions in charge of their implementation. The decisive turning point was the "Emergency Plan" in 1993 and the devaluation of the CFA Franc in 1994. In the face of the growing protests sparked by these two events, it was difficult for the government to continue excluding social and economic actors (private sector, unions, civil society etc.) from policy-making.

Poverty reduction strategy put a new emphasis on this involvement. Among the structuring elements of this strategy were good governance and participatory approaches in defining and implementing economic reforms. This new approach grew out of two major lessons drawn from the experience of structural adjustment programs. First, it was clear that social actors (mainly trade unions, employers' associations, civil society) had to be part of the policy process and adhere to reforms since the structural adjustment programs carried out previously without their input and participation were–rightly or wrongly–held responsible for the degradation of the living conditions of the population.

Secondly, it was now clear that the State's ability to implement the poverty reduction strategy strongly depended on the administration's capacity to manage public resources transparently, equitably and efficiently. For this reason, the main reforms touching on policy formulation and implementation focus on decentralization, capacity-building in public administration, streamlining administrative procedures and the availability of economic and social data. Such an approach could not work without the participation of the academic and research community as a component of the civil society.

CREA'S INVOLVEMENT IN POLICY FORMULATION AND IMPLEMENTATION

This section highlights some of the experiences through which CREA's research and work programs influenced public decision-makers' choices, more–or less–attracted their attention, or resonated with them.

MIMAP/Senegal program and CREA's work with poverty reduction

We now turn to CREA's participation in the international network known as MIMAP (Microeconomic Impacts of Macroeconomic Policies and Adjustment), which is one of the 22 case studies examined in Chapter Four of this book. MIMAP was initiated by the International Development Research Centre (IDRC). The MIMAP network brings together researchers from Canada, Asia, Africa and Latin America, and also operates in individual countries. As a participant in the MIMAP program in Senegal, CREA was able to contribute to the preparation of the country's Poverty Reduction Strategy Paper (PRSP) that was adopted in 2001, and has been considered since then as the reference framework for all economic and social policies in the country.

The Agreement Protocol of the first phase of MIMAP/Senegal was signed between the Dakar-based IDRC Regional Office and the Cheikh Anta Diop University of Dakar, in June, 2000, assigning CREA responsibility for the project's management during its first two years. Financing came from the IDRC and the Canadian International Development Agency (CIDA).

The overall objective of the program is to develop analytical tools for assessing the policy impact on the behaviours and living conditions of poor populations. Its purpose is to allow a better understanding of the profile and determinants of poverty and inequality in order to be able to pre-empt any possible negative effects of future economic reforms. In the long term, the project aims to develop a national analytical capacity for a better understanding of the mechanisms and determinants of poverty.

Apart from providing an opportunity for exchanges and cooperation among academic researchers and public administration experts in Senegal, the research program was also expected to document all decision-making aimed at poverty reduction. To undertake this program, CREA drew not just on its own staff but also on economists in the public administration and statisticians, notably those from the Department of Statistical Forecast, the Economic Policy Unit, and the Planning Department of the Economy and Finance Ministry. This diverse team permitted a rich mix of sometimes contradictory views and experience on a number of research topics, which were shared at MIMAP/Senegal to develop of policy dialogue between the administration and the academic community.

A MIMAP/Senegal Steering Committee made up of representatives of public and private institutions was set up to advise research teams on how to better integrate decision-makers' concerns in their work. A launching seminar was organized in January 2001, at which the Minister of Economy and Finance presided.

Because MIMAP/Senegal was established before the poverty reduction strategy process began, researchers involved in the program were able to play an important role in the process, as shown by the many quotations and references to the work of CREA in the official document. Indeed, to date the main impact that MIMAP/Senegal has had on economic policy has been through its involvement in the preparation of the country's PRSP (Tuplin 2003).

The MIMAP network served as a key communication forum; through MIMAP the Department of Statistical Forecast in Senegal–which managed the PRSP–was well informed about the research on poverty conducted by CREA and sought to make use of the skills the Centre possessed. With support from CIDA and IDRC, the Department then called upon CREA to prepare a document taking stock of the poverty situation, which could serve as a basis for discussion in the PRSP process.

The CREA study (CREA, 2003) was to focus on the need to "better grasp the contours of the poverty phenomenon, measure its scope, understand its distribution and characteristics in Senegal, identify its determinants and manifestations, and assess the impacts of the policies pursued so far". A dozen CREA researchers working on the PRSP study focused on a series of issues, such as: measuring monetary and non-monetary poverty; characterizing the forms of poverty affecting Senegal and identifying the zones and social groups most affected by them; identifying the determinants of poverty in Senegal; and the link between economic growth, poverty and inequalities. These analyses allowed CREA researchers to define the main lines of a poverty reduction strategy.

CREA was also designated as a member of the Committee in charge of the technical supervision of PRSP preparation. In addition to the Ministry of Economy and Finance and Planning, other members of this Technical Committee included the Ministries of Health, Education, Agriculture and Mining. Based on the research done by the CREA researchers, the Committee prepared a synthesis document entitled "Poverty Diagnosis", which served as a basis for discussion at the PRSP-launching seminar.

CREA not only led the five thematic groups set up during the launching seminar but its researchers also contributed to the work of all these groups. They helped clarify and explore issues that are rarely addressed in the definition of economic policy, namely inequalities, gender dimension, and the links between access to basic social services, productivity, and economic growth.

Discussions among the participating thematic groups made it possible to approach the poverty reduction strategy from a wide range of perspectives. These exchanges led to consensus on a number of points, notably the idea that growth is necessary but not sufficient for poverty reduction. To reduce poverty, growth must also be fostered in the sectors where the poor intervene, particularly in primary activities since 80 percent of poor households live in rural areas.

For the CREA researchers, the main achievement here was that they were able to contribute to and influence the PRSP preparation process, as most of the recommendations of the country's Poverty Reduction Strategy Paper were drawn from their research. This demonstrates the important point that national economic policies can be formulated without foreign expertise. Local research capacities, when given the chance and support, can develop appropriate policy strategies that can be implemented more easily and more effectively because they have been made to fit the needs and realities of the country. But a prerequisite is local capacity in research, which must be developed and sustained, and called upon when needed in policy development.

On the strength of the achievements made during the first phase of MIMAP/Senegal, CREA launched the second phase of the project in August 2003 by associating more researchers and public decision-making organs in the formulation of the new research program–Department of Statistical Forecast, National Poverty Reduction Unit, the Ministry of Social Development and the Ministry of Agriculture. An inaugural seminar helped identify new areas of research centred on the analysis of the impact of poverty reduction programs. The purpose was to lay the foundations for a more accurate knowledge of the conditions of PRSP implementation, so as to better monitor both its impact and the relevance of the selected indicators used to target poverty.

Lastly, it is important to mention that on two occasions (in 2002 and 2004), CREA acted for Senegal as the coordinator of the "Action Forum on Public Financial Policy for Poverty Reduction in Africa," organized by the World Bank Institute. This focused mainly on streamlining and targeting public expenditure for poverty reduction. These meetings, which were attended by public administrations, social partners, local authorities and researchers from all over Africa, were coordinated both by academic researchers and experts from the Ministry of Economy and Finance.

CREA's role in educational policy formulation and implementation

In 1997, CREA and the Ministry of National Education began an exemplary partnership that would ultimately transform the centre into the "institutional consultant" for formulating and implementing the Ten-Year Education and Training Program (PDEF), the implementation of which started in 2000.

CREA's involvement in PDEF

This partnership began when the education ministry involved CREA in the formulation of the *Programme d'Amélioration de l'Enseignement Supérieur (PAES* or Program for the Improvement of Higher Education) and the review of public expenditure in the education sector. The analyses proposed by the CREA researchers engaged in these two exercises radically changed the perspective from which traditional actors of the educational system addressed educational issues. Till then, public decision-makers had paid little attention to education costs and CREA's studies revealed that as in other areas of public policy, there was a problem in the way scarce resources were allocated to try to meet so many needs.

Naturally, CREA was later called upon to help the government formulate its Ten-Year Education and Training Program and to complete a series of studies intended to help shape this plan. In turn, these studies and the presence of CREA researchers at all stages of the PDEF, led the Ministry of Education to propose that the Centre assist it in the implementation of Phase I of the program. Table 1 lists the 19 studies that CREA produced between 1996 and 2004 for the Ministry of National Education.[2]

Table 1: CREA studies carried out on behalf of the Ministry of Education of Senegal, 1996–2004

1	1996. Cost of diploma at Cheikh Anta Diop University
2	1999. Cost-effectiveness in middle and secondary education
3	1999. Public expenditure in education and equity
4	1999. Evaluation and simulation model of the PDEF, (SIMULPDEF)
5	1999. Evaluation of the costs of financing the PDEF
6	2001. Review of public expenditure on education
7	2001. 2002, 2003, 2004 CREA Annual economic and financial report
8	2004. Revision of the SIMULPDEF model
10	2003. Analysis of educational tenders in primary education
11	2003. Socio-cultural obstacles to the demand for education
12	2003. Economic analysis of the demand of education
13	2003. Decentralization and the management of education
14	2002. Reform of the budgetary nomenclature in the Ministry of Education
15	2003. Feasibility study of the integrated development program for young children
16	2000–2003. Budgeting by objective in the education sector
17	2003. Step-by-step follow-up in the education sector
18	2003. Survey of secondary education institutions
19	2004. Analysis of the education sector

Among the studies CREA carried out between 2000 and 2004, each year it produced the "PDEF Economic and Financial Report", an assessment of the performance of the educational system. CREA, as an independent and external institution, was best placed to play the essential role of neutral assessor to monitor the PDEF implementation, separate from government, technical and financial partners, unions and other actors of the educational system. This annual report has become the basic document for the PDEF annual review, which brings together all actors of the educational system.

But perhaps the most important contribution CREA made to the preparations and implementation of the first phase of the PDEF was the 2004 report called "Education Sector Analysis". This report synthesizes a series of CREA studies[3] commissioned by the Ministry of National Education with a view to deepening various issues to be included as priorities of PDEF Phase II. CREA was asked to ensure technical oversight and administrative steering for this second phase. The conclusions of the report, which were discussed by all the actors of the educational system at a national seminar, thus constituted the basis for the formulation of PDEF Phase II.

Another intervention by CREA in the education sector was the training of staff of the Ministry of National Education in the financial monitoring of PDEF, in "budgeting by objective" and the new budgetary nomenclature for public expenditure developed by CREA on behalf of the Ministry (Table 2).

Table 2: CREA training for the Staff of the Ministry of Education, Senegal

1	2002. Design and implementation of a capacity-building plan for the Department of Planning and Reform of the Ministry of Education, Senegal
2	2002. Training the staff of Senegal's Ministry of Education in "Budgeting by Objective"
3	2002. Reform of the budgetary nomenclature of the Ministry of Education, Senegal

But CREA's activities in education policy research were not limited to Senegal. In 2004, the Republic of Guinea (Conakry) called upon CREA to help build staff capacity there. The Medium Term Expenditure Framework Unit of Guinea's education sector asked CREA to help build the capacities of its staff in modern public resource management methods. The training program was inspired mainly by the Centre's experience in budgeting by objectives.

What CREA learned from its work in the education sector

Many lessons were learned from the long and fruitful partnership of CREA and the Ministry of National Education. First, the Centre's researchers finally and successfully relieved foreign (especially French) experts in all economic and financial analyses devoted to the education sector. Secondly, CREA has shown that a research centre can play an expanded role in the policy process. The Centre provided not just analysis that provided a framework for educational strategies and policies but it also drafted documents leading to policy formulation and monitoring, as well as the assessment of PDEF implementation strategies. So CREA's experience is important in that it showed how a research unit can be involved through all stages and levels of the educational policy formulation and monitoring process.

In this case, the concept of a "policy-making community" (Tuplin 2003) can be used to understand the nature of the links being established between the different actors or groups of actors who have an influence on the decision-making process. Before the PDEF, national researchers were almost totally excluded from the spheres where educational policies were formulated. The analyses focusing on the education sector were done by foreign consultants directly recruited by donors and technical partners such as French Cooperation, the World Bank, the United Nations Educational, Scientific and Cultural Organization (UNESCO).

And thirdly, the involvement of CREA in PDEF implementation introduced a fundamental change in the "policy-making community". This change implies that henceforth, Senegal's and indeed other African countries' educational policy[4] options and orientations can be founded on the results of research done by local rather than international researchers.

Comparing lessons learned in education and poverty reduction strategy

It is useful to compare the influence exerted by CREA on the development of poverty reduction strategies and on Senegal's Ten-Year Education and Training Program. While MIMAP/Senegal's influence on PRSP was rather passive, as this research program had not been expressly designed to assist in developing a poverty reduction strategy, CREA's intervention in the education sector was proactive from the start. For the Centre, the purpose was to provide, through written contracts, its technical assistance in formulating, monitoring and assessing the education policies put forward by the Ministry of National Education. Later, the centre drew up and implemented research programs with the support partners such as IDRC, in order to expand the academic bases of its expertise.

A single fact illustrates the important role played by CREA in the appropriation of educational policies. Teachers' unions were often reluctant to accept some of the measures in the PDEF (the need for more contract teachers, for example), and the Centre had to defend the validity of these measures. It was able to succeed by demonstrating that these measures were not being imposed on the country from the outside, by foreign consultants of international institutions (in this case, by the World Bank); rather they were the result of an objective analysis in and for Senegal of the country's education situation. Needless to say, this is another advantage of using local research to formulate policies.

The abortive experience with the Scientific Focus Days on Senegal's economy

Every year, many studies are produced on Senegal's economy by both national and foreign researchers, but their results are rarely made known to public decision-makers, not even to other researchers, let alone the general public. The major obstacles to the dissemination of research on economic policies include their non-publication and the absence of a permanent framework where researchers, public and private decision-makers, members of the civil society as well as technical and financial partners, can freely exchange views on research findings.

For two years (1995 and1997), CREA and the Economic Policy Unit at the Ministry of Economy, Finance and Planning attempted to create such a framework by organizing the Scientific Focus Days on Senegalese economy. The two events were clearly successful; they were presided over by the Minister of Economy, Finance and Planning and each was attended by more than 200 participants over two days, including senior officials from the ministries in charge of the various sectors of the economy, representatives of the employers' organizations and unions.

The Scientific Days that focussed on Senegal's economy provided government authorities a special occasion to welcome new ideas and critical appraisals of their policies. They also gave researchers a golden opportunity to listen directly to the public and private decision-makers, and raise questions at the core of their concerns. Debates on potential research topics such as poverty, governance of public and private firms, or human capital development then led to subsequent research programs. Indeed, each event concluded with a session during which public and private decision-makers and members of the civil society shared the research issues of concern to them, which they wished to be addressed by researchers. So these scientific days were an informal way of communicating research results. They certainly influenced decision-makers' perceptions of priorities, the nature of policies to pursue and how to assess the performance of their policies.

But all was not rosy. Unfortunately, the Scientific Focus Days on Senegalese economy took place at a time when CREA did not have sufficient organizational capacity. The preparations for and organization of the events took too much of the researchers' time as they were forced to handle most of the logistical tasks. It was difficult to reconcile this workload with research activities. The event was so broad in scope that it largely exceeded CREA's human, organizational and material resources, and had to be discontinued after the second year. However, the principle remains valid, and such roundtable days are an important tool for interaction and communication among policy-makers, civil society and the researchers whose work links the two.

CONCLUSIONS

Since the end of 1990s, economic research has made significant progress in Senegal. The studies and surveys carried out on poverty, education, agriculture or economic growth have had considerable influence on the development of poverty reduction strategy papers as well as on educational policy design and implementation. However, this influence could have been even greater had research work been more broadly diffused to actors other than those who belong to the sectors directly concerned. The pursuit of Scientific Focus Days on Senegal's Economy could provide an ideal forum for such diffusion, provided the organizers have sufficient human and time resources to take on such an activity. To win the confidence of those who are at the heart of decision-making in Africa, researchers must produce quality research that goes hand-in-hand with the diffusion and application of their findings.

This analysis of CREA's institutional framework has revealed that the degree to which a research centre is involved in the policy process depends on both on its own orientation and the conditions of economic policy formulation in the country. Among the many factors determining this degree of influence are good governance and the credibility of the research institution with decision-makers and donors.

As for CREA, the scope of its influence has been hindered by at least three major obstacles. First, the research activities of the Centre required more coordination effort than had been anticipated. The Director, supported by CREA's Scientific Coordinator, were responsible for this coordination, which required a good deal of time that could therefore not be devoted to the regular monitoring of research programs.

Secondly, as its research activities expanded, CREA had to grapple with considerable administrative duties to establish good governance, including producing progress reports, minutes of the Scientific Committee and Board of Directors meetings, follow-ups of the application of procedures manuals, and drafting technical reports on progress made under research programs. For the Management of CREA, this administrative workload was incompatible with research activities and studies, lecturing, fund mobilization and institutional representation.

Thirdly, the status of the institute within the Faculty of Economics and Management at the Cheikh Anta Diop University meant it had no legal footing for its own autonomous development. Although a Board of Directors was established and has great influence over the orientation of CREA's strategy, it had no real decision-making power. The Faculty Assembly, all the members of which are not necessarily involved in CREA's activities, retains the latter. Regardless of these obstacles, the positive experiences of CREA that we have analysed in this chapter show without a doubt that the development of quality and policy-oriented research is possible in African countries–not only possible but extremely important in shaping their future by designing public policies adapted to their socioeconomic context and responding to their own needs and interests.

Notes

1. The analyses in this section have been inspired mainly by Daffe and Diop (2004) and Touré and Nourou (2004).
2. With the support of SISERA and IDRC, CREA prepared about a dozen "Policy Papers" drawn from these studies, which are being printed for publication.
3. These are the 2003 and 2004 studies listed in Table 1.
4. An illustration of this change is provided by the PDEF Economic and Financial Report 2002 , which revealed that while significant progress had been made by broadening access to schooling at all levels of education in Senegal, the same could not be said of education *quality*. These analyses, which were shared with education technical and financial partners, led the Minister of National Education to modifying the 2003 Annual Operational Budget Plan so that greater emphasis was placed on improving quality of education activities.

References

CREA 1996–2004. various studies carried out on behalf of the Senegalese Ministry of National Education.

______, 2001, 2002, 2003. Rapports techniques pour MIMAP/Sénégal.

CREA 2003. Appui Institutionnel de SISERA au CREA – Phase II, Rapport technique pour la période du 01 avril 2001 au 30 avril 2003.

Diagne, A. and G. Daffé (eds.) 2002. Le Sénégal en quête d'une croissance durable, CREA/Karthala.

Daffé G and Diop MC. 2004. Réformes économiques et environnement institutionnel : la politique commerciale et industrielle, *IN :* Diop MC (ed). *Gouverner le Sénégal.* Paris: Karthala.

Touré EH and Nourou Seydou. 2004. L'administration publique à l'ère des politiques d'ajustement structurel, *IN:* Diop M C. (ed.). *Gouverner le Sénégal.* Paris: Karthala.

Tuplin Tracy. 2003. The influence of research on policy: the case of MIMAP Senegal. Study prepared for IDRC (unpublished).

Chapter Eleven

RESEARCH AND POLICY-MAKING—THE UNIQUE EXPERIENCE OF *NEPRU* IN NAMIBIA

Dirk Hansohm

ABSTRACT

The Namibian Economic Policy Research Unit (NEPRU) is this southern African country's leading economic policy research institute. It was established at Namibia's independence in 1990 to support economic policy-making through applied research, provision of information and training. Since then, NEPRU has grown, both in quantitative and qualitative terms. This chapter reviews the policy-making process in Namibia and the role of economic research in the country. It examines where NEPRU fits in that process and offers a general analysis of various channels that influence policy. It shows that NEPRU's continuous and multi-focused involvement in poverty policy has contributed in a major way to meaningful policy changes. On the other hand, due to the institutional weakness and a lack or urgency, the work on industrial policy has still not managed to influence policy to a substantial degree. This chapter also draws lessons from NEPRU's work that illuminate the challenges and opportunities researchers have to influence economic policy.

INTRODUCTION

The governments of nations that are rich or on the way to becoming rich generally allow researchers to advise them. Conversely, one could argue that the lack of systematic input of economic analysis and research is a significant reason for the lack of progress in many poor countries (Olson 1996). However, there is little systematic evidence on how research influences the policy-making process, either in rich or poor countries (Klein 1999).

Nevertheless, the interest in the link between policy research and policy making is surging (Phillips and Seck 2004). Our intention here is to offer experience from Namibia to contribute to the discussion on the link between policy research and policy-making.

We start with a brief review of the literature on the link between research and policy, particularly in Africa. That is followed by an introduction to Namibia's economy and policy-making process, which leads into the main discussion of the role that the Namibian Economic Policy Research Unit (NEPRU) plays in this process and a general description of the policy channels. We focus on two policy fields—poverty reduction and industry policy—to illustrate the challenges of influencing policy. We conclude by drawing lessons that can be taken by researchers to improve their influence on policy.

THE GAP BETWEEN RICH AND POOR—AND ITS LINK TO POLICY RESEARCH AND POLICY-MAKING

The quality of governance, in particular economic policies and institutions, is increasingly recognized as a powerful explanation for the vast and increasing differences in wealth among countries (Olson 1996). Virtually all industrialized countries and newly industrialized countries (NICs) have systems of economic information and analysis in place that feed the economic policy-making process. In most developing countries these systems are notably absent.

The importance of economic policy research and advice arguably lies in three areas. First is in the provision of hard data about the economy and about its expected development. Second is in the interpretation of these data according to economic principles. Together, these form the basis of an informed process of decision-making, of a discussion of the costs and benefits as well as risks of particular courses of action. The third area of importance is to inform the public on the economy and on policy options, to underpin public discussion and thus strengthen governance.

This reasoning gives rise to two arguments for the need for independent research institutes, independent from the direct control of government bureaucracy.

1. Independent agencies can be expected to operate more flexibly, efficiently and effectively than those within the government.
2. They have a higher credibility, both to government (rather than departments evaluating themselves), and to the public.

Industrial countries have a sophisticated structure of economic policy research, based on a solid foundation of basic academic economic research. There are clearly defined channels for transmission of economic advice to policy-makers, as noted in the literature that has developed to describe this research structure and the channels of transmission (Blinder 1987, Haveman 1989, Peacock 1991, Aaron 1992, Eizenstat 1992, Hamilton 1992, Stiglitz 1997, Klein 1999, Mohr 1999).

In general, developing countries have a limited capacity for economic management and policy research. And yet the achievement of national social and economic goals requires well-developed economic management capacity within the public sector and beyond, if human, financial, and material resources are to be effectively deployed. A comprehensive strategy for training government economists to use the tools of economic analysis is needed to fully develop this capacity. And this, in turn, requires national strategy to build economic capacity.

It has been noted by Goldsmith (2001) and Wohlmuth (1998) that in general, research systems of poor countries have four main problems.

1. weak institutions for economic research
2. little systematic research on the economy
3. little access to recent international insights of economists
4. economic policy interventions are based to only a small degree on these insights.

NAMIBIA AND ITS POLICY-MAKING PROCESS[2]

Namibia, independent since only 1990, has a favourable system of political and economic governance. It had a peaceful transition from a highly inequitable apartheid system to a democratic society: repealing discriminatory legislation; setting up an independent judiciary and establishing the rule of law; a free press; a market-oriented economic policy; as well as high investment in education and health. Its development plans aim for economic growth, employment creation, poverty reduction, and alleviation of inequality. Its Vision 2030, issued by the

Office of the President in 2004, lays out its ambitions of becoming an industrial country by 2030.

Despite this favourable policy environment, the record of economic growth has been dismal. From 1990 to 2001 its annual average per capita growth has been 1.7 percent. During the years from 1995 to 2003 that growth rate averaged only 0.7 percent. This falls far short of what is necessary to reach the development goals. High growth will be required to attain the ambitious development objectives.

The weakness of institutions in the country is one explanation for this poor economic growth. Overall, economic policy has a refreshing degree of autonomy. Namibia is not subject to externally imposed economic reform programs such as structural adjustment, and the government looks critically at policy proposals by international financial institutions. Neither the International Monetary Fund (IMF) nor the World Bank has a permanent presence in the country, or any leverage over the economic policy. In this sense, Namibia's policies are home-grown.

At the same time, the cadre of indigenous economists is extremely limited. This results in two interacting drawbacks.

1. Policy is not based on a consistent set of economic information, analysis, and policy choices.
2. There is a high degree of dependence on expatriate advisors, mostly short-term in the country. This, in turn, creates more problems:
   - As no long-term relationship exists, there is little opportunity to build a relationship of trust between expatriate and national researchers, essential for knowledge transfer.
   - As consultancy services tend to take the form of "turnkey" reports, prepared outside the national research sphere and then handed over to government officials, their ability to make effective use of these is generally limited.
   - Little—if any—local capacity for policy analysis is built up in the public sector.

Cases in point are Namibia's National Development Plans (Republic of Namibia 2001a, 2001b, 2001c, 2001d) and the official Vision 2030 document. Although considerable resources are spent on those documents and they are important points of reference in the debate and action on development, the documents have significant weaknesses in common:

- The stated objectives are not based on economic data and analysis.
- While cross-sectional references are made in the various sections of each plan, they do not relate to each other in any systematic manner.

As a result, these supposedly policy-guiding documents remain limited to the level of good intentions unlikely to result in good results.

Another serious problem is the lack of capacity of government institutions to coordinate their activities, given the multitude of donors. This is partly compensated by donor coordination, notably by EU countries. However, when donors themselves handle donor coordination, usurping this from government, problems arise. First, it limits domestic ownership. Second, the priorities of donors in Namibia are not necessarily the same of those of the government.

After 14 years of independence, Namibia still faces a serious shortage of trained economists. This threatens the success of the country's development plans. Many ministries have failed to fill important economic management and planning positions with qualified economists. Often positions had to be filled by expatriate technical advisors. There has been little transfer of skills from expatriate advisors to the Namibian counterparts.

Skill transfer has not been satisfactory for a number of reasons. One key reason is that very few Namibian economists have been employed in economic policy management positions. Expatriate advisors have been required to carry out line functions rather than to train their counterparts to perform these duties. Furthermore, the training gap between the expatriate advisor and the Namibian counterpart has often been too wide to allow the counterpart to effectively absorb the skills and lessons of experience from the advisor. The time the advisors must spend providing basic technical training in computer skills, quantitative methods, and economic principles reduces significantly their opportunity to train counterparts in more sophisticated techniques of economic management and planning.

Namibia's educational system has not yet been able to provide the economic training to the extent that it is required to produce enough competent government economists. Furthermore, the stark gap between availability of skilled economists and the huge demand results in a high mobility and substantial scarcity premiums that have to be paid. Public sector salaries are not competitive with the private sector.

The prime institution for tertiary education, the University of Namibia, has difficulty attracting qualified and senior staff because it cannot offer them competitive remuneration packages and conditions. Donor-provided fellowships to government economists for training abroad have reportedly increased the country's economic management capacity, but not in a comprehensive fashion (van Niekerk and Samson 1995).

Institutional weakness is a national problem that extends beyond the public sector. The general weakness of business as well as labour organizations contributes to the lack of intermediation and the lack of trust between the social partners.

Several institutions have been set up to achieve wider participation in policy-making. These include the National Planning Commission (NPC), existing since independence. The NPC comprises five key ministers and eight personalities from public and private sectors, all of whom are appointed by the Namibian president. It leads the National Planning Commission Secretariat that is a key ministry, responsible for development planning and aid coordination. However, in practice, its role is rather limited because of the high workload of the members (who are all full-time professionals) and a lack of clear rules of operation.

Another institution is the President's Economic Advisory Council (PEAC), set up in 1997. The PEAC mainly operates through its six committees, and its overarching aim is to promote exchange of information and strengthen cooperation, collaboration and coordination between the public and private sectors. This is an important function in Namibia's society, which is characterized by deep divisions and a low level of trust among various population groups, most notably between labour and business. In economic terms, a low level of trust implies high transaction costs, dampening competitiveness of an economy.

The PEAC started off with high levels of expectation and motivation. However, its function was compromised by several factors, including its lack of clear rules of operation, large size, unclear selection mechanisms and relationship to other consultative and advisory bodies, as well as its weak coordination. These factors diminished members' motivation and only some committees continued to operate. Plans and ideas to remedy these problems have been made and circulated, and members as well as key policy-makers repeatedly point out the importance of the Presidential Economic Advisory Council and the need for its reform, but so far no change has occurred (NEPRU 2001).

In recent years also more research bodies have come into being. The most important are the Labour Research and Resource Institute, founded in 1998, and the Institute for Public Policy Research. The Labour Research and Resource Institute is aligned with the trade unions and its role is to carry out research with a view to providing continuous training and policy research in areas such as labour legislation, collective bargaining, gender equality, affirmative action, Namibia political economy and globalization. The Institute for Public Policy is independent of government, political parties, business organizations, trade unions or any other interest groups. It is guided by a board of independently-minded trustees and its mission is to deliver independent, analytical, critical, and constructive research on social, political and economic issues that affect Namibia.

And, of course, there is also NEPRU, the Namibian Economic Policy Research Unit, which is the focus on this chapter.

NEPRU's role in policy-making

NEPRU was set up in 1990, and it is the leading independent institute for economic research in Namibia. The Unit is an autonomous institution, governed by a Board of Trustees, with the following main objectives:

1. Assist the government of independent Namibia through applied research for policy formulation and decision-making in strategic economic and socio-economic areas.
2. Build an information resource base on socio-economic issues in Namibia.
3. Train Namibians in relevant research skills.

The latter two objectives arise from the first. All three are destined to support the economic policy process in a direct or indirect—but no less important—way.

A high-profile Board of Trustees, including both public personalities and representatives of the key economic policy-making bodies—the National Planning Commission Secretariat, Ministry of Finance, Bank of Namibia—as well as the Chamber of Commerce and Industry, governs NEPRU. This secures a degree of government influence on NEPRU's agenda, but is also one way for NEPRU to influence the thinking of policy-makers and serves as a connection to private sector decision-makers.

NEPRU works on the principle that the most important means to influence and improve governance is through research. NEPRU's primary client is the government, including the National Planning Commission Secretariat and various line ministries, most importantly the Ministries of Trade and Industry (MTI), Finance, Basic and Higher Education, Agriculture, Water and Rural Development, and Land. Other clients include multilateral and bilateral development organizations, and to a small degree, the private sector and NGOs.

Although NEPRU's work concentrates on Namibia, the institute is increasingly involved in research in the southern African Region. It co-operates with other research institutions in the region and beyond. NEPRU is part of various regional research networks, including the Southern and Eastern Africa Policy Research Network (SEAPREN) described in Chapter Six, which comprises six institutes from Botswana, Namibia, South Africa, Tanzania, Uganda, and Zambia, and of which NEPRU is the secretariat.

The changing structure of the kind of projects that NEPRU executes reflects its growing relevance. Dominant among its earliest projects were speech writing, workshop reports, and rather descriptive reports, and opinion pieces. More analytical work—if any—was done by academics attached to the unit on a short-term basis. During its growth process, projects of an increasing relevance became important. These are

1. joint projects with government agencies, so that skills are transferred in the work process
2. joint projects as local partners of international consultants, so that skills are transferred to NEPRU staff
3. projects involving elements of public consultation
4. projects involving quantitative analysis
5. projects involving monitoring and evaluation

NEPRU's research is predominantly driven by demand, ensuring the relevance of its research activities. At the same time, it limits the scope to move the research agenda forward, and to deepen competence in identified fields of importance, as budgets and deadlines for this kind of research are normally tight. To overcome this problem of demand-driven funding, the institute is developing research programs in identified key areas. The programs receive seed funding that is used to identify priorities in basic research underpinning applied research, to follow the academic discussion through literature and conferences, to contribute to local discussion, establishment and maintenance of relations to relevant other research and training institutes, and to prepare and supervise academic studies of research staff.

NEPRU has developed research competence, particularly in the following fields:

- macro-economic planning, policy analysis and governance
- fiscal policies and public sector reform
- poverty and employment
- rural development, agriculture and land
- regional integration, trade, and private sector development
- financial economics

NEPRU transfers its research results to the policy-making process not only by providing its research reports to the clients—mainly government—but also with targeted policy briefings, participation in numerous government committees, advice to and interaction with senior government officials, information dissemination to the public (policy briefs with non-technical language, press statements), and public seminars. It certainly helps that NEPRU's director is a member of the National Planning Commission, Chair of the Statistical Advisory Committee of the NPC, and also a member of the Presidential Economic Advisory Council.

In the process of conducting its research, NEPRU trains Namibian economists. Its training activities concentrate on Namibian Bachelor Degree holders in economics, with the aim of producing professional economic researchers. They are employed as junior researchers, and in the first phase are part of research teams in various fields. Later they attend MA courses in economics at first-class universities abroad. After this, they are given extended responsibilities in project management. At the end of this period they are promoted to researchers. In 2003, NEPRU decided to move from MA to PhD level of training, and from full-time sponsorship to a part-time study system, whereby the incumbents do research degrees related to NEPRU's research programs with joint supervision by senior researchers who lead the respective program. This is to ensure greater relevance of the research they undertake and more rapid career development,

NEPRU also provides training to clients in economic policy and research methodology. However, this function, envisaged to be a major activity, remained in its infancy. It was only in 2001, with the employment of a training co-ordinator, that this task was given systematic attention. Two important elements are an internship program for middle-level policy researchers and managers, and a regular series of policy seminars.

In addition, over the years, many Namibian and foreign students and guest researchers have been attached to the Unit. This resulted in additional publications, seminars, and skills transfer through joint projects.

No less important is the dissemination of information about economic developments to the public; NEPRU has published about 270 documents. All new publications are presented in press releases, some in press conferences.

NEPRU's library with some 6,000 accessions and an extensive stock of information, includes "grey literature" on Namibia, current literature on economics, and key periodicals. The library is also accessible by the public.

NEPRU has an economic database and an expanding literature database. Its growing website provides information about its past, current and upcoming activities, staff, employment opportunities, publications, and press releases. Publications such as its Working Papers, Viewpoints, Quarterly Economic Reviews and its newsletter can be downloaded from the website. Abstracts of other publications are available. Selected information is continuously sent by email to interested parties. The website has recently been redesigned to increase its accessibility.

We now move to two case studies focussing on the link between NEPRU research and policy-making. As research is only one influence on policy-making, it is difficult to determine exactly how and to what extent it has contributed to a given policy. Nevertheless, the following studies of NEPRU's work in the areas of poverty reduction and industrial policy in Namibia do offer insights into research programs that are successful—and also less successful—in shaping policy process.

Research and poverty reduction in Namibia

The reduction of poverty was one of the four major goals of the First National Development Plan (NDP1). The mid-term review of this plan revealed that sector-based strategies were not sufficient to reach this goal (Republic of Namibia 1998b). The government then opted for an integrated approach to address poverty, known as the Poverty Reduction Strategy (PRS; Republic of Namibia 1998a). This was based on economic research. Two local institutions—NEPRU and the Social Science Division of the University of Namibia—were part of an international research team led by the World Bank.

Namibia is a frontrunner among African countries in terms of policy formulation on poverty and its reduction, having both a poverty strategy and a poverty action plan, based on the former, in place. NEPRU played a key role in the development of poverty reduction policy in Namibia.

This involvement began when NEPRU undertook its own Poverty Research Program in 1994–1996. Financed through a grant from the Ford Foundation, this research program consisted of three projects, each led by one of the three senior researchers NEPRU had at the time.

The first project aimed to build a consistent database on poverty by making different data sources comparable, including the National Household Income and Expenditure Survey and a number of field studies of the Social Science Division of the University of Namibia. This project did not advance past its first steps for three reasons:

- delays in the availability of the National Household Income and Expenditure Survey data
- little effective demand from either state administration or other academics for the findings
- the departure of the leading senior researcher, an expatriate who worked at NEPRU for one year.

The second project, based on field research, intended to explore the role of intra-family transfers in the alleviation of poverty. Again, it suffered when the expatriate senior researcher left NEPRU, and it did not move past its initial stage, which was a pilot study of 70 families.

The third and most comprehensive component analysed the impacts of government policy on poverty. This project also made use of the results of the first two components and was the basis for further academic and policy-related work. The retention of the leading senior researcher and the high level of direct relevance to policy were key contributing factors to the continuing work in this field. Several academic studies, some of them published in peer-reviewed journals and books, came out of this first work on poverty and policy (Hansohm and Presland 1998; Hansohm, Schade and Wiig 2001).

The established track record of NEPRU led to its contract with the World Bank-led team that developed the Technical Report for Namibia's Poverty Reduction Strategy. The World Bank contracted NEPRU to execute three background studies for that technical report: on the trade with Angola (Schade 1998); on the construction and brick-making industries (Hansohm 1998); and on agricultural processing (Presland and Pomuti 1998). The joint research team identified the themes of these studies. Beyond this, NEPRU advised on the conceptual development of the overall strategy.

After the government policy-makers developed and adopted the Namibian Poverty Reduction Strategy, the Permanent Secretary of the Commission tasked the NEPRU team leader, also a member of Namibia's National Planning Commission, to oversee the development of the Namibian Poverty Reduction Action Plan. An external consultant was hired for this task, but NEPRU staff members participated in the work.

Building on its academic track record, NEPRU also carried out several other studies of an applied character. Among these, the Namibian trade and poverty program, the export-led poverty reduction program, the United Nations Development Program (UNDP) poverty program, a literature review on poverty, a medium-term research program on poverty, a study on livelihoods and employment, another on poverty and land reform, an assessment of the UNDP poverty reduction program, poverty research training, and poverty diagnostics training.

Despite all these research-driven policies to combat poverty, severe capacity constraints in Government and also across the society, have limited the effectiveness of planned policies. The mid-term review of the National Development Plan concluded that many ministries poorly conceptualized poverty. None of the sectors or ministries had departments devoted specifically to poverty reduction. Until now, Namibia's poverty situation has not been monitored. No comprehensive and consistent data are available, as the idea developed by NEPRU to develop a consistent database on poverty had not been taken up by government or donors (as reported above). Yet these are needed to monitor the extent and characteristics of poverty over time. We do not know if the extent and severity of poverty have improved or worsened since the first Household Income and Expenditure Review of 1993–94. Consequently, it is impossible to know how successful—or unsuccessful—measures to reduce poverty have been (Schade et al. 1998). This is a severe shortcoming, as poverty is widespread and its reduction is a key policy objective. This data deficit has been recognized and the monitoring of poverty has been envisaged in the Poverty Action Plan (Republic of Namibia 2000).

There are several channels through which NEPRU has had a substantive role in influencing the policy-making process on poverty reduction in Namibia:

- *Membership of its director in the NPC:* Key cabinet members and other senior policy-makers, as well as representatives of business and civil society are members. The meetings of the National Planning Commission are important fora for policy discussion. Resolutions are made that either directly determine work at the National Planning Commission Secretariat, or are forwarded to cabinet. That Secretariat is the line ministry dealing with poverty issues. The director himself has key experience in poverty research.
- *NEPRU's Board of Trustees:* Board meetings and meetings with Board members, in particular the Permanent Secretary of the NPC.
- *Programme Advisory Committee to NEPRU's Board of Trustees:* NEPRU presents its research agenda for discussion and members evaluate and may add new priorities. Poverty has continuously been a key issue.

- *Publications:* Several publications on poverty were presented to the press, at policy seminars, and on the website.
- *A stream of meetings* with policy-makers and bureaucrats by the director and staff members:
- *Meetings with donors* who finance much of development expenditure. Poverty has for many years been a key issue. At such meetings the NEPRU director and staff members present research insights and their policy implications.

Research and industry policy in Namibia

Pre-independent Namibia was a "fifth province" of South Africa and an integral part of the South African economy. Before 1990, Namibia had very little industry. Instead, it was mainly exporting raw materials and receiving manufactured goods. The government of independent Namibia identified industrialization as a key instrument to achieve economic development.

In 1992, the Ministry of Trade and Industry launched the White Paper on Industrial Development (MTI 1992), a medium-term policy for the development of an industrial sector. NEPRU played a major role in the formulation of this policy (Isaksen and Shipoke 1992, Orford 1992, Moorsom 1991). The White Paper was the first official recognition of the important role of industry in the economy, as well as the need for a strategy for industrialization. Furthermore, it identified many relevant issues for an industrial policy.

In 1998 NEPRU was asked to lead an MTI team to review the White Paper (MTI 1998). The review found that the effectiveness of the 1992 policy had been limited by many factors: little knowledge of the policy both in the public and the private sector; lack of specificity of the proposed approach; the general nature of many statements; little explanation of links to other policies; lack of an objective assessment of the human and resource capacity of the MTI; several strong assumptions about the economic environment; lack of targeting of specific sectors; little recognition of Namibia's international economic environment; little mention of technology, labour and labour relations, and the role of non-state actors; and lastly, a lack of comprehensive assessment of the situation. NEPRU presented the review the MTI management and it was accepted.

Because of the analysis and of changed international circumstances, the review had recommended that a new industrial policy be formulated. NEPRU was asked to lead an MTI team for this task (MTI 1999). Based on the analysis of the review, the policy began by setting the context of industrial policy, then formulated objectives and principles, distinguished general and specific policies as catalysts for industrial development, and identified implementing institutions and committees. Before drafting the policy, three background studies were executed on successful industrial policies elsewhere, on relevant regional agreements, and on the relationship of industry policy to other policies.

The draft policy was discussed at a workshop with high-profile political and technical participation and a final draft was delivered and accepted. However, immediately afterwards there was a change in MTI leadership. This resulted in the shelving of the document, and the recruitment of another consultant to formulate the policy, and another one to comment on the new draft and the abortion of the formulation of a new policy.

Two years later, NEPRU was approached again to formulate an industrial policy. The MTI accepted this document, but it had still to be ratified by Cabinet. Meanwhile, on 15 July 2004 the new agreement of the Southern African Customs Union (SACU) became effective. The agreement stipulated the formulation of a common industrial policy for SACU. NEPRU and the Trade Law Centre for Southern Africa (TRALAC) submitted a project proposal to the SACU Secretariat that, at the time of writing, is under consideration.

One can conclude that the influence of NEPRU's research on Namibia's industrial policy has not been as strong as could have been expected on the basis of its involvement. The key reasons for this are:

- institutional weakness of the line ministry
- no institutional link of NEPRU to the MTI
- some difference in the view on industry policy (While NEPRU presents an economic view emphasizing the role of the private sector, government—and particularly the MTI—tend to have a more public sector view, emphasizing stronger involvement of government itself in the economy).
- industrial policy is not prominent, neither in the eyes of government nor of donors (Thus, they are not as receptive to research

ideas as, for instance, in poverty. As a result of this, NEPRU did not have the funds to build up as much in-house competence in the field of industry as it had on poverty).

LESSONS FOR STRENGTHENING THE POLICY–RESEARCH LINK

The following lessons for policy research institutes seeking to strengthen the policy–research link emerge from NEPRU's experience.

- Long-term employment of senior research staff who lead research programs is a favourable condition for policy influence.
- Institutional links of researchers to policy-making institutions (governing body of the research institute, key government economic policy making institute) are favourable.
- A long-term perspective of research institutes is favourable. Sustainable funding and the development of research programs are favourable.
- A large parliamentary majority of a ruling party should be favourable of the pace of policy reform, but it may also slow the process because of a lack of urgency for reform.
- A non-partisan approach is advisable, one that limits itself to analysis, shows economic implications of different policy choices, gives balanced judgements explicitly mentioning costs and benefits, differentiates between interests groups, and focuses on the national interest in the first place, rather than lobbying for specific positions, mixing economics and politics.
- It is important to establish a climate of trust with government. This can be built up only over a period of time, as a number of systematic differences between policy-makers and researchers exist. For trust to develop, continuous direct communication with top policy-makers is important. They tend not to appreciate advice on what they are supposed to do appearing in the press.
- At the same time, it is important to establish and maintain a reputation of independence, professionalism, and integrity. Important building blocks for this are publicity (press releases, seminars, interviews etc.), as is the quality of research output. A fine line has to be walked between the imperatives of trust of policy-makers and public credibility.

Notes

1. The author would like to thank Mohamed Ali Marouani and Klaus Schade for their useful comments.
2. This section is based on the author's experience as director of NEPRU and as a member of Namibia's National Planning Commission (NPC) and the President's Economic Advisory Council (PEAC), and as chairman of the Statistical Advisory Committee to the NPC. See also Hansohm (2002).

References

Aaron HJ. 1992. Symposium on economists as policy advocates. *Journal of Economic Perspectives* (6)3: 59–60.

Blinder AS. 1987. *Hard heads, soft hearts—tough-minded economics for a just society.* Cambridge, Mass: Perseus Books.

Eizenstat SE. 1992. Economists and White House decisions. *Journal of Economic Perspectives* 6(3): 65–71.

Goldsmith AA. 2001. Risk, rule and reason: leadership in Africa. *Public Administration and Development* 21: 77–87.

Hamilton LH. 1992. Economists as public policy advisers. *Journal of Economic Perspectives* (6) 3: 61–64.

Hansohm D. 1998. Construction and brick-making in North Central Namibia, NEPRU Working Paper 66.

______. 2002. Economic policy research, governance, and economic development: the case of Namibia, *IN:* Olowu Dele and Sako Soumana (eds). *Better governance and public policy: capacity building and democratic renewal in Africa,* Bloomfield: Kumarian Press, pp 195–213.

______. 2003. Economic policy research as an input to good governance in Africa. Windhoek, NEPRU Working Paper 91, December.

______ and Presland C. 1998. Poverty, inequality and policy in Namibia: the state of knowledge and the way ahead in poverty research, *IN: In search of research: approaches to socio-economic issues in contemporary Namibia.* Windhoek: NEPRU, pp 51–102.

______, Schade K and Wiig A. 2001. Trade policy, poverty and inequality in Namibia, *IN:* Francis Wilson, Nazneen Kanji and Einar Braathen (eds). *Poverty reduction: what role for the state in today's globalized economy?* London/New York/Cape Town: Zed Books/NAEP:164–195.

Haveman R. 1989. Economics and public policy: on the relevance of conventional economic advice. *Quarterly Review of Economics and Business* 29(3): 6–20.

Isaksen J and Shipoke P. 1992. Some notes on an industrial policy for Namibia, NEPRU, unpublished.

Klein DB. (ed). 1999. *What do economists contribute?* New York: New York University Press.

MTI (Ministry of Trade and Industry). 1992. White Paper on industrial development. Windhoek, Namibia.

______. 1999. Industrial policy beyond 2000. Final draft, March. Windhoek, Namibia.

______. 1998. Review of the 1992 White Paper on industry policy. Windhoek, Namibia.

Mohr E. 1999. *The transfer of economic knowledge.* Cheltenham/Northampton: Edward Elgar.

Moorsom R. 1991. Indicative industrial plan for Namibia, NEPRU, unpublished.

NEPRU. 2001. Reform of the President's Economic Advisory Council (PEAC), confidential report to the Prime Minister.

Office of the President, 2004, Namibia Vision 2030. Policy Framework for Long-Term national Development, Windhoek.

Olson M. 1996. Big bills left on the sidewalk: Why some nations are rich, and others poor. *Journal of Economic Perspectives* 10(2): 3–24.

Orford J. 1992. Industry policy statement, NEPRU, unpublished.

Peacock A. 1991. Economic advice and economic policy, *IN:* David Greenaway, Michael Bleaney and Ian Stewart (eds). *Companion to contemporary economic thought.* London/New York: Routledge.

Phillips LC and Seck D (eds). 2004. *Fixing African economies: policy research for development.* Boulder, Colorado and London: Lynne Rienner Publishers.

Presland C and Akiser P. 1998, The market for mikllet and millet products, NEPRU Working paper 63.

Republic of Namibia (RoN). 1998a. *Poverty Reduction Strategy for Namibia.* Windhoek: National Planning Commission.

______. 1998b. Mid-term review of First National Development Plan (NDP1). Review. Volume 1. Windhoek: Office of the President.

______. 2000. National Poverty Reduction Action Programme 2001–2005. First Draft. Windhoek: National Planning Commission.

______. 2001a. National Development Plan II, volume 1, Windhoek, Namibia.

______. 2001b. National Development Plan II, volume 2, Windhoek, Namibia.

______. 2001c. National Development Plan II, volume 3, Windhoek, Namibia.

Schade K. 1998. Namibia's trade with Angola, NEPRU Working paper 64.

______, Hansen M, Hansohm D, Motinga D, and Erastus-Sacharia A. 1998. Overview of Poverty in Namibia, NEPRU.

Stiglitz J. 1997. Looking out for the national interest: the principles of the Council of Economic Advisors. *AEA Papers & Proceedings* 87(2) 109–113.

Van Niekerk I and Samson M. 1995. A discussion document for a Namibian economic policy capacity building strategy, unpublished report.

Wohlmuth K. 1998. *Good governance and economic development: new foundations for growth in Africa.* Bremen: University of Bremen, Berichte aus dem Weltwirtschaftlichen Colloquium der Universität Bremen.

Chapter Twelve

INFLUENCING DEVELOPMENT POLICIES THROUGH RESEARCH: THE KENYAN EXPERIENCE

Thomas N. Kibua and Lineth N. Oyugi

ABSTRACT

This chapter examines the policy-making process in Kenya and examines the divergence between theory and practice in policy-making. It looks at the role that the Institute of Policy Analysis and Research (IPAR) plays in influencing policy and presents the methodology used to influence policy. It also gives an account of a success story, and highlights, based on experience, the challenges facing the institution as well as the opportunities available for strengthening its role. It concludes that for a research institution to play its rightful role in influencing policy, it needs to recruit and retain highly qualified and credible researchers, have at its disposal adequate financial resources and establish a good working relationship with various stakeholders, particularly the government, without compromising on its independence.

INTRODUCTION

In the 1980s and 90s, Structural Adjustment Programs (SAPs) were brought in to shape most African economies. These were not based on solid research on which policies would work, and where they might best apply, if anywhere on the continent. According to Phillips and Seck (2004), governments were generally bankrupt, and most state-driven economies had experienced economic stagnation or even decline for several decades. Hence, international financial institutions (IFIs) generally imposed the first round of structural adjustment policies that were based on theoretical models and their self interest. The results of the reform process were generally dismal. This led to a re-thinking of the continent's development approach and to a consensus among African policy-makers that a market economy is a legitimate goal. Moreover, to deal with the vagaries of market-driven development dynamics, and given governments' limited capacity to conduct sound research and policy analysis, the need arose to establish research and policy institutes across Africa. These institutes conduct policy research to seek and develop home-grown solutions and bargaining positions that take into account local institutions and the political economy. They inform the policy-making process, but with varying degrees of success.

Kenya's negative experience in 1980s and 1990s with the design and implementation of structural adjustment programs made it abundantly clear that there was a need to build capacity in the country itself. This is because, during the SAPs regime, university departments and institutes of development studies remained distanced from policy- and decision-makers. In addition, the policy-makers themselves did not recognize the need to interact with professionals with the analytical capacity to share insights on various developmental issues. When the government recognized the urgent need to redress the detrimental effects of SAPs, it also realized that it must consult closely with local experts on policy issues. Consequently, the country mandated a number of policy research institutions (both government owned and non-governmental), to conduct research and policy analysis and advise the government and its development partners on home-grown solutions to local problems.

Our purpose here is to examine the experiences, challenges and opportunities that these institutions face in influencing economic policies. We do this by looking at the policy-making process in Kenya, the role of the Institute of Policy Analysis and Research in informing the policy debate, approaches to influencing policy (both successful and unsuccessful cases), and lastly, the challenges and opportunities for influencing policy. It also gives a synopsis of the key characteristics of other players in the policy–research arena.

THE POLICY-MAKING PROCESS

Policy has broadly been defined as the translation of a government's political priorities and principles into programs, projects and actions to deliver desired changes within a given time frame (Comptroller and Audit General UK 2001). According to Killick (1981), policies and their implementation are expressions of political processes and the distribution of power. Obviously policies are made by policy-makers, who can be defined as the persons bestowed with the power, either by society or a group of people in a society, to make decisions (Gitu 2001). The policy-making process is circular, largely iterative and involves interrelated stages (Juma and Clark 1995; Ng'ethe 1998; Bardach 1996). Policy-making defines the process by which broad government statements are developed. It involves issues of identification, analysis of available policy options, and actual policy choice or legitimization (Ng'ethe 1998). Policy research and analysis examines the policy-making process by systematically evaluating the technical and political implications of alternatives proposed to solve public problems. It encompasses both the process of examining and assessing policies or programs, and the product of that analysis. Research and policy institutions and institutes of development studies are assumed to play a role to inform decisions, acting as an important intermediary between the policy problem and the policy solution(s).

The theory of policy-making

A number of theories have been advanced on how governments should make public policies. One, which has been highly criticized, is the standard welfare optimizing model, emanating from the theory of consumer behaviour. According to the model, a government is able to maximize the society's welfare by ranking society's preferences among alternatives–with potential conflicts between them removed by the application of a consistent set of priorities and weights. Such a set of societal preferences forms the "social welfare function" that the government satisfies by reviewing all alternative lines of action before selecting the policy, which theoretically will achieve the stated objectives with maximum efficiency. If such a process is applied to all problem areas, the economy will achieve a "pareto optimality" condition, whereby no sector of the economy can be made better by a change of policy position without reducing the welfare of another sector.

The model is based on several assumptions, starting with the existence of a mechanism through which the government can translate community preferences into a social welfare function and then adopt this function as expressing its own policy objectives. It also assumes that: society is broadly agreed in its objectives and priorities; governments have sufficient concentrated power at the centre to ensure that the public interest prevails over special interest groups within society; and the existence of a huge volume of information about the nature of the problems confronted, the possible ways of responding to these problems, and the consequences of adopting each of the feasible alternatives. However, these assumptions may not be tenable in practice, rendering the applicability of this theorem impracticable in the real world.

As an alternative, there is the "satisficing" model of decision making, which is based on the modern theory of the firm. It postulates that governments search not for optima but for solutions that are "good enough"–solutions that will command the necessary minimum of group, organization and individual support without provoking violent resistance from those who are opposed. Philips and Seck (2004), citing HA Simon (1957), note that according to the theory of bounded rationality, most decision-makers are "satisficers", more interested in merely satisfying than in optimizing. That is, because exhaustive research of all viable options for each decision would be prohibitively costly, the search is usually interrupted early with the selection of the first option that is good enough. In a hierarchical organization like government bureaucracy, those at the top have the privilege of putting forth their options first, and they forge alliances to ensure their adoption. Claims regarding the rational quality of a policy option are made in the process of implementing it, despite the fact that it is usually arrived at in the context of a limited search for alternatives.

Odhiambo-Mbai (1998), citing (Lindblom 1968), notes that according to the theory of "disjointed incrementation", the day-to-day process of policy-making is a conservative exercise. As such, policy-makers often do not drastically alter the existing policies; instead they merely incrementally improve on the existing policies.

These models acknowledge the existence of many players in the policy arena. Phillips and Seck (2004) call this arena a market of ideas fuelled by actions and pronouncements reflecting the preferences of distinct groups of actors who seek to maximize their welfare. Regardless of this acknowledgement, a policy outcome cannot satisfy everybody and as such, it is hard to establish a social welfare function. There have to be winners and losers in the policy-making process. In practice, policy outcomes can be influenced by a small number of actors with strong preferences, regardless of the costs and the losers in the process.

Policy-making in Kenya–how it works and how it could work better

The policy-making framework in Kenya has a mixture of bottom-up and top-down approaches, and is largely dependent on the nature of specific policies. The extreme in policy-making is when policies are adopted by a decree of the president, as was the case in January 2003 with the policy of free primary education in the country. In normal circumstances, policies undergo a process of discussions and are adopted, based on expected costs and benefits.

In Kenya, the Ministry of Planning and National Development is responsible for the employment of all planning officers and gives broad policy direction through the coordination and writing of district development plans, national development plans and sessional papers. The national planning officers (usually chaired by the heads of Macro-economic Planning and Rural Planning departments) give circulars to district development officers, which outlined the broad theme of the government's development strategy for a period of five years and the specifics within which they have to design their district development plans. Under the leadership of the permanent secretary in the Ministry of Planning, a secretariat involving senior planning officers is formed to coordinate the writing of the plans. The district plans are written before the national ones. Once the secretariat has received the drafts of district development plans, a stakeholders' workshop is held to deliberate on their design, content, clarity and workability.

One flaw in this planning process is the lack of full participation of the all district development officers in verifying, clarifying and justifying the inclusion of particular programs in their plans. Consequently, programs that the secretariat does not consider a priority are removed from the plans. Since the Medium-term Expenditure Framework became operational in the 2000–01 financial year, the macroeconomic working group[1], the secretariat for the Medium-term Expenditure Framework, and eight sector working groups[2] were formed. The sector working groups draw their membership from various line ministries and government agencies. The secretariat for the design and writing of the ninth national development plan (2001–2006) made use of the macroeconomic working group and the eight sector working groups to write the plan. The chapters of this plan coincide with the working groups, with the addition of a chapter on monitoring and evaluation, a chapter that had not been in the earlier development plans.

The macroeconomic working group defines the resource envelope for the planning period, based on the forecasts of a model, jointly developed by the Ministry of Finance and Planning and the Kenya Institute of Public Policy Research and Analysis (KIPPRA) in 2000. In addition, the macroeconomic working group projects the movements of optimal level of targeted macroeconomic variables, such as gross domestic product, balance of payments, inflation, and interest rates. This group also stipulates growth of all sectors that is necessary to achieve the macroeconomic targets. The various sector working groups analyse the various proposals from the district development plans and synthesize the various policy initiatives that the government needs to formulate if it is to achieve the macroeconomic targets. The Mid-term Expenditure Framework secretariat puts together all the sector working group reports that form the national development plan, which gives policy focus for a period of five years. In the event that the government changes the broad policy focus, a sessional paper is written to direct the new focus. The national and district development plans spell out the broad government policy objectives that the annual budgets make operational.

During the preparation of the development plans, the government does not seek expertise from independent research and policy institutions. KIPPRA participates by virtue of its affiliation with government as a government think-tank. An all-inclusive participatory approach to budget formulation is important to enhance transparency. Inclusiveness of civil society organizations (CSOs), researchers, academics, media, government and the corporate sector in the budget process is vital in improving budget formulation, ensuring efficient resource allocation and better oversight of the budget process. Although the budgeting process is generally participatory, the level and quality of participation is limited by time, human and financial resources.

Participation in the budgeting process is by invitation to submit proposals. Policies that require government finances for their implementation are discussed, designed and adopted through the budgeting process. In 2003, a study by the Institute of Economic Affairs in Kenya rated the overall participation in the process as dominated by the government with minimal outsider contribution (Mwenda and Gachocho 2003). The guidelines given for the budget proposals, especially to research and policy institutions, are restrictive and the time period is short. For instance, for the 2004–05 financial year, the invitation from the Ministry of Finance to IPAR to submit policy proposals for consideration was sent on 26 January 2004, with a deadline of 29 February 2004. Its guidelines stipulated, "In order to remain focused on the need for change, we suggest that your submission includes: the nature of limitations the current framework provisions have on your organization; improvements or the benefits the proposed changes will have on your organization; and benefits and/or contributions the proposed changes will have on the economy." In addition to the three questions above, the Ministry of Finance further required that the proposal submitted must highlight limitations of the current policy, propose remedies and provide an analysis of how the proposed policy would benefit both the government and the organization in particular.

Before 1999, such proposals were to be presented to the budget steering committee. These days, they are to be presented to the Medium-term Expenditure Framework secretariat in the budgeting department of the Ministry of Finance, chaired by the director of the Fiscal and Monetary Affairs Department. All institutions and organizations that are invited to make proposals, and which are willing and capable of doing so, are given audience as long as they are able to meet deadlines. However, the budget secretariat reserves the right to incorporate or reject the concerns raised in the proposals. The budget defines the direction of national policy, the plan of action, and the cost implications of government programs and projects during the fiscal year, while at the same time identifying the resources required to implement them. The Minister for Finance presents the budget to Parliament annually on or before 20 June. Parliament legitimizes the policy proposals by approving the budget.

The policy proposals that a research institute needs to make for consideration in the budget are not necessarily geared to benefit the research institutes, but rather the various sectors of the economy at large. Research institutes conduct research in different fields and on the basis of domestically available data and best practice elsewhere. More often, they do not have a vested stake in policy issues. As think-tanks, they need more time and latitude to make informed proposals and to interact with the government.

Policies that are not financed through the budget, especially those implemented by non-governmental organizations, are not articulated in the development plans and are not deliberated during the budgeting process. Thus, NGOs make policy proposals to probable financiers and if they are accepted and financed, the NGOs implement them. Currently, this sector is not properly regulated and quite a number of NGOs have mushroomed in the country, with most of them being "briefcase NGOs". That is, they often represent individuals rather than true and credible organizations, and they have no clear and accessible address or operational set-up. The government is not responsible for monitoring and evaluating programs and projects implemented by NGOs. They account directly to their financiers for funds allocated to them.

From the foregoing discussion, it is evident that research and policy analysis institutions may not effectively influence policy either because their inputs are not provided in a timely manner and at the right intervention point in the policy formulation process, or because they may not be acceptable and respected institutions.

Mechanisms for monitoring policy implementation in Kenya

Though the Ministry of Planning and National Development is responsible for setting out the broad policy direction in Kenya, different ministries and government agencies formulate their own policies and push for their implementation through their budget allocation. There is no established body in government responsible for monitoring the implementation of all government programs. The various government agencies oversee the implementation of their own policies.

With increased realization that there is gross misappropriation of funds on various policy programs, the Ministry of Planning and National Development, in the 2004–05 financial year, established a Monitoring and Evaluation Department within the ministry, to develop guidelines on monitoring and implementation of national policies.

Research and policy implications–theory versus practice

Ideally, research institutions are supposed to generate intellectual capital, which becomes a critical input in the policy-making process. In theory, the issue of what constitutes intellectual capital and the technological process of feeding it into the policy production process remains basically unresolved. However, in practice, in an effort to define their locus in the policy process, research institutions have evolved into five almost distinct categories (Table 1).

Table 1. Types of research institutions and types of research

Institution type	Type of intellectual capital
Basic research	Research findings with policy implications; university type research
Policy research	Policy scenarios analysis; internal research agenda; internal human resources capital; balancing between supply-driven and demand-driven activities
Clearing house	Generally contracted work and outsourced researchers
Advocacy	Pooling research findings and championing a course of action
Briefcase	Non-institutionalized and personality-centred

Once this fundamental distinction among institutions has been made, the logical issue that arises is one of the theoretical versus practical mechanisms of policy influence. It is assumed that the intellectual capital, notwithstanding its varying shades as outlined in Table 1, is the desired input for the policy-making (influencing) process. When the input is available, then two other considerations arise. First is the issue of how the inputs are linked to policy outputs and policy impacts (outcomes). Second is the question of *how, i.e.* through what transmission mechanism, policy inputs are turned into policy outputs and impact–something that remains abundantly *un*clear. The corollary to this is the question of whether the relationship between policy input and policy output–impact is an event or a process, and consequently whether the situation is ordinarily and simply deterministic (predictable) or stochastic (random and unpredictable) in nature.

The pressure has been great on research and policy analysis institutions to treat their outputs–discussion papers, policy briefs, dissemination workshops and participation in committees–as direct inputs to the policy process whose outputs must be determinable, or predictable at any point in time. From this perspective, the input–output relationship is considered deterministic and hence measurable. This is arguably unrealistic.

The practical situation is that the relationship between policy input and output relies on a diffuse transmission mechanism. As such, the process has a complicated aggregation of measurable *and* non-measurable, immediate *and* long-term, definite *and* indefinite, desirable *and* undesirable outputs and outcomes. So realistically, an institution would have to persistently generate policy inputs directed to specific policy concerns to make it possible to assess whether or not it influenced policy–except of course, when the institution is basically an advocacy organization. The success of the institution may be gauged by the demand for its output, such as the purchases of its publications, visits to its website, number of persons using its library, requests by government departments to participate in government activities.

INFORMING THE POLICY DEBATE IN KENYA

The role of IPAR

IPAR works to strengthen the national capacity to develop and to implement and evaluate public policy by undertaking independent, objective research and policy analysis, and by sharing the results with the Kenyan government and its development partners. It also seeks to serve as an institutional and resource centre by offering technical, research and information support for national development. It provides objective data-based findings and recommendations, and articulates them at national and other fora for the benefit of interested parties. These include government, NGOs, the private sector and the donor community. Four programs make these aims operational: Governance and Development; Macroeconomics; Real Sector (Agriculture and Industry); and Social Sector (Education and Health). The activities of each program are designed to fit within a broad theme of the institute that is derived with due recognition of current political, economic and institutional developments in the country. Research output is documented as Discussion Papers, Working Papers and Policy Briefs. IPAR also produces Occasional Papers and thematic books.

Researchers identify policy issues and prepare initial concept papers. They present these at stakeholders' workshops, where they learn which additional concerns that stakeholders may wish incorporated into the study. The researchers then incorporate views of the stakeholders and carry out the study. Once the study is finalized, another stakeholders' workshop is held to disseminate the findings. The researchers then write a policy brief to spell out policy proposals for stakeholders' actions.

IPAR's objective is to furnish the government and its development partners with policy proposals based on objective research, policies whose implementation would improve the welfare of Kenyans. The implementation of the policy has largely remained a prerogative of the government; there is always a limit as to how much the institute can do to ensure the implementation of recommended policy.

Besides carrying out objective research and policy analysis, IPAR has designed a capacity-building or internship program that specifically targets middle-level officers working in government. The officers are recruited through a competitive interview. They stay at the institute on a full-time basis for a period of six months, during which they are trained on how to identify policy concerns, analyse them and make recommendations. Because the interns are from government, they offer a good conduit for interaction and communication linking the institute and government. This helps to disseminate most of the findings, especially when they pertain to issues in studies in which they have participated.

In addition, the government and/or independent organizations commissioned IPAR to carry out research on urgent policy issues and advise on the best way forward. Such ad hoc commissions indicate that the institute has a reputation for being credible.

The IPAR approach to policy influence

The success or failure of the institute to influence policy hinges on its approach and perception of stakeholders about its credibility. In addition to the wide distribution of its refereed publications, it also influences policy in other ways: its internship program; peer review; research associates; workshops and policy briefs; participatory research, participation in policy committees and university linkages.

Internship program

Its internship program, described briefly above, is a key institutional capacity-building component of IPAR's mandate. It is designed for government officials and young professionals from universities and other institutions. Through this competitive internship program, the institute contributes to capacity-building for young professionals seeking to enhance their careers in policy research and analysis within government, in the private sector and in other institutions. The trainees are attached to researchers in specific programs for a period of six months. During this time, the interns receive hands-on training in different aspects of policy analysis, including data collection, data management, analysis and report writing. The expected outcomes are:

training in understanding policy analysis frameworks; proposal formulation; data collection; data analysis; report writing; and seminar presentation. Each intern participates fully in all the activities of IPAR. Interns are expected to produce an inception report specifying clearly the distinction between policy research and policy analysis and how the attachment is likely to impact on the intern's professional engagement with the government. They are also to produce a concept note that includes: identification of a policy problem that needs to be addressed; objectives of and justification for the study to address the problem; a literature review, and methodology to address the problem. The interns carry these activities under the supervision and guidance of senior researchers. Once the concept is accepted, the interns are trained on how to collect, organize and analyse data. Further, the interns present their completed work in a staff seminar or colloquium. Before IPAR will publish an intern's work, internal and external peers subject the report to rigorous review.

After six months, interns from government return to their ministries and generally become contact persons for IPAR in government and research associates of the institute. This guarantees continuity in policy analysis, dialogue and influence in the parent government departments.

Besides young professionals from government ministries who are trained on policy analysis and research, the institute also allows attachments for PhD students who have their own financial support for the period they are carrying out their field work. Such students are expected to be carrying out research in an area relevant to IPAR's research programs. While at IPAR, they are supervised by the relevant program coordinators. IPAR has also been hosting and participating in the supervision of students, who are government junior economists and are sponsored to pursue Masters degrees in economic policy management at various universities in Africa. Once they accomplish their programs, these students eventually find their way either to the government, research institutions or institutions of higher learning where they impact on policy issues.

Since the inception of the internship program, the institute has trained 26 young professionals: nine from Kenyan universities and one from Oxford University; four from the Ministry of Finance; three from the Ministry of Labour and Human Resource Development; two each from the Ministry of Agriculture, the Ministry of Education, Science and Technology and the Ministry of Planning and National Development; one each from the Ministry of Health and the Ministry of Trade and Industry; and one intern from the National Hospital Insurance Fund.

Currently, three of the former IPAR interns are pursuing PhD programs, 14 are working in other research and policy institutes and ten are working in different government ministries.

Peer review

All policy papers prepared by IPAR researchers go through two important stages. First is an internal discussion session to which relevant government officials interested in the particular area are invited. Second and once the internal issues raised are incorporated into the paper, three peer reviewers assess the final output. One of these reviewers is usually a senior government technocrat dealing with the subject. This is considered to be an effective way of disseminating research findings to key policy-makers.

Research "associate-ship"

Besides acting as Peer Reviewers, some of the more qualified and experienced policy-makers in relevant government departments are associates of the institute. They undertake independent research and policy analysis or collaborative work with IPAR staff to produce both Discussion Papers and Policy Briefs. Subsequent discussions and recommendations form an important channel for influencing policy.

Workshops and Policy Briefs

The end product of any IPAR research is the production of a Discussion Paper and a Policy Brief. As a routine, these documents are distributed to all relevant departments of government as well as other interested parties. Besides sending the documents to the various institutions such as universities, development partners, embassies, and civil society organizations, copies are also sent to targeted consumers in government, including permanent secretaries, heads of departments and their technical staff. In addition, dissemination workshops are held to discuss the findings with invited stakeholders, among them government policy-makers. Experience has shown that for these documents to have significant influence, the participation of Permanent Secretaries, principle ministry officials and Members of Parliament is important. The media are also an effective way to transmit research findings to policy-makers. However, experience shows that there are serious limitations to this, as media tend not to report findings unless they are presented in a sensational way.

Participatory research

When researchers and stakeholders come together in focus group discussion on a research activity, research then draws wide stakeholder participation and this enhances achievements of impact and promotes effective targeting of research inputs. Besides, dialogue increases understanding of both parties on the nature of the problem that research addresses. This approach ensures that research activities are comprehensive and keeps stakeholders aware of on-going research. This approach gives rise to timely, need-driven research with high potential of influencing policy. However, researchers must take care to maintain objectivity in their undertakings and resist any attempts by stakeholders to influence the outcome of their findings.

Participation in policy committees

The participation of individual researchers on various policy committees and in government-arranged meetings is an effective way of influencing policy. So is the presentation of policy proposals, particularly budgetary ones, to the government. Of course this method also has its limitations; it depends on the extent of intellectual capital accumulated in a particular area and on the willingness of the institution to contribute to policy without financial compensation from the government.

University linkages

A less immediate and somewhat long-term mechanism for influencing policy can be established through linkages with universities. These can include lecturing by institute researchers, supervising post-graduate dissertations, compiling teaching materials, peer reviews, research "associate-ship" (as above), and collaborative work. IPAR has used and continues to use this multi-pronged approach to enhance its capacity to influence policy.

Research and policy–a success story

All these activities have been successful to varying degrees. But the level of success has to be considered at many levels, namely: institutional; program (sectoral); project (publications) and individual researcher. Further, there are many diverse factors affecting how successful research is in informing policy. Among these factors: the number of top government officials attending dissemination workshops; the diversity of representation in dissemination workshops; media coverage; incorporation of research findings in government policy documents; intensity and interest of participation in the discussion of the findings; the number of publications purchased; stakeholder participation in research; request for publication by government departments and development partners; the number of other parties asking for publications; interest shown by government technocrats wishing to join the institution as interns; frequency of requests by government departments for researchers to contribute to and/or participate in policy discussions; and the number of requests by universities to host and supervise post-graduate students.

There is no single index for measuring success, indeed just attempting to do so can be a daunting task. Nevertheless, IPAR can say that it has had two very successful cases. The first came with a paper produced by one of its research associates on privatization of security in Kenya. The paper did not meet the rigorous publications criteria set for all IPAR publications, so it was published as a Working Paper entitled " Kenya's Insecurity Problem: How can the Role of Privatized Security be Enhanced?" since the subject was extremely important as the issue of insecurity is considered to be of national importance. As soon as the paper was published, the Ministry of Internal Security requested 150 copies and requested that IPAR nominate a person to join a Ministerial Committee working on a regulatory framework for the provision of private security. This was an instant success in influencing policy.

The second success story came when the Ministry of Transport decided to implement rules and regulations governing the operation of the *matatu* (pro-poor mode of public transportation) sector, which was considered by the people who used it to be badly organized and extremely dangerous. These new rules caused a serious confrontation between the government and the *matatu* owners, which led to a *matatu* strike that paralysed public transport in the country. In the ensuing confusion, the owners approached IPAR and asked its researchers to undertake a number of studies on the sector, hoping they could come up with reasoned recommendations that would bring tranquillity and restore understanding in the sector. IPAR acted as an arbitrator and brought the stakeholders together. The stakeholders were drawn from the Ministry of Transport, the traffic police, the *matatu* owners' association, the *matatu* welfare association, the city council and research institutions. After deliberations, the stakeholders agreed on the implementation of the transport policies that had hitherto triggered chaos in the sector. The sector has since attained sanity and tranquility.

Both of these successful experiences in which IPAR helped government develop appropriate policies–for private security and also public transit in Kenya–demonstrate that research institutes can be extremely influential in helping to solve policy crises. In our view, there are three factors to which these research–policy success stories can be attributed.

1. They involved timely and need-driven research.
2. The research institute had the requisite institutional capacity and was perceived by stakeholders to be credible.
3. There was substantial donor interest in the issue at hand.

CHALLENGES AND OPPORTUNITIES FOR INFLUENCING POLICY

Research and policy-making are complementary and mutually reinforcing. Research can constructively inform policy and learn from it (Phillips and Seck 2004). Though this has been acknowledged as evidenced through the creation and nurturing of research and policy institutions in sub-Saharan Africa, these institutions are faced with a number of challenges in their endeavours to inform the policy process.

Challenges

Acceptability

Research results, no matter how good they are, remain nothing better than a wish list if policy-makers do not accept and act on them. Besides doing research, researchers need to package their findings in a language and format that can easily be understood by, and accessible and *acceptable* to policy-makers. Quite often, researchers make policy recommendations without necessarily knowing how, by whom and when the recommendations are to be implemented. The recommendations themselves may also fail to distinguish between short-, medium- and long-term interventions or to determine the costs of implementation. This leaves the policy-maker with a dilemma as to how to implement the recommendations, which reduces their acceptability.

Accessibility and quality of information

The information that is readily available to researchers and policy analysts is secondary data. For Kenya, a comparison of locally-collected data documented in the government-published Economic Surveys, and globally-available data on Kenya in the World Development Indicators and at the United Nations, shows significant variation. This divergence casts doubt on the quality and validity of available data on any one issue. Furthermore, accurate published information may not be readily available on some emerging issues, such as corruption. Some data sets are general and probably not disaggregated to facilitate individual scrutiny of research issues. Therefore, depending on which data the results are founded and the government's perception of those sources, policy-makers may decide to accept or reject research results. In addition, some government data are classified and thus confidential. Access to such data is obviously limited, involving a lengthy process that can delay research activities.

Capacity

There are clearly high costs involved in attracting and maintaining high-calibre staff for a period long enough to make an impact on the policy realm; for this the institute must pay competitive salaries. In addition, sourcing experts for work on current research fields such as economic governance, health and poverty, is proving to be difficult. National researchers in Africa often use local research institutions as platforms from which they can move on to highly rewarding jobs in international research institutions. So each time a senior researcher leaves an African research institute his or her departure can spell a long hiatus of a particular program, until such time as another expert is found and recruited.

Policy reversals

Government policy is often ambiguous and subject to reversals. This has a lot to do with the country's status and its relationship with development partners, initiators and the financiers of the policy. In the event that the government changes the policy focus or reverses a particular policy, on-going research on the same is rendered indefinitely irrelevant. This has high costs and it kills the morale of researchers.

Independence

The challenge for a research unit is to be acceptable to policy-makers and yet remain an independent think-tank, and it is a delicate one. Sometimes, the government may think that the institute is anti-government, especially if it publishes dissenting findings on important national policy issues. In such a situation, the litmus test for the institute is when government representatives decline to attend dissemination workshops for fear that their participation may be construed badly by their superiors for political reasons.

Collaboration with peers

In Kenya, there is only minimal collaboration among the various research and policy institutes, despite the fact that they may be financed by similar institutions. This has led to duplication of efforts, unnecessary competition, and conflicts of interest, especially when it is realized too late that two or more institutions have invested a lot of time and finances in a similar study. Usually, the soft option is that one of the institutions has to abort the study. This problem comes up as a result of independence of program design within competing institutions and inability to be very clear on the "intellectual niche" of the institutions.

Timeliness

Timeliness in carrying out research is important if its findings are to influence policy. Because it is hard to predict the focus of government policy, a number of researchers may work on fundamental problems without policy agendas in mind and their works are reflected in professional journals or they may gather dust on book shelves. According to Ryan (2004), a perfect solution that is late is a wasted effort.

Donor interests

When a research institute is donor-funded, then the agenda of the donor may become a binding constraint on how much influence the institution can have on government policy. If the donor platform shifts, the research agenda of the institution becomes non-compatible with the donor's principal interest, jeopardizing the institution's financial sustainability and weakening its influence.

Moral hazard

Because of the limited supply of qualified and experienced researchers in the African labour market, research institutions tend to get most of their research staff from university faculties. The researchers are motivated to work for research institutions because of the higher remunerations that they offer, as well as the opportunity to publish. However, a majority of researchers use these institutions as avenues for actualizing their self-interests and ambitions, which may not necessarily be the same as those of the institutes. Often the feeling of ownership and allegiance is minimal. Conflicts of interest arise and are compounded by the fact that contracts for researchers do not usually exceed three years.

Countering the challenges: recommendations

Acceptability

The purpose of policy research is to assist and advise policy-makers. So in addition to doing their studies, researchers need to package their findings in a language and format that are simple and can easily be understood and implemented by policy-makers.

Accessibility and quality of information

Establishing credible in-house resource centres to organize data and create databanks in consultation with national statistical offices can solve this problem. The same institutes can help governments design comprehensive data-collection instruments and also help in decoding them.

Local capacity

There is little an institution can do to stop researchers from looking for better opportunities. However, the best can be made of local human resources if institutions can build capacity and establish networks with researchers both in the public sector and in academic institutions, who can readily be available do conduct collaborative research.

Policy reversals

Policies generally do not change abruptly, but occasionally they do when government brings in a policy reversal. Researchers must take this into account, remembering that if their research drags on too long it may fail to input policy because the policy context itself has changed.

To mitigate this contingency, researchers could ensure that credible preliminary findings should be made available to policy-makers as soon as possible and certainly when the need arises.

Independence

Independence is a very important component that determines credibility of an institute. Though the government may reject the research results in the short run, as long as they are well researched and therefore reputable, they should be widely disseminated to other stakeholders and to the public, who will in turn negotiate with the government on an informed basis.

Collaboration

Institutional independence in program design and execution is likely to persist in the short run. However, as research institutions identify their niche areas, then build capacity and credibility around particular issues, various institutions will be identified with comparative advantage for research in particular fields, and there will be minimal or no overlap of research mandates; complementary institutions can collaborate rather than compete or replicate each other's work.

Timeliness

In policy research and analysis, topicality, timeliness and proper dissemination are very important and should be taken into account if research is to inform policy.

Donor interests

Institutions should strive to diversify their sources of financing and above all, put in place mechanisms to ensure that once the donors withdraw their support, they are can be independent and able to finance their own programs. Building an endowment fund may be a reasonable way out of this problem.

Moral hazards

To avoid any moral pitfalls associated with conflicts of interest, researchers should adhere to yearly research programs while maintaining the leeway to undertake need-driven research. They should set up minimum quality standards for publications and ensure that the peer-review mechanism is credible.

Emerging opportunities

Close consultation

As the Kenyan government recognized the need for home-grown solutions to domestic problems and with the mushrooming of research institutions, there is also goodwill in government to work closely with experts on policy issues. Research institutions need to prove their worth and they can do this by conducting well-focused and objective research above that which government departments and universities are capable of conducting. In this way, research institutes can convince the government that they have value to add to the policy process and enormous opportunity for close consultation with government.

Consensus-building

The government in Kenya has recognized that the ownership of a policy is important if its implementation is to be successful. Increasingly, the government is involving stakeholders in both designing and implementing policies. This has opened up a forum that researchers can exploit to build consensus in the country, which they can do if they educate stakeholders by informing them on the policies, based on their research findings.

Intellectual capital

As a research institution matures and accumulates a wealth of intellectual capital in some areas, it becomes more visible to policy-makers and other stakeholders and is increasingly viewed as a reputable organization, and a partner in the policy process. This is certainly the case for IPAR in Kenya, where its non-partisan research agenda and findings are becomingly increasingly marketable to the government.

CONCLUSIONS

Research must continue to shape policy-making. Independent think-tanking and research are key in national development. In Kenya, the Institute of Policy Analysis and Research has endeavoured to influence policy by finding just the right distance from government, being close enough to ensure its input is used yet far away enough that it is not unduly swayed or influenced by government policy-makers. IPAR has consistently created capacity and credibility in various areas of policy. Consequently, the government has increasingly recognized it.

However, its efforts to undertake sellable research findings have met with various challenges in the areas of capacity, resources and credibility. The institute has identified these challenges and continues to tackle them. At the same time, the institute has identified opportunities for increasing its visibility and influence in the policy-making arena. To increase its success as a producer of high-quality research to feed into and help shape sound policies, it must meet several conditions, including: the recruitment and retention of highly qualified, respected and committed researchers; the consistent build-up of credible intellectual capital, and; the availability of sustainable financial resources.

Notes

1. The macroeconomic working group comprises representatives from various institutions, including the Ministry of Finance, Ministry of Planning and National Development, Central Bank of Kenya, Kenya Revenue Authority, Central Bureau of Statistics, and Kenya Institute for Public Policy Research and Analysis.
2. Early in the 2000–01 financial year, six sector working groups were created, namely: (1) public administration; (2) public safety, law and order; (3) human resource development; (4) physical infrastructure; (5) agriculture and rural development; and (6) trade and industry. Later that financial year, National Security (7) and Information Technology (8) were added, making eight sector working groups.

References

Bardach E. 1996. *Policy analysis: a handbook for practice.* Berkeley: University of California, Graduate School of Public Policy.

Comptroller and Audit General. 2001. Modern policy-making: ensuring policies deliver value for money. London: National Audit Office.

Gitu K. 2001. *Strengthening the link between policy research and implementation.* Kenya Institute of Public Policy Research and Analysis, Occasional Paper No. 1/2001. Nairobi: KIPPRA.

Juma C and Clark N. 1995. Policy research in Sub-Saharan Africa: an exploration. *Public Administration and Development* 15: 121–137.

Killick T. 1981. *Policy economics: a text book of applied economics on developing countries.* London: Heinemann Publishers.

Lindblom Charles E. 1968. *The Policy Making Process.* Englewood Cliffs, New Jersey: Prentice-hall Inc.

Makokha Joseph (2004). Kenya's Insecurity Problem: How can the Role of Privatized Security Providers be Enhanced. IPAR Working Paper NO. 01/2004.

Mwenda A and Gachocho M. 2003. Budget transparency: Kenyan perspective. IEA Research Paper Series No. 4. Nairobi: Institute of Economic Affairs.

Ng'ethe N. 1998. Public policy, policy analysis and reforms, *IN:* Ng'ethe Njuguna and Owino Wassunna (eds). *From Sessional Paper No. 10 to structural adjustment: towards indigenising the policy debate.* Nairobi: Institute of Policy Analysis and Research.

Odhiambo-Mbai C. 1998. The nature of public policy-making in Kenya: 1963–1996. *IN:* Ng'ethe Njuguna and Owino Wassunna (eds). *From Sessional Paper No. 10 to structural adjustment: towards indigenising the policy debate.* Nairobi: Institute of Policy Analysis and Research.

Phillips LC and Seck D. 2004. Fixing African economies: the research–policy nexus, *IN:* Phillips LC and Seck D (eds). *Fixing African economies: policy research for development.* Colorado and London: Lynne Rienner Publishers.

Ryan TCI. 2004. Kenya: policy research and policy reform, *IN:* Phillips LC and Seck D (eds). *Fixing African economies: policy research for development.* Colorado and London: Lynne Rienner Publishers.

Simon Herbert Alexander. 1957. *Models of man: social and rational.* New York: Wiley.

Chapter Thirteen

THE NEW SOCIAL CONTRACT BETWEEN ECONOMIC RESEARCH AND DECISION-MAKERS: LESSONS FROM CÔTE D'IVOIRE

Mama Ouattara, Kalilou Sylla, Souleymane S. Diallo and Yaya Ouattara

ABSTRACT

In a rapidly changing world environment shaped by globalization, economic research centres in Africa are confronted with a dilemma. They must continue to carry out fundamental research and produce publications as they have always done, but they must at the same time conduct research activities that increase their relevance and importance to policy-makers, donors, the private sector and civil society. And they must also sustain their funding through consultancy, which relies in large part on exogenously-determined topics, the problematics of which do not always coincide with theirs. Globalization demands increasingly complex and multi-disciplinary research, which most research centres were not set up to handle. This chapter focuses on the exceptional case of the *Centre Ivoirien de Recherche Economique et Social,* the Ivorian Centre for Economic and Social Research (CIRES), to demonstrate how this research structure has managed to broaden its research programs to successfully feed into a wide range of policies and train executives both in Côte d'Ivoire and throughout Africa. This study describes the changes as well as the challenges that this centre had to take on to succeed, and describes the new social contract between CIRES and the Ivorian society, an experience that ought to be shared with other research centres on the continent.

INTRODUCTION

Economic research in Africa is at a crossroads, trying to reconcile the new and complex requirements for research in an increasingly globalized world environment. Globalization brings complexity that makes the analysis generally offered by mono-disciplinary research centres ineffective–population issues have become a highly complex mix of policy, economics, sociology, history and technology. To tackle such complexity, researchers must adopt a multidisciplinary approach, something they were not originally set up to do.

Research centres are increasingly torn between their original calling to conduct research and publish, and pressure to justify and sustain their own existence with consultancy research. Indeed, consultancies and other work not directly related to the main research interest of these centres increasingly preoccupy their time. This altered role disturbs their own internal dynamics. More and more it seems as if their research programs consist only of consultancies, the topics of which are formulated by external partners, which in some cases could cause research centres to "lose their own souls". As a result, the type of research they undertake is not rooted in the concerns of the population. This widens the gap between researchers and their own people, which in turn means that the research is of no great benefit to national decision-makers looking to make appropriate policies for the population.

In this new context, characterized by the complexity of the problems linked with globalization, they also have to grapple with the enormous challenge of finding solutions to the multidisciplinary problems that arise in Africa because of globalization. As if that were not enough, they must also try to function with reduced funding from the public sector under strict budgetary policies.

All of this alters the social contract between research centres and decision-makers in African countries. This chapter analyses the changing nature of that social contract in the context of globalization. Its purpose is to identify the major challenges facing economic research centres in Africa.

Focusing on the case of CIRES, the study demonstrates how a research structure can develop from a simple centre set up to facilitate the application of economic theories to the Ivorian society into a centre trying to provide alternatives to Ivorian and African decision-makers.

Our study is in four parts. The first analyses the lessons that research centres can draw from globalization. The second part focuses on the current logic governing the role of research centres and their attempts to adapt to changing times and realities. The third part provides an in-depth study of CIRES' experience, and the fourth offers recommendations on the reforms necessary to make research centres competitive in the context of globalization. This helps identify avenues that need to be explored for economic research centres in Africa if they are to position themselves to increase their influence on decision-making, while retaining their prerogatives.

THE GLOBALIZED CONTEXT–CHALLENGES FOR AFRICAN RESEARCH CENTRES

Globalization alters the nature of the relationship between research and decision-makers. Increasingly, researchers are called upon to shed light on vastly more complex issues. Problems become more complex as globalization impacts on every aspect of life in Africa–economic, political, social and technological. The implication for research centres is that there will be a growing demand for multidisciplinary reflections on their part. This growing demand for diversified studies will also be followed by a demand for "inter-disciplinarity".

In addition to the increased complexity of issues that research centres must tackle, they have also to adjust to the new demands of the state, and their role as contractors in managing economic activity. The government alone cannot adapt to the rapidly diversifying world (Bates 2002) and it must revisit its role and status, and position itself to meet new demands (Sylla 2003). This means that research centres must incorporate a new set of concerns and actors that they may have previously neglected.

These concerns and actors include the civil society, private sector concerns and studies that transcend traditional disciplinary boundaries. Previously, economic research centres in Africa tended not to involve civil society or inter-disciplinary approaches in their studies.

The donors increasingly view civil society and the private sector as major actors in all aspects of decision-making, and presses for inter-disciplinary work that will involve them. Similarly, for a research centre to be able to show its legitimacy, it must involve these actors and their concerns in its work if it is to contribute to democracy in the country (Sylla 2004).

To establish their legitimacy, research centres must not just publish and undertake consultancies but they must also engage all the main actors in their society in shaping their research and disseminating the results. Their legitimacy also depends on how their leaders are chosen; they should choose leaders on the basis of qualifications to demonstrate good governance. Political appointments are no longer acceptable.

Another challenge for research centres is competition, which will sooner or later come to stay in the sector. They should be prepared to face this competition by changing ineffective bureaucratic behaviours (N'guessan 1996). To achieve this, the researchers' incentives will have to be improved and the centres management streamlined. At the moment, research centres have an acute problem in retaining their researchers. This becomes even more crucial as researchers witness steadily reduced public funding.

To illustrate this, Table 1 shows funding sources 1986 and 1991 within the agronomic research sector, to which African countries allocate the most important part of their research funds.

Table 1: Sources of funds allocated to agronomic research in sub-Saharan Africa *

Sources of funds	Years	
	1986	**1991**
Government	55.9 %	47.5 %
Owned funds	6.5	4.9
Specific tax	2.3	4.2
Foreign partners	34	47.2
Other	1.4	0.8
Total	**100**	100

Source: Pardey et al. (1995)

Until 1991, public sources and foreign partners remained the main sources of funding for agronomic research. But with structural adjustment policies, the share of public contribution to agronomic research declined from 55.9 percent in 1986 to 47.5 percent by 1991. Furthermore, the capacity of research to mobilize funds from private sources remained weak, falling from 6.5 to 4.9 percent over the same period. Factors explaining this decline include the research centres' failure to reach out to the private sector and conduct research that would in turn result in more private support for their research. Paradoxically, agronomic research centres tend to overlook the enormous potential of the private sector in Africa. This can also be said of economic research centres, which tend to cling to public funding even as its shrinks with structural adjustment programs and declining official development assistance from outside.

As a result, research centres have become increasingly weak and unable to fulfill their mandate of conducting research. This raises an important challenge that all research centres in sub-Saharan Africa will have to overcome, namely mobilizing resources without losing their autonomy in formulating their research programs. In other words, what strategies are required if they are to successfully adapt to the new global environment? In the following section, we try to come up with some answers to that crucial question.

Adapt to the new global environment–or perish

One strategy for adapting to the new global environment is to improve governance through the democratic election of directors. This measure would ensure that researchers within the centres would feel their interests are being better served and represented by the leadership, and it would send an important signal to partners about good governance and accountability.

Another strategy is to disseminate research with a view to creating a greater impact on decision-makers in the running of country business. The constraint here is the mode of communication between researchers and the administration. The two entities use different methods of communication. The administration, which is searching for information and well-documented advice for decision-making, very often blames research centres for providing theories rather than concrete solutions. On the other hand, researchers argue that even when they provide the administration with documented advice from their research, this is often relegated to office drawers and never used in decision-making.

Research centres should also be more pro-active. As it is, they often await budget allocation by the government on the assumption that the state should give them preferential treatment in view of their importance. This behaviour is detrimental; research centres must prove their importance. They should not forget that the state is ruled by rational consumers, and they should instead strive to maximize their relevance and usefulness to the people they are there to serve (Tullock 1978). Those who govern will be interested in–and support and consult with–research centres only if the latter prove that their findings provide workable policy options which allow decision-makers to focus their actions and impact positively on their constituents.

Researchers need to make themselves not just useful but also competitive, if they are to be fully appreciated by decision-makers. They must dispense with complacency; a prevailing spirit of expectation should be transformed into a culture of contributing and a motivation to produce useful results. Without that transformation, they may not just publish but they may also perish, along with their research centre.

It should also be said that the challenges of the new global context can be turned into great opportunities for researchers; today research is–or should be–at the core of decision-making. The negotiations within the World Trade Organization (WTO) and Economic Partnership Agreements (EPA) are good examples in point. For negotiations in these bodies, African governments need to refer to research to clarify their positions, following the example of those of developed countries that rely heavily on research to assess the impact of multilateral trade. This is a key entry point for researchers.

The CIRES experience

The Ivorian Economic and Social Research Centre (CIRES) is an example of an African research centre originally created to facilitate research in the economics faculty at the University of Cocody. Very quickly though, CIRES was transformed into an autonomous research centre, which performed relatively well and was supported through grants similar to those accorded other academic centres.

CIRES built its reputation on a network that brought it in contact with American and European universities. This partnership initially focused on the training of its researchers, the majority of whom had not yet attained their doctorates when the network was set up in 1971.

With this partnership network and its regional rural economy doctorate program, CIRES was able to invest in and train a new generation of bilingual researchers. One objective of the program was to maintain research impetus through the massive presence of doctoral graduates from countries in West Africa, and also open CIRES up to the sub-region. To date, about 120 rural economy PhD-holders have been trained through this program and CIRES gained international recognition in research and training.

While setting up its research program, the Centre approached the government with research proposals covering the latter's needs. The result was government interest in CIRES activities. Thus, all CIRES directors have held high responsibilities in planning ministries, employment ministries and in the office of the Prime Minister. CIRES' researchers have also been involved in the implementation of various government programs, holding high-level positions. Many officials in the current Ivorian administration holding posts of Ministers and Directors in different sectors of the economy are former CIRES researchers. In turn, their participation in these programs or administrative positions offered these researchers invaluable insight into how government formulates policies and understanding of how these are implemented. However, this also meant temporary drains of the Centre's human resources.

CIRES' relative success can be attributed to the fact that it carries out several projects expressly for government and donors. CIRES provides advice to the government of Côte d'Ivoire through its Economic Policy Analysis Unit, trains African executives under an Economic Policy Management Program, and contributes to the design of an agricultural policy, notably in the coffee and cocoa sector.

The CIRES Economic Policy Support Unit conducted studies on economic policy management and surveys on the pricing and marketing of the all-important coffee–cocoa sector commissioned by the *Bourse du Café et du Cacao (BCC)*. Given that Côte d'Ivoire is still the world's largest cocoa producer, such research is crucial to the country and these projects have contributed to major economic policies. Since 2002, the BCC's pricing policy has relied principally on the recommendations of this CIRES research.

CIRES maintains a relatively flexible organization of research units and divisions, as well as fairly autonomous entities such as its Economic Policy Support Unit. This cohesive diversity has allowed the Centre to expand its audience with public authorities, and subsequently its influence on the definition of economic policies. Thus, many of the studies undertaken by its Economic Policy Support Unit in the education and monetary sectors helped the government build the national education and training policy, and define its position on the devaluation of the CFA Franc in 1994.

In addition to its role as a council through its Economic Policy Support Unit, over the past few years CIRES has opened itself up to the private sector, civil society and the semi-public–or parastatal–sector. To do this, it established a framework for cooperation and exchanges that would allow the centre to better publicize its research findings. In fact, CIRES established a partnership with some state and parastatal structures, which resulted in the realization of several fundamental studies for Côte d'Ivoire. It is worth mentioning three of the studies that we believe have been particularly significant in their scope.

The first of these focuses on the study of the "Industrialization Plan" for Côte d'Ivoire. The objectives of this study, commissioned by the Ivorian government in 1997, include the diagnosis of the country's existing industrial policy and the definition of a new industrialization plan. The government adopted that plan, which became the roadmap of the country's industrialization policy.

The other two significant studies were completed in 2002 and 2004 within the framework of a convention signed between BCC and CIRES as well as the *Bureau National d'Etudes Techniques et de Développement (BNETD or the National Office of Technical and Development Studies),* the *Centre National de Recherche Agronomique (National Centre for Agronomic Research, CNRA)* and the *Centre de Recherche sur la Microéconomie du Développement (Centre for Research on the Microeconomics of Development) of the Unité de formation et de Recherche en Sciences Economiques et de Gestion (Unit for Training and Research in Economic and Management Sciences).*

One of these two studies was assigned solely to CIRES and its purpose was to determine coffee and cocoa production costs, as well as the minimum income required to cover coffee and cocoa producers' production costs. The study, which required a survey of producers in all major coffee and cocoa growing zones, made it possible to determine the production cost structure as well as the minimum income required for farmers to be able to recover their production costs. The Ivorian government adopted the findings of this study. The CIRES' recommendations have allowed the establishment since October 2002 of a framework for setting producer prices, and this document today constitutes a reference for setting the suggested producer price, and for negotiations between Côte d'Ivoire and development partners.

The second study, on which CIRES collaborated with BNETD and with a private firm, was undertaken between July and October 2004. Its main purpose was to determine the handling costs of the coffee and cocoa industry and to survey the costs of the major cocoa-and/or coffee-producing African countries. This work supplements the first study and its purpose was to determine the cost structure along the marketing channel from farm to the export stage, and to compare marketing costs in Côte d'Ivoire with those of other African countries.

To grasp the full importance of these studies for Côte d'Ivoire, it should be mentioned that coffee and cocoa account for 15 percent of its GDP and 60 percent of exports. The liberalization of this sector completely destabilized the economic environment and the institutional framework for coffee and cocoa production and marketing activities. This was all the more important as the structure put in place after liberalization to manage these industries needed objective information on production and marketing costs in order to better define the development policy for the coffee and cocoa sector in general, and the marketing policy in particular. To achieve this, the framework of the convention signed between the management of the Coffee and Cocoa Stock Exchange and CIRES envisages additional studies focusing on the design of a harvest projection model, the study of the quality of coffee and cocoa, and the definition of a development plan for the Professional Farmers' Organizations of the sector.

Apart from these studies, and considering the on-going crisis situation in Côte d'Ivoire, CIRES is now developing some expertise on the war economy and good governance sector that could be instrumental in helping Côte d'Ivoire to pull itself out of the crisis that began in 2002 with a rebellion that effectively divided the country in half. Such expertise in conflict economics and good governance is also crucial for the post-crisis period, when CIRES may be called upon to help with development options and the reconciliation process.

This involvement of CIRES in a diverse range of research projects requiring a wide range of expertise in complex and inter-related areas of interest to policy-makers has translated into the formulation of a new generation of projects that directly involve stakeholders in project formulation and more importantly in their implementation.

The centre drew up three projects that demonstrate the value of this approach: (1) a governance and development institute; (2) a democracy and development observatory, and; (3) a task force on corruption, with the support of the European Union.

These projects reflect the Centre's will to meet more of the decision-makers' needs by involving them in finding solutions to problems such as corruption, information deficit and the weak democratic culture of the population. These projects also show the growing capacity in CIRES to undertake research that transcends traditional disciplinary boundaries.

To insure against the disruption in the financing of the centre's research activities, CIRES created a 25 percent institutional levy on the projects, using the centre's institutional capital to raise funds for research. The tax was used to refurbish office buildings, to provide incentives to the scientific committee and to finance the library. Starting in 2005, the new management of the centre has reassigned these funds to financing research divisions.

CIRES has been able to establish its credibility and usefulness, and build its reputation and influence through a network that reinforced the capacities of its research staff, and maintained dynamic contacts with the government through monthly seminars and making the findings of its work available widely to potential users.

But, like all research centres in Africa, CIRES still confronts the weighty problems of finding ways to retain its research staff by offering them competitive incentives, and finding sustainable funding for its research activities.

IMPROVING THE PERFORMANCE OF RESEARCH CENTRES—SOME SUGGESTED REFORMS

The essential dilemma for research centres in Africa is how they can attract funding without losing their independence to powerful foreign or other interests. The basic answer is that they need to reform themselves, both institutionally and managerially. Research centres should behave like "planetary institutions", meaning they should develop and reinforce their credibility through the scientific quality of their work and their capacity to have decision-makers adopt their recommendations, thus adding to their legitimacy and their importance in the realm of national life that includes a multitude of actors.

Clearly, the primary role of a research centre is to do research, so every "serious" centre should publish a progress report indicating all the publications of its researchers and a detailed record all the centre's other activities as well. Academic credibility will increase if these publications appear in respected, peer-reviewed journals. Academic credibility is necessary but not sufficient. A centre must also be credible in decision-making circles. Generally, a research centre can earn this credibility through mechanisms such as lobbies (using leaders to approach government and respond to population needs and to disseminate results), its consideration of the administration's needs in research, as well as the involvement of the administration in research formulation. A simple way a centre can strengthen its credibility outside academic circles is by including stakeholders and especially the administration on its board of directors. Stakeholders must be included so that they can formulate, implement and assess the centre's research program. The involvement of these partners in the governance of the centre is an important element in making the institutional architecture viable.

Furthermore, a research centre must handle its own marketing by disseminating its research findings. However, these findings must be diffused in a format that decision-makers can easily access and digest; otherwise they may be useless to them. Another useful marketing strategy is to organize and host important meetings to explain the activities of the centre and more importantly to present research findings of interest to them.

Of course a marketing strategy is of no use at all unless the product to be sold is of good quality. So researchers must be motivated and able to produce quality research that meets the needs of its various partner clients. For researchers to be motivated, they must be adequately remunerated and given the resources they need for their work. Consultancies can help augment tight budgets and provide income for staff to expand their research capacities. In other words, part of the funds generated by consultancy services should be used to finance more academic research.

Clearly, research centres seeking funds for their work must not exclude the private sector, NGOs and especially decentralized administrations. With the advent of globalization, these actors provide the networks through which significant funds can be channelled into the economy–and into research networks. African governments and the development sector have based their strategy on these actors but researchers have not.

Till now, African economic research centres have been conspicuously absent from the crucial debates involving our states. These include international negotiations for Economic Partnership Agreements and especially at the World Trade Organization. Yet, these agreements are essential to the existence of our nations. Their purpose is to establish new rules to govern globalization. These new rules will commit our peoples and affect all aspects of their lives. It is unfortunate that Africa's decision-makers are not highly visible in these crucial debates and negotiations, but it is tragic that the continent's economic researchers are invisible at these fora.

At the same time that African research centres are desperately seeking funding, research related to these international negotiations and agreements benefits from substantial financial support and addresses major challenges. This kind of research is not sufficiently covered by African research centres. Yet there is a strong demand from administrations on the continent for research that would enlighten them and strengthen their bargaining positions at the international table. Here lies the challenge for research centres. They must seek resources to provide their administrations with the information they need to lead their people towards prosperity and to avoid traps inherent in the context of globalization and free markets, in which African negotiators must be equipped to defend the interests of their own populations.

Much in the same way as companies compete, so do nations and blocks of nations at international negotiations. African research centres should rise to the exciting challenges in this process, produce the databases and policy suggestions that will strengthen their administrations' positions in these negotiations and even out the playing field. If African research centres produce the ideas and data that African governments need for these negotiations, they will not only prove their ability to be competitive but also their credibility not just in the global context but also at home.

Every day, researchers are expected to propose alternatives to improve the welfare of the general population. But the demands of the population in much of Africa are so high that researchers can hardly meet them all. Such a situation calls for a social contract between research and the general population. Research programs should be designed to incorporate and deal with the concerns of the citizenship, as well as decision-makers and stakeholders. Thus, research centres will have a contract binding them with *all* stakeholders and they will be assessed on the basis of this contract alone. In the absence of such a contract, the populations have unrealistic expectations, expecting answers to all of their concerns.

This is not to say that research centres can afford to abandon their strategic watchdog role. While remaining cognizant of and attentive to the current and real concerns of the populace, centres must also maintain a long-term vision for the future, and the need for theoretical research. In the African context where the short-term and immediate plight of the population tends to dominate, where political expedients and structural adjustment programs tend to limit a government's long-term planning, it is crucial that research centres continue to address both present *and* future problems. Researchers who prefer to remain locked in their ivory towers, contemplating only the future, will inevitably find themselves without funding for any research at all.

Finding sustainable funding for economic research is a problem for both applied and fundamental research. However, this does not mean that one of these can be abandoned for the other, even if applied research is currently easier to fund. Indeed, an economic research centre must continue to do theoretical research to feed scientific reflection and discussion, and to address the long-term concerns of the society. Otherwise, empirical research would lose its scientific base.

We propose an institutional mechanism for research centres, an institutional levy that would allow researchers to benefit from a consultancy service that would bring in resources to support empirical research, with enough to finance fundamental research as well. This consultancy levy should not exceed 25 percent of the research budget and should not concern small individual grants to researchers engaged in research networks and capacity-building. It should lead to the establishment of a package including scientific support and office building refurbishment.

CONCLUSIONS

This chapter showed that CIRES, like research centres throughout Africa, has had to grapple with many problems, including limited access to funding, weak incentives for researchers, limited allocation of support equipment and weak co-operation with decision-makers.

In a new and rapidly changing global environment, CIRES was able to adapt by developing a new type of social contract between the government and the other actors such as the private sector and civil society. This restructuring had a very positive impact on relations between our economic research centre and decision-makers in the country. Our conclusion is that economic research centres must change to confront the challenges of the times and to make themselves relevant and important to their main partners, the state and foreign donors.

Such a change is absolutely necessary in the face of globalization, with a strong demand for sound economic research on issues linked with international negotiations and integration. This study has demonstrated that economic research centres with their current configuration are unable to meet decision-makers' need for information, and that there is a need for reform. Drawing on CIRES experience, we have concluded that such reform is possible–and rewarding.

References

Bates R. 2002. Some thoughts about globalization. Paper presented at the international conference: Development Issues in the New Economy. 25–27 March 2002, Cape Town, South Africa.

N'guessan T. 1996. *Gouvernance et politique monétaire: à qui profitent les banques centrales de la zone franc?* Paris: Harmattan.

Pardey PG, Roseboom J and. Beintema NR. 1995. African agricultural research: three decades of development". ISNAR Briefing Paper No 19. The Hague: ISNAR.

Sylla K. 2004. Fund-raising from private sector to finance fight against Aids in Africa in globalization context: NGO approach of Côte d'Ivoire. Paper presented at the Halifax university conference: Mending the global economy: a role for economic participation, Halifax: 8–10 July 2004.

Sylla K. 2003. La société civile dans les démocraties naissantes en Afrique de l'ouest: "enfant gaté" ou alternative à l'Etat et au marché pour le financement du développement? cas des ONG en Côte d'Ivoire. Paper presented at the anniversary of CODESRIA – West Africa, Cotonou: 6–7 September 2003.

Tullock G. 1978. *Le marché politique: analyse économique des processus politiques.* Paris. Economica.

Conclusion

AN EMERGING CONTINENTAL CONSENSUS

Elias T. Ayuk and Mohamed Ali Marouani

The chapters in this book have examined the role of African economic research institutions in designing and formulating policies in several countries and regions in Sub-Saharan Africa. The emerging consensus emerging among the various and diverse authors is that African Economic Research Institutions (AERI) should occupy a central position in the design, development and formulation of economic policies in the sub-continent. They are uniquely placed to do this as they have a better understanding of the socio-economic and political environment in which they operate. The solutions that African research institutions propose will clearly reflect the most solid grasp of the issues. The contributing authors have examined at some length the key questions of whether research can influence policy, whose policy it is, and the different models of linking research and policy-making. They have also summarized the experiences of institutions – mostly in Sub-Saharan Africa that have as their primary objective to undertake economic research to influence policies – and identified the challenges that they face in accomplishing this mandate.

The authors of the narratives in this book detail experiences that come mostly from economic research centres, not just those that are university-based but also some that are independent. Most of these centres were created in response to the need to develop policies that are home-grown, given the context of the failures of imported policies associated with the implementation of the structural adjustment programs in Sub-Saharan Africa. The centres profiled here vary greatly in size; some having only about four researchers and others having as many as 60. Most of them depend on funds from external donors to carry out their work.

The emerging consensus among African economic researchers about the importance of African research input for African policy is a composite of many diverse lessons learned by AERIs, which are detailed in this book.

First, Africa's economic research institutions remain only peripheral to policy debate on the continent, which means their influence in that debate tends to be sub-optimal, even minimal. More often than not, these institutions are not directly involved in the design of policies and are called upon only when the policy development is already at an advanced state. Thus, rather than directly influencing policy, the centres are used as consultants to examine only certain components of policies that have already being developed and are in the process of being implemented. This runs counter to logic and to the interests of Africans themselves.

African economic policies should be spearheaded by African policy-makers on the basis of research undertaken in the African context that takes into account African realities. It is not obvious, for example, that the new poverty reduction strategy papers (PRSPs) are not just a reincarnation of the structural adjustment programs appearing in a different guise. The argument here is whether the goal of poverty reduction that is the current stated goal is similar to the concept of income or wealth creation that was the rationale behind and justification for the SAPs.

Second, AERIs need to improve their own credibility and thus their reputation so that they become and are also regarded as credible partners in the policy debate. They must play a more pro-active role that goes beyond the "firefighter approach", which means they should not wait to be summoned but put themselves in the forefront where they can participate from the start of any policy process. There is a need for strategic thinking within the research institutions that would enable them to position themselves to address second-generation problems. This means the institutions must develop clear strategic plans and unambiguous internal managerial procedures, and instil a culture of transparency in their institutional management.

Third, centres must produce evidence-based research, which is a critical element in the design, development and formulation of economic policies. Experience from SISERA-collaborating institutions furthermore indicates that there is clearly not a single blueprint or path that researchers can take to ensure policy influence. They must learn to adapt their practices to the environment in which they operate and take advantage of opportunities that present themselves.

Fourth, the link between policy research and policy-making is non-linear. Researchers must be flexible and agile in their timing and approaches if they are to influence economic policies. They should be willing and able to re-assess the situation at any point in time, and to re-visit their course of action or strategy.

Fifth, economic researchers should provide a set of policy options rather than policy recommendations to policy-makers. This distinction is extremely important. Policy options indicate to the policy-maker the various options available and the implications of each. Policy recommendations, on the other hand, usually do not provide the policy-makers with all the information they may need, or with solutions that are viable given their own political constraints. Policy-makers have different constituencies with conflicting needs and interests; when they are provided with various options they will use these to weigh the relative importance – and need – of each constituency, and generally take wise decisions. Policy options are more flexible – and thus more practical and more likely to influence policy – than are recommendations.

Sixth, it is extremely important for economic researchers to develop a communication strategy that ensures that research results are communicated to the various stakeholders in an appropriate and useable way. The information provided should be readily available and of good quality, and the links with policy-makers should be forged throughout the stages of the research process, from beginning right to the end when it results in policy options. This is a clear strategy to ensure that the research undertaken is relevant. A communication strategy that fosters constant dialogue between the researcher and the policy-maker is also a guarantee that results will be made available on a timely manner. A sound communication strategy also helps researchers identify the needs of policy-makers and the population through its feedback and dialogue, offering them a futuristic prism through which they can identify future policy needs before they arise.

Finally, it has been shown in this book that inadequate financial resources and a lack of critical mass of researchers at a given research institution can render the institute highly vulnerable to many risks – irrelevance, undue influence from interest groups, donors or governments, and near-sightedness, among others. Research institutions should differentiate between – and balance – their undertaking of consultancies and developing a coherent strategic research program. Research centres without a critical mass of researchers may feel compelled to restrict their own research scope, narrowing their focus to the detriment of their overall research capacity.

In discussions about the viewpoints of policy-makers during the roundtable discussions at the conference that gave rise to this book, it became clear that a number of factors are of particular interest to policy-makers in Sub-Saharan Africa and beyond. First is the importance of creating an atmosphere of trust between the policy-maker and the researcher; this is critical in establishing the credibility of research results. Policy-makers are sometimes wary of research results if they suspect they have been fine-tuned to create political difficulties for them, especially where the researcher is suspected to have an ideological difference with the policy-maker. Research centres must make their neutrality clear to all their partners, and ensure this in their communication strategy.

Second, policy-makers rely on researchers to maintain a keen interest in and awareness of changes taking place in the society, so that they can address current and imminent concerns. This means that researchers should focus more on problem-solving oriented research rather than on fundamental research, if they are to infuse the policy process with sound research results and African expertise. Policy-makers always appreciate it when researchers are able to respond to their needs within short notice.

Finally, researchers can strengthen the capacity of policy-makers by becoming their partners and enabling them to gain more insight into the complexities and difficulties that researchers confront in responding to the same problems that policy-makers need to deal with. A better understanding of the research process would ease any tension that may exist between the researcher and policy-makers.

In concluding, it is fair to say that most economic policies that have been implemented in recent years in Africa have not originated from the continent. This must change. Africa's own economic research institutions can play a key role in the development of policies that can solve the myriad problems facing the continent. The Bretton Wood institutions must recognize the role of these institutions and design a different strategy for collaboration that brings AERIs in as main actors rather than faint voices in the wings. African Economic Research Institutions must cease to be simple consultancy houses, and become leaders in the development of home-grown policies. This turn-around, long overdue, will help competent Africans – researchers and decision-makers – take charge of the policies that shape the future of their continent for the benefit of Africans.

ACRONYMS

ACBF	African Capacity Building Foundation
ACOA	Africa Growth and Opportunity Act
AERC	African Economic Research Consortium
AfDB	African Development Bank
AFSSRN	Asian Fisheries Social Science Research Network
AGOA	African Growth and Opportunities Act
ALOIS	Action in Language, Organisations and Information Systems
Arsaal	Project for sustainable improvement of marginal land in Arsaal, Lebanon
AU	African Union (surplants Organization for African Unity)
BCC	*Bourse du Café et du Cacao*
BNETD	*Bureau National d'Etudes Techniques et de Développement or National Office of Technical and Development Studies (Côte d'Ivoire)*
BIDPA	Botswana Institute for Development Policy Analysis
CAD	Canadian dollars
CAMES	*Conseil Africain et Malgache pour l'Enseignement Supérieur* (African and Madagascan Council for Post-secondary education)
CASS	Centre for Advanced Social Studies (Nigeria)
CIRES	*Centre Ivoirien de Recherche Economique et Social* (Ivorian Centre for Economic and Social Research)
CMI	Christian Michelsen Institute

CODESRIA	Council for the Development of Social Science Research in Africa
CNRA	*Centre National de Recherches Agronomiques (Côte d'Ivoire)*
CPI	Consumer price index
CSO	Civil Society Organization
DANIDA	Danish International Development Agency
DFID	Department for International Development (UK)
DIAL	*Développement, Institutions, Analyses de Long Terme*
DoL	Department of Labour
DPC	Development Policy Centre (Nigeria)
DPRU	Development Policy Research Unit (South Africa)
EAC	Eastern African Community
ECAPAPA	Eastern and Central African Program for Agricultural Policy Analysis
ECOWAS	Economic Community of West African States
EMDU	Environmental Management Development in the Ukraine (IDRC)
EPR	Economic policy research
EPRC	Economic Policy Research Centre (Uganda)
ERI	Economic research institutions
ESRF	Economic and Social Research Foundation (Tanzania)
EU	European Union
FAO	United Nations Food and Agriculture Organization
FDI	Federal direct investment
GATS	General Agreement on Trade in Services
GATT	General Agreement on Tariffs and Trade (replaced by WTO in 1995)
GDN	Global Development Network
GDP	Gross domestic product
HIPC	Heavily Indebted Poor Countries (debt-relief initiative)

HIVOS	International Humanist Institute for Cooperation with Developing Countries (Netherlands)
IAOS	International Association of Official Statistics
ICT	Information and communications technology
IDEP	United Nations African Institute for Economic Development and Planning
IDRC	International Development Research Centre
IFI	International financial institution
IFPRI	International Food Policy Research Institute
ILO	International Labour Organization
IMF	International Monetary Fund
INESOR	Institute of Economic and Social Research (Zambia)
INSTAT	*Institut National de la Statistique Malgache* (Madagascan National Statistics Institute)
IPAR	Institute of Policy Analysis and Research (Kenya)
IRD	*Institut de Recherche pour le Développement* (Institute for Development Research, France)
IT	Information technology
ITC	International Trade Centre
ITDG	Intermediate Technology Development Group
JITAP	Joint Integrated Technical Assistance Program
KIPPRA	Kenya Institute of Public Policy Research and Analysis
KVB	Kenya Veterinary Board
LATN	Latin American Trade Network
MADIO	Project Madagascar-Dial-Instat-Orstom
MAN	Manufacturers Association of Nigeria
MDA(s)	Ministries, Departments and Agencies
MDG	Millennium Development Goals
MIMAP	Micro Impact of Macroeconomic and Adjustment Policies (IDRC)
MoU	Memorandum of Understanding
MTI	Ministry of Trade and Industry (Namibia)

MTS	Multilateral trading system
NASI	Nigerian Association of Small-Scale Industry
NEPAD	New Partnership for African Development
NEPRU	Namibian Economic Policy Research Unit
NIC	Newly-industrialized country
NIPSS	National Institute for Policy and Strategic Studies (Nigeria)
NISER	Nigerian Institute of Social and Economic Research
NIIA	Nigerian Institute for International Affairs
NGO	Non-governmental organization
NORAD	Norwegian Aid Agency
NPC	National Planning Commission (Namibia)
OAU	Organisation for African Unity (surplanted by African Union)
ODI	Overseas Development Institute (London)
OECD	Organisation for Economic Co-operation and Development
OPEC	Organization of Petroleum-exporting Countries
OPS	Organized private sector
PAES	*Programme d'Amélioration de l'Enseignement Supérieur* (Program for the Improvement of Higher Education), Senegal
PDEF	Ten-Year Education and Training Program (Senegal)
PEAC	President's Economic Advisory Council (Namibia)
PRSP	Poverty Reduction Strategy Paper
PTCI	*Programme de Troisième Cycle Inter-Universitaire*
RAPID	Research and Policy in Development (ODI program)
SACU	Southern African Customs Union
SADC	Southern African Development Community
SAP	Structural Adjustment Program
SEAPREN	Southern and Eastern African Policy Research Network

SIDA	Swedish International Development Co-operation Agency
SIDA/ SAREC	Swedish International Development Co-operation Agency/Department for Research Co-operation
SISERA	Secretariat for Institutional Support for Economic Research in Africa
SRISTI	Society for Research and Initiatives for Sustainable Technologies and Institutions (IDRC)
SSA	sub-Saharan Africa
TEHIP	Tanzania Essential Health Interventions Project (IDRC)
TI	Transparency International
TRALAC	Trade Law Centre for Southern Africa
TRIPS	Trade-related Aspects of Intellectual Property Rights (WTO provision)
UCAD	*Université Cheikh Anta Diop* (Cheikh Anta Diop University, Senegal)
UNCTAD	United Nations Conference on Trade and Development
UNDP	United Nations Development Program
UNECA	United Nations Economic Commission for Africa
UNESCO	United Nations Education, Scientific and Cultural Organization
UNICEF	United Nations Children's Fund
UNRISD	United Nations Research Institute for Social Development
USAID	United States Agency for International Development
VAT	Value-added tax
WB	World Bank
WECAPREN	West and Central African Policy Research Network
WIPO	World Intellectual Property Organisation
WTO	World Trade Organization

LIST OF CONTRIBUTORS

David Olusanya Ajakaiye is the Director of Research at the African Economic Research Consortium, Nairobi since October 2004. Prior to that, he worked at the Nigerian Institute of Social and Economic Research (NISER), Ibadan for 29 years. He held several positions in NISER including Head, Research and Consultancy Unit (1988-92), Director, Economic Development Department (1993-98) and Head, Macroeconomic Modeling Unit (1998-99). In 1999, he was appointed Director-General of NISER, a position he held until he joined AERC in 2004. He obtained a PhD in Economics from Boston University in 1984. He has published 14 books, 15 monographs and several journal articles as well as chapters in books all in the area of economic development.

Elias Ayuk is a Senior Program Specialist for IDRC's Globalization, Growth and Poverty program initiative based at the Regional Office for West and Central Africa in Dakar, Senegal. He was the acting Executive Director of IDRC's Secretariat for Institutional Support for Economic Research in Africa (SISERA). Prior to joining IDRC, he worked for ten years at the International Centre for Research in Agroforestry (ICRAF) serving in Burkina Faso, Mali and Zimbabwe. He holds a PhD in Agricultural Economics from Texas A&M University and has published extensively. He currently serves in the Editorial Board of the journal Nutrient Cycling in Agroecosystems.

Haroon Bhorat is currently Director of the Development Policy Research Unit (DPRU), based at the School of Economics, University of Cape Town. Dr. Bhorat obtained his PhD in Economics in 2003 from the University of Stellenbosch, South Africa. He has published widely in the areas of labour economics, poverty and income distribution and has done extensive work for numerous South African government departments, international agencies and the donor community. He has recently co-authored a book on labour markets and poverty issues in South Africa. He sits on a number of advisory boards and official government commissions.

Fred Carden joined IDRC's Evaluation Unit in 1993 and became the Director in March 2004. He has written in the areas of evaluation, international cooperation, and environmental management. His current work includes assessment of the influence of research on public policy, and the development of use-oriented evaluation tools and methods in the areas of organizational assessment, participatory monitoring and evaluation, program evaluation and outcome mapping. Recent co-publications include "Outcome Mapping", "Organizational Assessment", and "Evaluating Capacity Development". He has taught and carried out research at York University, the Cooperative College of Tanzania, the Bandung Institute of Technology (Indonesia) and the University of Indonesia. He holds a PhD from the Université de Montréal and a Master's degree in environmental studies from York University.

Gaye Daffé is a senior lecturer and researcher, based at the Department of Economics and Management at the Université Cheickh Anta-Diop, Dakar, Senegal. He was for a long time in charge of the coordination of research programs at the Department's research center (Centre de Recherches Economiques Appliquées, CREA). Specialized in international economics, he has undertaken research in the fields of trade between developed and developing countries and on trade policy. For some years now, Dr. Daffé has been also working on the economics of education and on the micro- impact of macro-economic policies on poverty. He is the co-editor of the book entitled " Le Sénégal en quête d'une croissance durable", (CREA – Karthala, 2002). He holds a "Doctorat d'Etat en Sciences Economiques" from the Université Paris X- Nanterre.

Abdoulaye Diagne, professor of economics at the Université Cheikh Anta Diop of Dakar, is former Director of Centre de recherches économiques appliquées (CREA). He is now the Director of the

« Consortium pour la recherche économique et sociale (CRES) » ine Dakar. His main research fields are macroeconomics, monetary economics and human resources. He has published many papers on academic reviews, and books with Gaye Daffé. He is a holder of a "Doctorat d'Etat en Sciences Economiques".

Souleymane S. Diallo, a Ph.D student, currently based at CIRES, University of Cocody – Abidjan, Souleymane S. Diallo works on areas of trade and fiscal reforms, income distribution and poverty. His other fields of interest are technical efficiency and productivity theory in agriculture sector. Moreover he has participated in important studies on the cocoa, coffee and cotton sectors in Côte d'Ivoire. He is member of the PEP Research Network and the African Economic Research Consortium (AERC).

Dirk Hansohm was Director of the Namibian Economic Policy Research Unit (NEPRU) from 2000 to early 2006. He is an economist with more than 20 years of professional experience in research, advice, and training of government officials in various African countries. He is also member of Namibia's National Planning Commission (NPC) and the Council of Economic Advisors (CEA) to the President, co-ordinator of the Southern and Eastern African Policy Research Network (SEAPREN), and editor of the Monitoring Regional Integration in Southern Africa Yearbook. His areas of interest include economic policy reform, economic governance, the role of research in policy making, regional integration, labour market, poverty reduction, industry policy, and small industry promotion.

Afeikhena Jerome is with the Department of Economics, University of Ibadan, Nigeria. Until recently, he was with the National Institute for Economic Policy, Johannesburg as a Senior Researcher. He has had over fifteen years' experience in Economic Policy Research and lecturing in the University. He has consulted for numerous organizations, including the World Bank, African Development Bank, ILO, NEPAD and UNDP amongst others. Dr. Jerome has a PhD in Economics from the University of Ibadan.

Basil Jones is Senior Program Specialist with Globalization Growth and Poverty (GGP) program initiative of IDRC based at the Regional Office for Eastern and Southern Africa in Nairobi. He obtained his Ph.D. in Economics from the University of Hull, UK. He has research interests in the areas of trade and regional integration and poverty dynamics.

Thomas N. Kibua is the Executive Director of IPAR and coordinator of Macroeconomic Programme. He holds Masters degrees from the University of Nairobi and Yale University and a PhD degree in Economics from University of Nairobi. Prior to the current appointment he worked as Economic Advisor to the Kenyan Ministry of Health, was Deputy Governor of the Central Bank of Kenya, served as Advisor to the President of East and Southern Africa Trade and Development Bank. His areas of specialization include banking, finance, quantitative methods and development economics.

Mohamed Ali Marouani is *Maître de Conférences* at the *Institut d'Etude du Développement Economique et Social* (IEDES) of Paris1-Panthéon-Sorbonne University. He is Research Associate at DIAL (Paris) and of the Economic Research Forum of the Arab Countries, Turkey and Iran (ERF). He also lectures at the *Institut d'études Politiques* de Paris (Sciences-Po). His research focuses on the impact of public policies on employment, income distribution and poverty in developing countries. His experience as officer of the Saga Program within SISERA/IDRC gave him the opportunity to work closely with African economic research institutions. He holds a Ph.D in economics from Montpellier University, and a Master in Agricultural Economics and Development Administration from the International Centre of Advanced Mediterranean Studies (Montpellier). He received many awards, including the silver medal of the Food and Agriculture Organization of the United Nations (FAO).

Erwin Naimhwaka is currently lecturer at the University of Namibia. He previously worked as researcher at the Namibian Economic Policy Research Unity. His research interests are public finance, poverty and inequality and governance issues.

Aderibigbe S. Olomola is a Research Professor at the Nigerian Institute of Social and Economic Research (NISER) where he has been conducting research for the past two decades. He has been Head of the Macroeconomic and Strategic Modelling Unit and the Research and Consultancy Unit of the Institute during the past five years and has coordinated several research projects. He has numerous publications to his credit and was listed in the Marquis 2004 edition of Who's Who in the world. He has served as consultant to various organizations nationally and internationally in the field of agricultural and development economics. Currently he is at the Head of a research team working on the Nigerian budget process and also the coordinator of a Comparative Research Network on Public Service Reform in Africa. He holds a PhD from the University of Ibadan.

Mama Ouattara is an Associate professor and is currently Director of CIRES (*Centre Ivoirien de Recherches Economiques et Sociales*) based at the University of Cocody – Abidjan. His main field of research is dynamical system theory. He has published in the areas of optimal economic growth in relation with health economics, macroeconomic stabilization policy and optimal decentralized systems. He is vice president at CIEREA (*Conference des Institutions de Recherche Economique en Afrique*). He holds a "Doctorat d'Etat en Sciences Economiques".

Yaya OUATTARA is a Ph.D Student and research fellow in economics and is currently based at CIRES (*Centre Ivoirien de Recherches Economiques et Sociales*). His main fields of research concern trade theory and poverty analysis. He has participated in studies on the UNDP Human National Development Report of Côte d'Ivoire. He is member of Globalization Studies Network (GSN) and African Economic Research Consortium (AERC).

Lineth N. Oyugi is Researcher, Macroeconomics Programme. She holds a Master's degree in Economics from University of Nairobi. Previously, she worked as an Economist in the Ministry Finance and Planning Her research interests are in the following areas: poverty, public policy, budgetary processes and reforms, debt, project management and decentralization.

Mireille Razafindrakoto, Researcher at IRD (*Institut de Recherche pour le Développement*) and member of DIAL (*Développement, Institutions et Analyses de Long terme*), a Paris-based research centre specializing in development economics. She is the author of numerous articles on poverty issues (monitoring and evaluation of poverty, the voice of the poor, the many facets of poverty, redistribution and the role of the State). She did field work in Madagascar from 1994 to 1999. She graduated from ENSAE-CESD (*Ecole Nationale de la Statistique et de l'Administration Economique, Paris*) and obtained a Ph.D. in economics at EHESS (*Ecole des Hautes Etudes en Sciences Sociales*) also in Paris.

François Roubaud is Research Director at IRD (*Institut de Recherche pour le Développement*) and member of DIAL (*Développement, Institutions et Analyses de Long terme*), a research centre based in Paris specializing in development economics. He graduated from ENSAE and obtained a Ph.D. in economics at the University of Paris. He has been in charge of several cooperation programs with national institutions in Mexico, Cameroon and Madagascar, where he was stationed for several years. He is the author of numerous papers in scientific journals and has written various books (on the informal sector in Mexico, macroeconomic perspectives of Cameroon and Madagascar, the new international strategies to fight poverty).

Kalilou Sylla is a Senior lecturer the University of Cocody – Abidjan and former deputy director of CIRES, he was a UNDP expert at the prime minister office and technical councillor at agricultural minister in his country. During these five last years, he was chief negotiator for his country on agricultural issues at WTO ministerial conferences. He has published several articles on development and globalisation issues. He holds a "Doctorat Troisième Cycle en Sciences Économiques".

John Young joined ODI in May 2001 after 5 years in Indonesia managing the DFID Decentralised Livestock Services in the Eastern Regions of Indonesia (DELIVERI) Project - an action-research project to promote more decentralised and client-oriented livestock services. Before that he was ITDG's Country Director in Kenya, responsible for managing the group's practical project and research work on a wide range of technologies to ensure that lessons were effectively communicated to government and non-government policy makers. Since joining ODI he has been involved in projects on decentralisation and rural services, information and information systems, strengthening southern research capacity, and the research-policy interface. He leads ODI's *Research and Policy in Development* Group, and also manages the *Civil Society Partnership Programme.*

INDEX